AN INTRODUC1
WORLD ANGLICAN...

What is the nature of world Anglicanism in a postcolonial, global age? With talk of fragmentation constantly in the media, what does it mean to be 'Anglican'? This book presents Anglicanism as a conversation over time amongst a community of people held together by sets of practices and beliefs.

The first part describes the emergence of Anglicanism and its foundations in older Christian traditions. The second looks at Anglican practices within the framework of changing understandings of mission, and focuses on liturgy, patterns of engagement with others, organisation and power in the church, and ministerial offices. There are two separate chapters on the ordination of women and homosexuality in the public life of the church. The third part, on beliefs, addresses the central question of knowledge and authority in Anglicanism, as well as ecclesiology, the nature of the church itself. A final chapter looks to the future.

BRUCE KAYE was General Secretary of the Anglican Church of Australia from 1994 to 2004. He is a cosmopolitan scholar and priest who, after studying in Sydney and taking his doctorate in Basel, held a post in the Theology Department at the University of Durham in the UK for twelve years before returning to the University of New South Wales in Australia. His visiting fellowships include periods in Freiburg-im-Breisgau, Cambridge and Seattle, and he is a regular visitor to North America. He is the author of eight books, editor of ten further volumes, and has written some sixty journal articles as well as contributing to newspapers, radio and TV. He is also the foundation editor of *The Journal of Anglican Studies*.

AN INTRODUCTION TO
WORLD ANGLICANISM

BRUCE KAYE

CAMBRIDGE
UNIVERSITY PRESS

CAMBRIDGE UNIVERSITY PRESS
Cambridge, New York, Melbourne, Madrid, Cape Town, Singapore, São Paulo, Delhi

Cambridge University Press
The Edinburgh Building, Cambridge CB2 8RU, UK

Published in the United States of America by Cambridge University Press, New York

www.cambridge.org
Information on this title: www.cambridge.org/9780521618663

First published 2008

Printed in the United Kingdom at the University Press, Cambridge

A catalogue record for this publication is available from the British Library

ISBN 978-0-521-85345-3 hardback
ISBN 978-0-521-61866-3 paperback

Contents

Acknowledgements

Writing a book of this kind presents enormous challenges. The material is so vast, the scope so indeterminate and the interested parties amongst potential readers almost infinitely varied. Having been general secretary of the Anglican Church of Australia for ten years and a member of a number of Anglican Communion bodies is a partial preparation. Having been a life-long theologian with an interest in history, and editing the international *Journal of Anglican Studies*, was also a help. But the sheer magnitude of the material encompassed by world Anglicanism renders it completely impossible to be aware of, let alone cover, everything. More than that, the material demands an interpretative standpoint. Simple definitions are bound to be inadequate. I have taken the view that it is best understood as an ongoing story of a tradition of Christian faith. Some may find such a category of explanation too vague, and others may think it antiquarian. But it seems to me to best fit what is a very distinctive form of Christianity that has survived a number of significant crises. As a good historian I have tried to view my subject with an eye of compassion, and as a theologian with what Michael Ramsey once referred to as one foot on the ground and one foot in the kingdom of heaven. How far these ambitions have been achieved is for others to judge.

Whatever an author proposes as an interpretation of something in which most of his readers will be directly involved will never commend itself to all. Therefore I invite my readers to be co-workers in understanding the life of the scattered, curious and extraordinary community of worldwide Anglicans. Here I acknowledge those co-workers. A friend told me that to undertake such a task at this point in time was a sure-fire way of pleasing no one and probably losing your friends. But I think this is overdramatic. One of the consolations of working on the book has been to confirm many friendships around the world and to make new ones. Despite the fractious tribalism that is currently on such dispiriting display in world Anglicanism, I have found face-to-face encounters with fellow Anglicans from all corners of the globe to be not just civil, but encouraging and in the totality inspiring. It has been one of the privileges of my life to have placed my foot on every continent on earth, and furthermore to have friends and colleagues on all of those continents. It is this far-flung community of Anglican believers, and the nearer and more intimately connected community of my own parish church, that I wish to acknowledge as the foundation of this book. It has been written for them and their communities. The nearest, most immediate and important of these people is my wife Louise, who has borne the brunt of this project while maintaining her own ministry in medicine and community service, and to whom I express my profound gratitude. Our children, who are grown-up and wise, initially thought the project to be a bit of Dad's hubris, but I hope that in the event they will see it for what it has been – a midlife education for their father.

Special thanks are due to the librarians and archivists, too numerous to mention, who have been sources of generous goodwill and assistance, and to various friends who have had meals overgarnished by conversation about some obscure aspect of world Anglicanism, or read things on subjects which at first they did not think would be interesting. For my part I have found the journey endlessly fascinating. Anglican Christianity never ceases to amaze me by its capacity to get so many things wrong while still being able to confront us with the face of the crucified Christ. It is truly crooked timber being broken into the shape of a cross, no matter what silly things we might have done or might do in the future.

Abbreviations and sources

ACC	Anglican Consultative Council
ACO	Anglican Communion Office
ARCIC	Anglican–Roman Catholic International Commission
Bede EH	Bede, *A History of the English Church and People* (London: Penguin, 1968). References are given by book and chapter followed by the page in this edition.
CCEA	Council of the Churches of East Asia
CMS	Church Missionary Society
CSI	Church of South India
Eames	Anglican Consultative Council, *Women in the Anglican Episcopate: Theology, Guidelines and Practice: The Eames Commission and the Monitoring Group Reports* (Toronto: Anglican Book Centre, 1998)
ECUSA	Episcopal Church of the United States of America. Its name changed in 2006 to the Episcopal Church (TEC).
ELCA	Evangelical Lutheran Church of America
IASCOME	Inter-Anglican Standing Commission on Mission and Evangelism
IATDC	Inter-Anglican Theological and Doctrinal Commission
LC	Lambeth Conference
MISAG	Mission Issues and Strategy Advisory Group
MISSIO	Anglican Communion Standing Commission on Mission
NIFCON	Network for Inter-Faith Concerns
SPCK	Society for Promoting Christian Knowledge
SPG	Society for the Propagation of the Gospel
WCC	World Council of Churches

Lambeth Conference and Anglican Consultative Council resolutions are indicated according to the year and the resolution number, e.g. Resolution 16 of the Lambeth Conference of 1988 is LC.1988,16. In general the text of these resolutions is taken from the electronic version provided on the official website of the Lambeth Conference. Reports such as the Eames Commission Report are given by the short title and the paragraph number.

Introduction

At the turn of the century the synod of the diocese of New Westminster in western Canada considered whether to approve liturgies for committed same-sex relationships. There were strong divisions within the diocese, but after a lengthy debate the synod voted in favour of the move on 22 June 2002. The bishop, Michael Ingham, was personally in favour of such a step, and as the diocesan bishop he had the responsibility of giving final authorisation for these liturgies. He delayed, perhaps in some degree wanting to be responsive to the furore which the proposed step had created in Canada and the rest of the Anglican Communion.

The issue was not new. Gender relations had been debated in Canada since 1976 and was on the agenda of the Lambeth Conference in 1988 and 1998. Indeed in 1998 it was the occasion of an unseemly row in which some bishops distinguished themselves in the public eye by the racist language they used to characterise their opponents. So the issue clearly had a lot of explosive potential.

Since 1998 the primates had decided to meet each year for consultation and fellowship. They had a meeting scheduled to be held in the diocese of Southern Brazil on 19–25 May 2003, at the Serrano Conference Centre in Gramado. It was to be the first such meeting for Rowan Williams as the new Archbishop of Canterbury. The pre-meeting press release stressed that it was to be a private meeting. The gathering was to take the form of a retreat, with Eucharist and Bible study being the framework of their being together.

As it turned out, some aspects of the meeting were anything but private. An official letter was released at the end of the gathering which described something of the topics which had been discussed. Not the least of these was human sexuality. With moderated understatement the primates declared:

The question of public rites for the blessing of same sex unions is still a cause of potentially divisive controversy. The Archbishop of Canterbury spoke for us all when he said that it is through liturgy that we express what we believe, and that there is no theological consensus about same sex unions. Therefore, we as a body cannot support the authorization of such rites.[1]

That statement was made on 27 May 2003. During the Primates' Meeting Michael Ingham, in New Westminster, Canada, issued a rite for blessing committed same-sex unions and the first such blessing took place the day after the primates made their announcement. It was a globally public snub to the position of the primates and still ripples around the world amongst Anglicans. It reflects issues at the heart of the turn-of-the-century institutional crisis facing worldwide Anglicanism.

What kind of religious tradition can create such a public confrontation? Clearly one that includes questions about the relationships between centres of authority and the extent of jurisdiction. It is manifest that the primates have no jurisdiction over Michael Ingham. They did not claim it and he certainly did not concede it.

The primates did, however, intervene in the debate and as a group sought to exercise some authority. If that authority weighed with Michael Ingham, it was not enough to change his course of action. So again we are confronted with this question: what kind of religious tradition could lead to such a situation? The language of authority and jurisdiction occurs throughout the history of Anglicanism. It is precisely reflected in exchanges with the Pope when he spoke the language of jurisdiction to William I in the eleventh century. Authority and jurisdiction were implicit in the debates at the synod of Whitby in AD 664. Notoriously Henry VIII and the papacy engaged on issues of jurisdiction. If Henry and the Pope spoke the same jurisdictional language, that commonality of language was apparently absent from the exchange between Michael Ingham and the primates. Clearly the institutions of the Anglican Communion did not have, and do not appear to wish to have, any kind of Tudor/papal jurisdictional role.

So without jurisdictional authority how did such a religious tradition come to be a worldwide phenomenon and with such a character? How does such a religious tradition sustain itself? To what does this tradition testify? These are important questions and point to the odd history and character of the community of Anglicans worldwide. That story has been told on a number of occasions and with different lines of interpretation. Kevin Ward has written an excellent account of global Anglicanism by regions.[2] His book is different from earlier accounts in that it highlights the local

---

[1] Primates' letter from meeting of May 2003, available at: www.aco.org/acns/articles/34/50/acns3450. html (accessed 25 March 2007).

[2] K. D. Ward, *A History of Global Anglicanism* (Cambridge: Cambridge University Press, 2006).

initiatives which led to the spread of Anglican Christianity around the world. In this respect his book represents a welcome change in historiographical approach, an approach which has been to some extent anticipated in postcolonial historiography generally.

This book is not a history of worldwide Anglicanism. It is an introduction to world Anglicanism and seeks to set out a way of understanding world Anglicanism as it confronts the twenty-first century. In order to understand this Christian community we need to have some understanding of the foundations upon which the community faith is based and some sense of the dynamics that shape that faith. In order to do justice to the current dynamics and its heritage of institutions and activities I will be treating Anglicanism as a tradition. By this I do not mean a set of fixed habits from the past, but rather the more dynamic sense of being a conversation over time amongst a community of people held together by sets of practices and beliefs. Anglicanism is thus seen as having a story which provides a framework within which Anglicans understand and experience their practices and beliefs.

That story needs to be characterised so that the practices and beliefs of Anglicans can be seen in their appropriate perspective. There are some prominent markers in this tradition, pre-eminently a theological habit of focusing on the incarnation. This focus gives a quite particular construal for a notion of catholicity: it begins with the local expression of a universal faith in which the local is part of a larger whole. That local needs a larger community to save itself from being inadequate in its faith and practice.

This orientation explains why Anglicans have always thought that the complete ecclesial unit is a province with an archbishop. This practice provided two things: a manageable reach for effective catholicity and a reasonable framework for ecclesiastical order for ordination and discipline of all ministerial orders – deacons, priests and bishops. Anglicans regard this as the model of the early church and therefore as having an important pedigree. Archbishops are not an order, but hold a part-time temporary job and are subject to discipline as bishops. This system of provinces is the reason why the Anglican Communion has historically described itself as a fellowship of churches and not as a church. In this respect it is similar to the world federation of Lutheran churches, and in some contrast to Roman Catholicism which begins its ecclesiology with the magisterium and the pope as the Vicar of Christ. It thinks of itself not as a fellowship of churches but certainly as a universal church. We shall see that each model has its problems.

The idea of a supra-provincial structure is not necessarily impossible for Anglicans, but the tradition lacks resources to provide a clear rationale for it.

For this reason I describe the moves since 1988 as an ecclesiological experiment. The story of the Inter-Anglican Theological and Doctrine Commission (IATDC) reports is a tale of attempts to find resources from the tradition to provide shape for the experiment. A number of options have been canvassed along the way: regional conferences and structures, international congresses of all the churches, and an international study centre for theological education and research with appropriate resources on Anglican identity. This is to name just a few options that have been considered or tried but have now been discarded for the time being.

The current line of experiment follows the suggestions of the *Windsor Report* and moves in the direction of a covenant which would provide more manifest authoritative power than the present arrangements to restrain deviations from some central norm. This line of experimental development has come in the context of very significant conflict over the institutional actions in the areas of gender relationships. It is interesting to observe that the currently discarded experiments have tended in the direction of persuasive authority and the currently pursued experiment moves in the direction of jurisdictional development. So the experiment is really quite innovative, if not revolutionary.

This book focuses on the global experiment that Anglicans are engaged in. This means that activities at the world level occupy a large part of this account. The records of the Lambeth Conference are therefore very important sources, not because they report decisions that apply in the regions – they do not, and do not profess to do so – but because they are taken as reasonable evidence of what is going on in the world community. Throughout the book I have tried to refer to the Anglicans that live around the world and their local institutions as part of world Anglicanism. The term 'global' has for some the connotation of western domination.[3] The current struggle among Anglicans around the world, and the post-1988 institutional experiments, seem to many to be a form of globalism.[4]

There is a distinction between the institutions of the current experiment and the well-established regional and local institutions. The latter form the framework for the life and faith of Anglicans everywhere. They are where the practices which sustain the tradition of faith operate and where the faith is lived out and expressed in the lives of individuals and communities. There are literally thousands of such institutions and organisations, just as there are

---

[3] L. O. Sanneh, *Whose Religion Is Christianity?: The Gospel Beyond the West* (Grand Rapids, Mich.: W. B. Eerdmans, 2003), p. 22.
[4] See J. R. Saul, *The Collapse of Globalism: And the Reinvention of the World* (London: Atlantic, 2005).

hundreds of worldwide networks and institutional relationships which keep these dispersed Anglicans in touch with each other. A mere fraction of these connections are visible in the institutions of the Anglican Communion. When we look at the Anglican Communion and its organisational arrangements we need to remember this wider network of living connections between Anglicans around the world. Yet it is the organisational arrangements of the Anglican Communion which are the subject of the current ecclesiological experiment in Anglicanism, and they must therefore occupy a good deal of our attention in this book.

It is completely impossible in a single book to describe the vast extent of the activities in this world community. Being selective about which topics to include has been inevitable and it is also certain that readers will know of examples which could or should have been used. A book like this is an open invitation to upset almost everyone because I have left out what they know is important. My only hope is that what I have written will be of interest, and help the reader to have some idea of what this thing called world Anglicanism is, and something of what the current experiment is about.

PART I

Foundations

CHAPTER I

The nature of the story as a tradition

The fact that a community has had such a long history raises some important questions about how best to tell its story. This book is not a history of Anglicanism. Rather it is an introduction to a particular tradition of Christianity. In order to enter into the nature of contemporary world Anglicanism we need an interpretative standpoint from which to make some sense of what we see today. There are a number of different frameworks that could be used: Marxist class struggle, a study of social power and manipulation, conflict between nationalist sentiments, the impact of modernity and the fragmenting effects of postmodernism or postcolonialism, to name just a few. This book is written from a theological standpoint. It sees Anglicanism as part of the response to the presence of God in the person of Jesus of Nazareth and of the struggle to give expression to that presence in the life circumstances of the Christian community and the believer. The contemporary encounter with Jesus Christ is not just a process of leaping from the present to the first century. We make that encounter within the framework of a living tradition of faith and life.

Within Christianity there are a number of discrete traditions of faith, and Anglicanism is one of them. What Anglicans bring to the contemporary encounter is thus a complex mix of practices and beliefs that have developed over many generations. These provide the framework for understanding contemporary world Anglicanism.

The Anglican tradition is a continuing response to God in particular circumstances and is a dynamic force. The foundations of world Anglicanism are thus not easily set out in simple descriptive terms. Rather they are best captured in narrative form: not as a simple story of what Anglicans have done through the centuries but as a narrative of the continuity within the tradition in its various manifestations.

The construction of such a narrative faces very significant hurdles in the case of Anglicanism. Precisely how tradition is conceived affects the nature of the narrative and needs to be identified clearly. The horizon for the narrative is itself a contentious matter amongst Anglicans and other Christians, not least Roman Catholics. Did it begin with the reformation of Henry VIII or does its pedigree date from an earlier time, even from Jesus of Nazareth himself? And what might it mean to say that it began at a certain point anyway?

The idea of a Christian nation, which has influenced the understanding of Anglicans for a thousand years, has little currency in the modern world, yet it is a crucial part of the Anglican story. To enter into what it meant for Anglicans to live in a self-consciously Christian nation over a long period of time requires a significant imaginative endeavour for inhabitants of the twenty-first century. These are issues to which we must turn first, before offering a narrative within which to locate our understanding of world Anglicanism.

THE NATURE OF A TRADITION

The terminology of tradition is found in the earliest documents of Christianity. Paul wrote to the Corinthians in the following terms, 'I handed over to you as of first importance what I in turn had received' (1 Cor. 15.3). This is an activity construed along a temporal line with a view to sustaining some kind of continuity in the community within which these matters are being handed on. That dynamic notion of tradition persisted in earliest Christianity. With the passing of generations the content of what was being handed on came to be identified as tradition. That process made it possible for a conflict to emerge between the expressions of this tradition at different times and in different places and what was perceived as the original meaning. We can see this concern clearly in Irenaeus (*c.* 130 – *c.* 200), who argued for what we would regard as a historical use of the early Christian texts in combination with an appeal to the public tradition of gospel-preaching in the church in Rome. During the second century a collection of texts from the earliest period inevitably came into existence as a benchmark. This collection in due course became a rule or canon, and was accepted in early Christianity as authoritative testimony to the original message of the faith: the texts were apostolic. There was always a dynamic between past tradition and present experience of the God testified to in the tradition. As Christians developed institutions of greater complexity that dynamic increasingly shared the cultural assumptions and problems of each generation.

In modern western culture tradition has become a highly contentious idea. The internal impulses of romanticism and the rigorous new 'discovery mentality' of modernity have meant that in the west tradition has been under constant attack for nearly two hundred years. It has come to be seen as the past and to be a burden and an inhibition. The spirit of this is captured very nicely in Rousseau's 1762 book on education and upbringing, *Émile*. In the first sentence of Book I Rousseau declares: 'God makes all things good; man meddles with them and they become evil.' And so he appeals to mothers: 'Tender anxious mother, I appeal to you. You can remove this young tree from the highway and shield it from the crushing force of social convention.'[1] In this highly influential work Rousseau developed a sharp contrast between humanity and nature on the one hand and society and its institutions on the other. So he says to mothers: 'Forced to combat either nature or society, you must make your choice between the man and the citizen, you cannot train both.'[2] Thus on this account civilised man is a slave and freedom is gained only by learning from nature: 'take the opposite course to that prescribed by custom and you will almost always do right'.

The last quarter of the twentieth century witnessed a significant renewal of interest in these issues. Modernity appeared under severe threat and philosophers and social theorists were grappling with the challenges for humanity of a century of hot and cold wars and the apparent evaporation of confidence in the values of the western heritage. The struggle was finely represented in Alasdair MacIntyre's 1981 book, *After Virtue*. He rejected the Marxism of his earlier days and also contemporary liberal individualism.

MacIntyre claimed that the most pressing problem was that moral arguments were essentially interminable, in the sense that they cannot reach conclusions. The crucial test case for him was that of 'emotivism', in which any evaluative utterance has 'no point or use but the expressing of my own feelings or attitudes and the transformation of the feelings or attitudes of others'.[3] His argument challenged this disposition. He argued for a re-construction of our understanding of the western philosophical tradition and called for a return to a form of the predecessor model of Aristotelianism.[4]

The MacIntyre project has fallen like a bombshell into the contemporary debate about the nature of moral discourse, and how communities exist in historical particularity and at the same time have continuity through

[1] Jean-Jacques Rousseau, *Émile*, trans. Barbara Foxley (London: Dent, 1969), p. 5.

[2] Ibid., p. 7.

[3] Alasdair C. MacIntyre, *After Virtue. A Study in Moral Theory* (London: Duckworth, 1981), p. 24.

[4] Alasdair C. MacIntyre, *Whose Justice? Which Rationality?* (Notre Dame, Ind.: University of Notre Dame Press, 1988); Alasdair C. MacIntyre, *Three Rival Versions of Moral Enquiry* (Notre Dame, Ind.: University of Notre Dame Press, 1990).

history. According to MacIntyre that continuity is sustained by the practices of the community within the framework of a notion of tradition. MacIntyre has placed the serious analysis of moral practices and their modes of thinking squarely on the table. These aspects of his work are of direct importance in trying to understand the nature of the Anglican community in its various manifestations.

MacIntyre has not been the only person concerned about these matters. In the same year (1981) that MacIntyre published *After Virtue*, Edward Shils published his T. S. Eliot Lectures of 1974 entitled simply *Tradition*.[5] Like MacIntyre, Shils began with the disrepute into which tradition had fallen under the influence of the Enlightenment. He argued that tradition is what is handed down. He has a more developed sense of institution than MacIntyre and claims that in relation to practices and institutions what is handed down are 'the patterns or images of action which they imply or present and the beliefs requiring, recommending, regulating, permitting or prohibiting the re-enactment of those patterns'.[6] Tradition implies some continuity and identity with the predecessor handlers of the tradition and thus carries within it some tacit knowledge of the life and meaning of those in the tradition. In this sense Shils argues that tradition is the cohering force in a society.

Having begun his book with the disrepute in which tradition is held, Shils ends it with an evangelistic assertion of its value and importance:

I wish to stress that traditions should be considered as constituents of the worthwhile life. A mistake of great historical significance has been made in modern times in the construction of a doctrine which treated traditions as the detritus of the forward movement of society. It was a distortion of the truth to assert this and to think that mankind could live without tradition and simply in the light of immediately perceived interest or immediately experienced impulse or immediately excogitated reason and the latest stage of scientific knowledge or some combination of them.[7]

Shils' concept of tradition is cast in more static content terms than the more open-ended notion we find in MacIntyre. Even though the precise configuration of the character and role of tradition found in Shils and MacIntyre is not exactly the same, they were both attacking the same issue and seeking to assert that communities exist within a narrative of particulars, and that the continuity of that narrative is shaped and sustained by a tradition of practices.

---

[5] E. Shils, *Tradition* (London: Faber and Faber, 1981).   [6] Ibid., p. 12.   [7] Ibid., p. 330.

These preliminary engagements with the modern ambivalence about tradition are the starting point for our characterisation of Anglicanism as a tradition of faith within the broader tradition of Christianity. In this context tradition is the process which creates a story, or a narrative, for a community. It provides for a memory which is housed in institutions within which the life of the community flourishes and is sustained. Institutions here are the patterns of ongoing relationships through time between people and things which provide continuity through changes in the occupants of the offices of these institutions. They are not the people, nor are they the community. They exist to serve the community.[8]

Anglicans provide for institutions which yield status for certain texts (the canon of scripture pre-eminently, but also liturgies, canon law and constitutions), for persons (most obviously the whole community of believers in their various roles in the church but also in particular the orders of ministry and office holders in constitutions) and for practices (centrally the sacraments and habits of the moral life).

Such a tradition yields order and thus also meaning and rationality as the community conducts its life in constant conversation and engagement with the elements of these institutions and habits. Thus tradition is marked by practices which both express and shape our beliefs. Because Anglicans have been generally local in their priorities and insisted on the importance of the particular, there has been ample scope for conversation which, by its vigour and energy, could be characterised as argument. That kind of interaction is not only endemic in the tradition, it is fostered and encouraged by it.

Looked at in terms of organisational theory this is a somewhat understated version of the organisation of Anglicanism. That understatement is not mistaken, because it reflects something quite important about the nature of the tradition itself and the theological character of Anglicanism. The emphasis on the presence of God in the particular, together with the essential significance of the Christian vocation in that particular, is coupled with modesty about the extent and detail of our knowledge of God. Wonder at the essential central truth of God's redemptive incarnation is more the note than the confident articulation of sets of detailed theological propositions. This tradition of faith underlines a real presence of the divine in the ongoing life of the community, but yet with restraint, modesty and humility in the face of the wonder of the divine and a sense of the limited and fallible character of the human response to God.

---

[8] See B. Kaye, *Web of Meaning. The Role of Origins in Christian Faith* (Sydney: Aquila Press, 2000), pp. 115–59.

These instincts underlie the continuing ambiguities in the history of Anglicanism in the relation between the divine and the human. The history of the relation between secular power and spiritual expression in Christian England is an example of this tension. The most staunchly establishment-minded Anglican was never far away from a doubter on this point. Even the iconic Hooker accepted the notion of the Royal Supremacy only with significant qualifications, which taken in the longer run would inevitably undermine any attempt to give the supremacy enduring significance. The emphasis at the Reformation on human frailty resonated with a longer tradition visible in the patient trustfulness of Cuthbert and the detached confidence of Bede that God was at work in the nation of the English, even though events sometimes did not seem to suggest it. But that was the nature of the tradition as it was forming from the earliest times. It could be seen in the Celtic heritage which Bede's argument might have swept aside, but did not. The Celtic frame of faith had both a practical engagement with God in the particular and a capacity for strategic withdrawal in the face of violent attack. The dispositions of such a tradition yield values such as grace, resilience, patience and humility. The struggle to give expression to these things, and the manifest failures of individuals and the institutions of the church to exemplify them, constitute the ongoing history of penance. These themes underline the inadequacies in the community and thus the importance of failure, suffering and fallibility as marks of the community in this tradition.

WHEN DID THE ANGLICAN STORY BEGIN?

When to begin the story of Anglicanism is very contentious. What is at stake in this is the interpretative significance of the horizon for identifying the character of Anglicanism and other aspects of western Christianity. The point may be illustrated by the candid statement by the Roman Catholic writer Aidan Nichols about the Anglican Church: 'It was created by the sixteenth century English monarchy in an effort to avoid the religious disunity of the kind so notable in the Continental Reformation.'[9] This view yields a picture not only of the Anglican Church but also of Roman Catholicism. On this model Anglicanism is a sixteenth-century breakaway from Roman Catholicism and different from the continental Reformation

---

[9] Aidan Nichols, *The Panther and the Hind: A Theological History of Anglicanism* (Edinburgh: T&T Clark, 1993), p. xvii.

churches. Given the distance from the sixteenth century, Anglicans should now seriously be looking to rejoin the Bishop of Rome.

It is disappointing that some Anglican scholars have accepted the sixteenth-century Reformation as the starting point for the discrete tradition of Anglican Christianity. One also sees that practical assumption in reports from various organisational parts of Anglicanism such as the *Virginia Report* of 1997.

J. Robert Wright has helpfully reviewed the issues of terminology and the question of where to begin the study of Anglicanism. He pointed out that the English term 'Anglican' does not occur until the nineteenth century and he canvassed the meaning of the Latin phrase *Ecclesia Anglicana*, used most notably in Magna Carta (1215). He concludes that while the commencement in common usage of the English term Anglican begins in the nineteenth century, the 'terms "Anglican" and even "Church of England" in their various translations can be shown to have a continuous and consistent non-doctrinal use that stretches from the modern era well back into the Middle Ages'. As a consequence he concludes that the study of Anglicanism 'must finally go back conceptually and doctrinally to the New Testament and historically and geographically to the martyrdom of St Alban in the "patristic" period of "Anglican" church history'.[10]

This is a conclusion with which in general I agree, though I would put the matter a little differently, in part because I am interested in a slightly different question. Wright was answering the question of when the study of Anglicanism should begin historically. I am asking when the tradition begins in order to identify some of its characteristics. The answer to that question is when the English people begin to be identifiable as a discrete people, and that really begins with the account of them by the Venerable Bede in the eighth century. It would be a significant mistake not to recognise that the faith which came to formation amongst the English was in fact, as Bede points out, a faith which they received from their Celtic neighbours. What Bede conceptualised in the eighth century, Alfred made a political reality in the ninth, and this in turn was consolidated by the Normans under William the Conqueror in their own particular way.

There is another candidate for the commencing horizon and it has particular appeal in the contemporary world of Anglicanism, namely the period of the spread of the Anglican faith to the four corners of the world, mainly on the coat-tails of the expansion of the British Empire and some colonial expansion by the United States of America. That would place the

[10] J. R. Wright, 'Anglicanism, *Ecclesia Anglicana*, and Anglican: An Essay on Terminology', in S. Sykes and J. S. Booty (eds.), *The Study of Anglicanism* (London: SPCK, 1988), pp. 427ff.

horizon in the seventeenth century and shape it in a quite different way. Here the horizon would point to the movements which inexorably led to the phenomenon we know today as world Anglicanism. This horizon is appealing because it more directly points to the contemporary situation of Anglicanism, with the major growth in numbers occurring in the southern hemisphere, in the countries to which this faith was taken in the colonial period. It also gives priority to seventeenth-century Anglicanism as the 'classic' form.[11]

The problem with taking this phase as the commencing horizon is that it would significantly eclipse aspects of the tradition to which Anglicans around the world are committed. Almost all constitutions adopted by provinces of the Anglican Communion include in their recitals a statement of their heritage in the Church of England, and many include in their constitutions English Reformation documents such as the 1662 Book of Common Prayer and the Thirty-Nine Articles of Religion. These same constitutions generally locate the character of their Anglicanism in the one holy and catholic church and the faith which goes back to the apostles. These commitments are part of the threads of continuity which bring together the story of this tradition into a narrative and make it clear that the commencement horizon needs to be placed further back than the sixteenth century if the shape of that narrative is to be fully drawn.

I am not contending that Anglicanism is somehow unique as a tradition in Christianity. On the contrary, it is one of several traditions which have survived over the centuries. Some traditions are actually broad coalitions of traditions; indeed most of the larger traditions are. Orthodoxy, if it can be construed as a single tradition, is in effect a matrix of sub-traditions which can be reasonably well characterised, but which coalesce together in a kind of federation of traditions.[12] The Roman tradition of Christianity similarly contains a number of sub-traditions, though they are much more constrained and centrally ordered through the papacy than any other tradition of Christianity. Anglicanism is also large enough to share this quilt-like character as a broad tradition of traditions, and its expansion from the seventeenth century outside the land of its formation has only served to multiply those inner traditions.

---

[11] See the remarkable documentation in P. E. More and F. L. Cross, *Anglicanism: The Thought and Practice of the Church of England, Illustrated from the Religious Literature of the Seventeenth Century* (London: SPCK, 1957).

[12] See J. Binns, *An Introduction to the Christian Orthodox Churches* (Cambridge: Cambridge University Press, 2002).

THE CRUCIAL ROLE OF THE IDEA OF A CHRISTIAN NATION

The earliest Christians faced a very significant challenge in terms of the social framework of their lives. Jesus had come as a Jew, a member of the nation of Israel. His first followers had the same background, and when they became his disciples they did not immediately leave behind them the assumptions about God, the law and social institutions that provided the framework of their faith as Israelites. However, the confession of Jesus as Lord inevitably meant changes in those assumptions. The problem was magnified when gentiles became Christians because they did not bring these Israelite assumptions with them. The conflict in the early church about the observance of the law gives us a direct insight into these issues. This process deeply affected the way the Christians came to terms with the social order of their day. Judaism came with some very clearly established social institutional markers, such as Sabbath observance, family structures, a holy nation and religious institutions such as the temple and the synagogue. As the early Christians began to separate from these Jewish institutions, they had to find ways of relating to the broader social institutions of their surroundings according to principles that were relatively untested.[13] They were caught between the creative contemporary presence of God and the stories of their predecessors.

One aspect of the great achievement of Bede was to provide not just a story of the English, but a story of the English which was also a story about the activity of God. It was a theological telling and the English were portrayed as having a role as a Christian nation in the purposes of God. Adrian Hastings has pointed out that the model of the story of Israel in the Old Testament provided images not only for the people but also for rulers to understand their role in this Christian nation.[14] The journey from Bede to the Tudor Royal Supremacy was not straightforward and there were many byways and diversions. But throughout there was a persistent sense that this nation had a Christian character and carried Christian responsibilities.

This underlying strand in English life to remain enmeshed within the orders of the nation persists long in English and also in Anglican sentiment. Even to this day it is visible in the reluctance of the Church of England to give up an established relationship with the modern state of the United

---

[13] See further Kaye, *Web of Meaning.*
[14] See Adrian Hastings, *The Construction of Nationhood. Ethnicity, Religion and Nationalism* (Cambridge: Cambridge University Press, 1997).

Kingdom, or of the Episcopal Church to think of itself in terms other than those of a national church in the United States of America.

These general trends often covered significant dissent within each model. Anglican leaders often seemed to enjoy some imperial power in the land. Similarly, within the Roman jurisdiction Gallicanism has run like an underground river, rising to the surface from time to time to wash away the pretensions of structural imperialisms. The resurgence of 'new theology' in the run-up to Vatican II largely drew its dynamic from this stream of influence. Even given these exceptions the general trend in the Anglican tradition remains. It points to a particular orientation to social enmeshment and to the consequential issue of the social ownership of authority and jurisdiction.

All this worked more or less well until the nation itself began to change in ways which made the assumptions of this enmeshment increasingly unworkable. The growth of significant dissent from the mainstream religious tradition meant that the congruence of the nation with the religious assumptions of the mainline church was fractured. The process reached a peak of public plurality with the removal in the early nineteenth century of the legal disabilities of Roman Catholics and Dissenters, and eventually of Jews in 1858.

However, for Anglicanism worldwide this internal collapse of the notion of the Christian nation in England was simply a story from a distant galaxy. These Anglicans had to find ways of sustaining the character of their Anglican tradition in very different contexts. This transformation was all the more difficult because their religious sensibilities had been shaped by the framework of a Christian nation for over a thousand years.

This has been the situation of Anglicans around the world for the last hundred years. The demise of the Anglican version of the Christian nation, and the associated notions of authority and power which made that long history possible, has meant a profound tectonic movement for Anglicans. It is that convulsion which makes the present time so engaging for those who want to reflect on the nature of their faith.

How can a narrative of this faith be fruitfully and faithfully given? In the first place by focusing on the religion as a tradition of practices and beliefs with a horizon to the story going back at least to the distinctive formation of the idea of an English nation in the writings of Bede in the seventh century. Secondly, by recognising the key importance for the tradition of its social enmeshment and in particular its social enmeshment in the Christian English nation, the confines of which it has now left behind. On this basis a theological reading of the story of Anglicanism can be undertaken.

CHAPTER 2

Forming an Anglican nation in England

From the very earliest of times a Christian nation was being formed in England until it broke down in the face of modernity. That process formed not only the nation, but also the Christianity of the people. The creation of this Anglican nation was therefore the creation of an Anglican tradition of Christianity.

WALKING TOGETHER: THE IDEAL OF BEDE AND ITS INFLUENCE

After the departure of the Romans in AD 406, Anglo-Saxon Britain developed on its own terms for 200 years, and Christianity flourished in various ways. A second wave of Nordic invasions began at the opening of the ninth century. Alfred defeated the Danes at Ethendune in 878. Edward the Elder conquered the Danelaw and became the first king of all England. The following 150 years saw a second flourishing of the Anglo-Saxon civilisation and Christianity. The fateful year of 1066 saw the defeat of Harald Hardrada, king of Norway, by Harold, who had been made king of England, and then Harold's own defeat and death at the hands of William the Conqueror at Hastings.

Much of what we know of this period comes from Bede, especially his *Ecclesiastical History of the English People*. It is not surprising that we see on the pages of this account a view of the relations between royal power and spiritual authority, between king and bishop. The pre-eminent ideal is found in Bede's account of the life of Oswald told in close relationship with his account of Aidan. Of course they lived at the same time; indeed Aidan came from Iona when Oswald had asked the community for someone to be bishop in his kingdom. But there is more than this involved. They make such an attractive pair – monk and king working in unison – in part because Oswald is a king who resembles a monk. Bede tells us that Aidan 'never sought or cared for any worldly possessions, and loved to give away to the poor who chanced to meet him whatever he received from kings or wealthy folk'.[1] Oswald 'brought under his sceptre all the provinces of Britain speaking the four languages, British, Pictish, Scottish and English. Although he reached such a height of power, Oswald was always wonderfully humble, kind, and generous to the poor and strangers.'[2] At the beginning of his history Bede described the situation in Britain in his day as comprising four nations – English, British, Scots and Picts – and then goes on to describe the antecedents of these nations in the invasions and migrations of earlier times. Each had their own language, though they studied God's truth in Latin.[3]

Bede's conception of kingship was framed in his own monastic life and attitudes which he projected onto the political sphere. 'The king was a kind of Christ, and his life showed forth the virtues of his prototype as they were cultivated in monastic circles.'[4] Biblical imagery is often used by Christian apologists. Such images often presented the king as the representative of God and as one who should demonstrate the wise, caring qualities of the God who protects his people. Thus the king was responsible for his people body and soul.

Such ideal pictures, however, were not always the reality, even with Christian kings. Oswald died in battle at the hands of an alliance of the British king Cadwalla and the English kings Osric and Eanfrid. Clearly religious affinity did not necessarily override perceived political interest. Bede attributes the destruction of his hero to the 'callous impiety' of Cadwalla and the 'insane apostasy' of the Christian English kings.[5] The religious and moral ideals of the cloister were not easily assimilated to the harsh realities of political life. It was a lesson that was to recur for Anglicans throughout the whole of their history, and one that has not always been heeded. Indeed the struggle between faith and humility on the one hand, and politics and power on the other, are unresolved tensions in Anglicanism to this day. They are unresolved because the tradition lacks an eschatological vocation of humility and human frailty together with a commitment to living in the particulars of the social world. For Anglicans the relationship between the vocation of the crucified and the 'powers' of human society has been intensely ambiguous from a very early time.

Political issues were undoubtedly at stake in the synod of Whitby in 664. The synod was called by king Oswui of Northumbria. The presenting issue

---

[1] Bede EH, III,5, p. 148.   [2] Ibid., III,6, p. 150.   [3] Ibid., I.I, p. 38.
[4] H. Mayr-Harting, *The Coming of Christianity to Anglo-Saxon England* (University Park: Pennsylvania State University Press, 1991), p. 255.
[5] Bede EH, III,9, pp. 155f.

was conflict between the Irish and Roman practices for calculating the date
of Easter. Arguments were presented on both sides, Colman for the Celtic
tradition and Wilfrid for the Roman. Bede notes that during the lifetime of
Aidan variety of use was tolerated because of the respect in which Aidan was
held. When Oswui opened the debate he began with an essentially political
proposition. 'All who served the one God should observe the one rule of life,
and since they all hoped for one kingdom in heaven, they should not differ
in celebrating the sacraments of heaven.'[6] In the end Oswui decided the
issue on the grounds that St Peter had been given the keys to heaven. 'Then
I tell you that Peter is the guardian of the gates of heaven, and I shall not
contradict him.'[7] Behind the religious language is the king's undoubted
awareness of the influence of Rome and the wider western Christian
tradition. The king was making a decision with clear political connotations.

Five years later in 669, a Greek monk by the name of Theodore came to
England as Archbishop of Canterbury. The original candidate, sent by
Oswui and king Egbert of Kent, died in Rome, and Pope Vitalian took
the initiative and appointed Theodore. Though originally from Tarsus in
the East, Theodore was committed to the establishment of Roman ways of
doing things. Furthermore he did so with considerable exercise of personal
power. Bede regarded the twenty-one years of Theodore's tenure as a golden
age to which he could look back with affection and admiration. Bede relates
that Theodore visited every part of the island which was occupied by the
English and was well received. He was

the first archbishop whom the entire church of England obeyed and since, as I have
observed both he and Hadrian were men of learning both in sacred and in secular
literature, they attracted a large number of students into whose minds they poured
the waters of wholesome knowledge day by day . . . Never had there been such
happy times as these since the English settled in Britain; for the Christian Kings
were so strong that they daunted all the barbarous tribes. The people eagerly sought
the new-found joys of the kingdom of heaven and all who wished for instruction in
the reading of the scriptures found teachers ready at hand.[8]

Bede's enthusiasm for Theodore reflects his commitment to the idea of a
Christian English nation being born in line with the practices of the greater
western church and Rome. His monastic model for the nature of Christian
kingship is clear in his treatment of Oswald. But when it comes to Theodore
there is a new aspect to the model of the leader of the church. Here is an
archbishop who lives like a monk, but who acts out of a sense that his office as
a bishop implies personal power and jurisdiction. On his own initiative he

[6] Ibid., III,25, p. 189.   [7] Ibid., III,25, p. 192.   [8] Ibid., IV,2, p. 206.

deposed Chad, who had been irregularly made bishop of the Northumbrians and later became bishop of Lichfield. Theodore appointed bishops and consecrated them and called two synods, the first at Hertford in AD 673:

Theodore summoned a council of bishops and many other teachers of the Church who both understood and loved the canonical statutes of the Fathers. As befitted his authority as archbishop, when they were assembled, he began by charging them to observe whatsoever things were conducive to the peace and unity of the Church.[9]

In the records of the council Theodore is described as bishop of the see of Canterbury 'by the authority of the apostolic see'. As well as discussing the date of Easter, the council adopted the following Roman canons:

• No bishop was to intrude into the diocese of another.
• No bishop was to interfere in any way with monasteries.
• Monks were not to wander from place to place without letters dimissory from their abbot.
• Clergy were not to leave their own bishop.
• Travelling bishops and clergy were to be content with the hospitality they were offered.
• A synod was to be held twice each year, though because of practical difficulties it was actually agreed on an annual synod.
• Seniority of consecration was to be the only test of seniority amongst bishops.
• More bishops were to be appointed as required by numbers, but no actual decision was made about any new bishops.

But there are other things going on with Theodore which point to a shift in the character of the ecclesiastical tradition of the Anglo-Saxon church. We can see it in Theodore's determined action of dividing the large dioceses which coincided with the kingdoms. The bishops and others at the synod of Hertford declined to agree to the sub-division of any of their dioceses. Subsequently Theodore went ahead on his own authority, even though it caused him some difficulties. Edward Carpenter sums up Theodore's achievements in these terms:

He came at a time of crisis so severe that the future of the Roman church in Britain, and with it the see of Canterbury was uncertain. He left behind him a Christianity rooted in a Roman obedience, a diocesan structure firmly established and a metropolitan of greater authority and increased prestige.[10]

---

[9] Ibid., I,5, p. 214.
[10] E. Carpenter, *Cantuar. The Archbishops in their Office* (Oxford: Mowbray, 1988), p. 21.

There are real shifts in the political and ecclesial conceptions at work in these changes which are somewhat glossed over by Bede. When the dioceses coincided with the kingdoms, the Christian role of the king could be easily seen in relation to the work of the bishop in his kingdom. However, now the king's 'Christ-like' role was to be sidelined. Conversely the bishop, and we can see this in Theodore, exercises power more directly and personally. He deposes bishops, divides dioceses and appoints bishops. The canons at Hertford reflect the older model of independence and respect; Theodore's actions speak of something else. It is one more chapter in the emerging struggle in Anglicanism between the power to act and authority to persuade.

The older model, which we find in Bede, of pastoral care conducted by clergy, bishops and monks who travelled across wide areas of a kingdom, was now giving way to a diocesan territorial structure in which pastoral care is located and subject to contained jurisdictional authority. Bede tells us that in these times 'whenever a clerk or priest visited a town, English folk always used to gather at his call to hear the Word, eager to hear his message and even more eager to carry out whatever they had heard and understood'.[11] The more the territory of a bishop was closely defined and reduced in size, the more this peripatetic ministry must change, as change it did.

However these were not the only things going on in Anglo-Saxon Christianity at this period. There are the clear signs of the resilience which has so marked the general life of the faithful and which undoubtedly owes much to the Celtic fount from which this tradition was replenished. The monastic life and the discipline of prayer are beautifully demonstrated in the lives of Cuthbert and Patrick and their communities at Lindisfarne and Iona. They can also be seen in the flourishing of a Christianly informed culture during the time of Alfred and the creation of a vernacular literature of Christian faith and practice. These traditions of prayer and monastic discipline were increasingly centres of inspiration and sources of spiritual resilience.

The English church was itself beginning to take on some kind of identifiable shape. There were centres for prayer and penance, and women such as Hilda and Ethelreda found ways of marking out a place for themselves in the church. Joint monastic and convent houses were usually ruled by an abbess, as at Whitby. Boniface grew out of the English church and went to evangelise the Germans. The nation of the English was also taking on more shape by means of the self-same forces. These political and religious realities make sense within the framework of understanding which Bede outlined in

[11] Bede EH, IV,27, p. 260.

his *Ecclesiastical History of the English People*. It was a theological exposition of the Christian story of the English, and as such a foundation chapter in the story of Anglicanism.

There is more to be said of Bede, for his influence did not die with him on 21 May 735. His works were read and copied, and had a lasting influence on later generations. At the simplest level his work was reproduced in succeeding centuries. Antonia Grandsen[12] claims that according to Laistner and King's Hand-list of Bede MSS that were produced between the eighth and the sixteenth centuries, 31 per cent were made in the twelfth century, 10 per cent in the thirteenth, 17 per cent in the fourteenth and 12 per cent in the fifteenth. The figure drops to 1.2 per cent in the sixteenth century. M. B. Parkes' analysis of the work of the Scriptorium at Wearmouth led him to say that the monks had a bestseller on their hands, and that it created major copying demands for the monks.[13] This points in the direction also suggested from other sources that Bede became something of the teacher of the Middle Ages. Adrian Hastings locates the creation of the English nation with the translation of Bede's History into English by Alfred. 'It is with Alfred that we begin to move from perceiving the nation to establishing the nation-state.'[14] He goes on to argue that the Normans were assimilated on the basis of a strong and enduring sense of English nationhood, a sense that was in the first instance 'imagined' by Bede.[15]

The life of Cuthbert undoubtedly influenced the revival of monasticism in the tenth century, and again in the eleventh Bede was the inspiration for the revival of monasticism in the north. Bonner says that the story of 'the northern monastic revival initiated by Aldwin ... is the most dramatic illustration of the influence of Bede in the early Middle Ages'.[16] He goes on to say: 'Modern scholarship has confirmed and enhanced Bede's reputation as the teacher of the Middle Ages by exploring fields of study like his writings on Latin grammar and poetic metre and their influence on the schools of the Carolingian renaissance; the character of his biographical writings; and his qualities as a historian.'[17]

All of this points to the fact that by a remarkable combination of factors Bede not only imagined the new Christian nation of the English, but his

---

[12] A. Grandsen, 'Bede's Reputation as an Historian in Medieval England', *Journal of Ecclesiastical History* (1981), pp. 397–425.
[13] M. B. Parkes, *The Scriptorium at Wearmouth Jarrow* (Jarrow Lecture in Durham Cathedral, 1982).
[14] Hastings, *The Construction of Nationhood*, p. 39.
[15] Hastings is alluding here to B. Anderson, *Imagined Communities* (London: Verso, 1991).
[16] G. Bonner, 'Bede and his Legacy', *Durham University Journal* 78.2 (1986), p. 220.
[17] Ibid., p. 221.

influence went a long way towards bringing it into real political and social existence. In doing so he helped to shape the way in which the Norman Conquest reinforced the sense of Englishness by a political and ecclesiastical consolidation of the country. He facilitated a way of seeing the nation as Christian, with an ecclesiastical hierarchy and a monastic tradition, with its own English character and a sense of belonging to catholic Christianity in Europe. In the words of J. N. Stephens,

> He succeeded in doing what none of them [later historians] were able even to attempt: he gave his audience a new history. He gave the Anglo-Saxons first a British history; then by turn a Roman history, a Catholic and a Christian history. Finally he showed them that all this meant that they had a new history of their own, English history. Thereby he created it.[18]

All of this shows not just that Bede has had a deep and abiding influence on English self-understanding but that he brought to birth a conception of the English as a Christian nation in which political power and the church walked together. This church was catholic and it was national. It was monastic and it was diocesan. It was marked by a sense of immanence and located in a church calendar that referred it back to the birth of Christ. At the same time it showed that embedded in this tradition from the beginning was a continuing struggle between the exercise of power and its temptations and the resilience of the vocation to authority and persuasion. This form of Christianity, which took shape in the mind and writings of Bede and gained social and political expression after the Norman Conquest, is the seedbed of the Christianity later called Anglicanism. The persistent Celtic elements were grafted onto the form and substance of the English Christian nation. That national religion is the real immediate foundation from which a continuous tradition of Anglicanism is to be traced.

THE GODLY PEOPLE AND KING. THE NEW MONARCHY
AND THE LAW OF THE PEOPLE

The forces at play in the first five hundred years of the second millennium are dramatic and extend across the whole of western Europe. One useful way into the political and power forces which were being transformed is to look at the life of the Holy Roman Empire.[19] The title first begins to be used with the coronation of the German king Otto I in 962, and in strict terms

---

[18] J. N. Stephens, 'Bede's Ecclesiastical History', *History* 62 (1977), p. 13.
[19] For a general overview see F. Heer, *The Holy Roman Empire* (London: Phoenix, Orion Books, 1995).

continues until its renunciation by Francis II in 1806. In reality, however, it all came to an end in the treaty of Westphalia in 1648, when the sovereignty of the constituent states was recognised. Westphalia marks the effective demise of the international authority of the Holy Roman Emperor and a corresponding increase in the autonomy of the constituent nations. The result was that these states were increasingly coherent political units. This general pattern was part of the long transition from feudalism to modernity[20] and the states also had their own form of Christian faith.

From the eleventh century the notion of a Christian nation whose spiritual and secular rule was a joint affair was diminished by the reform movement in the papacy to establish a church centrally ruled from Rome, through a disciplined clergy and episcopate that were to be created by the pope and held under his jurisdiction. While *imperium* in the secular was becoming local, *imperium* in the hands of the papacy was becoming universal across these higher national borders and at the same time was narrowing in terms of its arena of jurisdictional control. In such a context it is not surprising that religious orders revived. They were after all another way of having authority which reached across national borders. They came in time to be subversive of the centralisation process. Relations with the papacy were not always easy because they provided yet another front in the papal struggle for power and jurisdiction. Within the nation they provided another way into religious knowledge and at the same time a different structure for pastoral care and thus presented a caveat to centralisation in the national church. This is the story of the emergence of centralised local nations and centralised universal papal claims. It is no wonder that such momentous changes in the configuration of power and authority in the human condition should produce conflict, dispute and wars.

While England had its own distinctive issues which became more apparent as time went on, it worked these out in continuous interaction with the broader European struggle, especially the struggle for the nature of the church and the authority of the papacy. In the first half of the second millennium some key foundations were established which began to mark England out from the continental countries. At the end of this period Sir John Fortescue laid out these issues with clarity and in the certain conviction that the English legal system was superior to the main continental alternatives because it reflected and promoted a distinctive and better form of human society. Fortescue (*c.* 1395–1477) was 'undoubtedly the major

---

[20] See for a general discussion R. J. Holton, *The Transition from Feudalism to Capitalism* (London: Macmillan, 1985).

English political theorist of the fifteenth century',[21] not because he reflected the actual state of fifteenth-century constitutional arrangements in England, nor because he provided a classic text for later seventeenth-century protagonists in the struggle between parliament and crown, but rather because he addressed in the fifteenth century a real crisis in government in a creative and at the same time traditional way. He reflects the issues and values of the past in a way which opens up the possibilities of the future – possibilities which in large measure came about. Furthermore Fortescue writes with the full commitment of an English churchman. He was an Anglican and what he describes is an Anglican nation.

It was always going to be difficult to follow Henry V, but Henry VI really showed up the contrast by losing Normandy, incurring huge royal debts, and allowing the abuse of royal patronage. There was disorder in the community which Jack Cade and his rebels saw as the result of the king's weakness and the maliciousness of his council. As a young man Fortescue had seen the glories of the reign of Henry V, but in middle life he lived through the tragedies of the reign of Henry VI. He prospered under Henry VI and was knighted in 1442/3. During the struggles between the Yorkists and the Lancastrians Fortescue seems to have joined the Lancastrian forces in February 1461, just before Edward IV was proclaimed king. Thereafter he stayed with them and went into exile with Queen Margaret, Henry VI's widow, and their son the young Prince Edward, first in Scotland and then in France. He returned to England in 1471, but after the battle of Tewkesbury he was taken prisoner and gave himself over to the cause of Edward IV, with the result that he was pardoned in October 1471. He wrote his great book on the laws of England, *De Laudibus*, in Scotland in the years 1468–70 and *On the Governance of England* in the period 1471–6. The *Governance* was most probably written with Edward IV in mind.[22]

De Laudibus contrasts the laws of England with those of France. The prince is enjoined to learn and appreciate these laws, not in their precise details but in the principles that underlie them. He treats trial by jury and the preservation and distribution of property as the two key institutional areas that reveal most about the nature of the English legal tradition and the social and political system which the laws serve.

[21] Shelley Lockwood in the introduction to her edition of Sir J. Fortescue, *On the Laws and Governance of England*, ed. S. Lockwood (Cambridge: Cambridge University Press, 1997), p. xv.
[22] See the discussion in J. Fortescue, *The Governance of England Otherwise Called the Difference between an Absolute and a Limited Monarchy*, ed. C. Plummer (Oxford: Clarendon Press, 1885), pp. 87ff. and Fortescue, *On the Laws and Governance of England*.

Governance on the other hand is concerned with a somewhat different range of questions. It begins with the same contrast between types of kingship, between 'regal dominion' and 'regal and political dominion', though in this instance he takes his starting point from the request of the Israelites for a king in 1 Sam. 7. The unfaithful Israelites are not content with a theocracy in which the prophets have only a derivate authority. Samuel warns them that such a king will have tyrannical tendencies. This text of scripture provides him with the basis for a comparison between England and France. He had used this text to similar effect in *De Laudibus*. Here in *Governance* the argument moves directly to money matters because this book is concerned with the issues of finance and the king's council. He contrasts the French and the English systems in terms of the social distribution of wealth, and in the process deals with the importance of the king having adequate finances. He remarks on both the fairness of the English system and its capacity to bring social contentment. The king's council, its membership and activities, takes up the final part of the book.

The first book deals with questions from the perspective of the common people and the ordering of social life, whereas the second book comes at these questions from the perspective of establishing the appropriate roles for the king and his support. The first moderates the ambitions of the king; the second underlines the importance of his position being secure. All this flows out of the initial scriptural imagery and the tyrannical tendencies of unrestrained power and authority which the scriptural text implies.

This contrast also probably reflects to some extent the proffered context for the accounts: advice to a putative future king in the first instance, and a general essay directed to the newly re-established position of the new monarch Edward IV in the second. If this is so then it is perhaps a tribute to Fortescue's immediate influence that Edward spent so much effort organising and securing the royal finances.[23] However, we should not imagine that Fortescue was simply addressing an immediate concern; he was seeking to lay down some principles about what he thought ought to be the case generally. In doing so he clearly brought together a number of interests: his extensive knowledge of English law, his reflections on scripture, his Christian faith, about which he had directly written on a number of occasions, and a conception of the way in which societies ought to work. He does not offer a theoretical ideal. Rather he identifies certain qualities in the human condition which are best restrained and accommodated in the

---

[23] C. Ross, *Edward IV* (London: Book Club Associates, 1974). See the discussion of finances in G. Elton, *The Tudor Revolution in Government* (Cambridge: Cambridge University Press, 1969).

interests of public good. In modern theological terms it is a classic example of contextualisation.

In that sense Fortescue is interested in a society which is ordered so as to enhance the good and restrain the evil. Such a society will provide for liberty of a kind not experienced by the peasants of France and an authority structure which is directed to the common good and not the private interests of the king. France is his *bête noire* in these documents. Whether his descriptions of France are accurate is not really the point. France performs a rhetorical function to highlight the character of law and society that he is propounding for England, much as the prophet Samuel describes the characteristics of the kings in the nations around Israel. In advocating his changes Fortescue has in mind issues of liberty, authority, order and public good, all of which are shaped for him in a Christian context of faithful social living. This Christian theme is of significant interest for us because it reveals a vision of social and political life which implies significant change in how the religious and the political are to be understood.

The image of the godly prince who is responsible for his people body and soul has not been left behind, though it has been modified in this argument. Fortescue operates within a framework which sees England as a Christian nation ruled by a godly prince according to laws that have evolved in such a way under the providence of God that they have a certain divine character. It is this framework which enables him to accommodate the notion of papal authority alongside that of the authority of the king and of the laws. The papal authority is to be respected, and indeed the Pope's words are to be obeyed, within the framework of the local expression in England of the persistent providence of God revealed in the legal and social order he has put forward.

It is apparent that Fortescue is committed to the view that the scriptures are authoritative in the matter of how England is to be governed, but they work that authority only indirectly. They show how kings were expected to rule in Israel and the evil consequences that flow from a failure to rule according to the law. England is a Christian nation which has been the object of a particular divine providence. As a consequence God is really ruling in England, albeit representatively. The agency of that rule is the law and its administration and the king whose judgements must be set within the laws that divine providence has provided. Such a conception sits within a set of understandings which are quite different from those that can talk about a divine right of kings to rule according to a *regale*. In relation to the position and practice of William I and Lanfranc, Fortescue has given more established place to the law and to the divine role in the history of the

English and the formulation of their laws. In this respect he treads more nearly in the footsteps of Bede. On the other hand, Fortescue sees the English situation in polar contradistinction to the sort of divine right of kings entertained by the later Stuarts. Were he able to see forward to it he would almost certainly have cast it in the same failed and evil terms as the *regale* of the French monarchy.

This is a just society because it operates in a way that most effectively works for justice. It is also a society which under the providence of God has been brought to such a circumstance. Shelley Lockwood is surely right when she says that there is no duality in Fortescue's political thought.[24] It is, I think, more than just that the king and his people are united in a common and unified society. Fortescue's society is also united in the sense that it is seen *sub species aeternitas*: it arises from the providence of God and operates as the representative expression of the justice and dominion of God. The church is the ecclesiastical element in this society and is set in the same conceptual framework.

In the context of the more centralised character of the 'new monarchy' such a conception operates as a form of restraint because it sets the crown and the exercise of power within a framework which both meets the empirical needs of the king and the people, and also carries with it the sanctions of history and divinity. Fortescue is both responding and advocating. He is responding to the focused power of the new monarchy and of the new papacy. His response is to set out a picture of England based upon a conception of order and good which is shaped by a notion of divine providence and of representative rule through human dominion. His focus is political, but it has an ecclesiastical and theological obverse to it throughout.

Fortescue thus represents here an Anglican approach to Christian society which is as much an ecclesiology. Because he is thinking of a Christian society, an Anglican society, he orders his thoughts in a way that reflects and is shaped by the Anglicanism of his day. The contrast between his vision of society and thereby also the church, and that of the papacy, is both sharp and historically important. The conflicts in the church which had so disrupted the papacy from the time of Gregory VII's reforms indicate a community moving in the direction of a *regale*. As an Anglican writer, Fortescue is clearly marching to a different beat. In ecclesiological terms it is more manifestly conciliarist in style and direction.

[24] In Fortescue, *On the Laws*, p. xxxix.

The particularities of the emerging English representation of the divine will are the attention to the scriptural examples and injunctions, a sense of balance in social systems that privilege the public good over private benefit, and a conception of order which by the certainty and continuity it creates facilitates and defines the liberty which Fortescue sees as the hallmark of the English laws and governance. In that sense he is vitally interested in the social values that lie behind each example of the empirical, and he is focused on the nature of institutions and institutionality that enables these values to flourish. It is throughout a theologically formed conception of society which is set in the utmost opposition to an imperial conception.

Of course there is an element of the ideal in Fortescue's portrayal of the English situation, but the fact that on the basis of these two works he was regarded as the great exemplar of English law of his time, and the continuing influence of his texts on subsequent generations, testifies to a widespread acceptance of this ideal. The balance between authority and a power which he presents would be challenged by the imperialism of the Tudors. It was only by the skin of their teeth and the exercise of significant theological subtlety and resilience that Anglicans managed to navigate the Tudor form of that imperialism and the residual imperialisms which the narrow terms of the Restoration of 1662 sought unsuccessfully to impose.

NEW IMPERIALISM IN CHURCH AND STATE: TUDORS AND THE CAVALIER SETTLEMENT

In an influential book first published in 1990 Eric Hobsbawm declared that 'The basic characteristic of the modern nation and everything connected with it is its modernity.'[25] His book thus sees the notion of nation and nationalism beginning in 1780. This view has been subjected to severe criticism and has been brought into doubt by recent early modern and medieval historical studies. The most sustained critique has been offered by Adrian Hastings, who builds a case for England coming to national consciousness almost a thousand years before the date set by Hobsbawm. We have already met this argument from a slightly different angle in discussing Bede and the origins of the idea of the English nation. Hastings rightly identifies Bede as the crucial figure in the creation of the idea of the English nation, and sees in Alfred 'the move from perceiving the nation to establishing

---

[25] E. J. Hobsbawm, *Nations and Nationalism since 1780* (Cambridge: Cambridge University Press, 1990), p. 14.

the nation-state'.[26] He also shows how, despite the disappearance for one hundred and fifty years of the English language in government in favour of French, the Normans in fact fused with the English in the twelfth and thirteenth centuries. In that fusing he claims that 'English nationalism would ever after have an imperialist tone that it did not have before'.[27] He suggests that throughout the formative period of English national self-consciousness religion had been a moderating influence. The connections with the wider catholicity of the western church had restrained the growth of independent national sentiment. This growth, and its associated institutions, was 'a quietly secularising process'.[28]

This portrait enables him to describe the English Reformation, or more particularly the assertion of the Royal Supremacy by Henry VIII in 1534, as the point at which that wider catholic restraint came to an end and from this point on the 'national principle alone would reign supreme'.[29] In other words the politics of the Reformation turned English nationalism Protestant. But the history of the previous five hundred years points in an altogether different direction. It is true that the new monarchy marked a consolidation and centralising movement in the political life of England. But, as we have seen, the constraints on that process came not from connections with the papacy or the wider European circle, but rather from the social and religious traditions which had grown up in England. The foundational influence of Bede and the representative work of Fortescue point to a tradition which dispersed authority and restrained power to a distinctive degree. That tradition, moreover, had emerged in conjunction with the nation's Anglican faith. The papacy did not represent constraint on imperial notions of power; on the contrary it had adopted just such an idea of jurisdictional power in the church. The evidence from as far back as William I and Pope Gregory VII points to papal commitment to imperial notions of power in the church.

The Reformation legislation of Henry VIII and Edward VI is startling in the English environment for the absolute claims it makes in both the political and religious aspects of society. The point is clear in the crucial act for the Restraint of Appeals (1533) whereby any jurisdiction of the Pope is strictly excluded from England.

Where by diverse sundry old authentic histories and chronicles, it is manifestly declared and expressed, that this realm of England is an empire, and so hath been accepted in the world, governed by one supreme head and king, having the dignity and royal estate of the imperial crown of the same, unto whom a body politic, compact of all sorts and degrees of people divided in terms and by names of

---

[26] Hastings, *Nationhood*, p. 39.   [27] Ibid., p. 45.   [28] Ibid., p. 51.   [29] Ibid., p. 53.

spirituality and temporality, be bounden and ought to bear, next to God, a natural and humble obedience: he being also instituted and furnished, by the goodness and sufferance of almighty God, with plenary, whole, and entire power, pre-eminence, authority, prerogative and jurisdiction, to render and yield justice, and final determination to all manner of folk, residents, or subjects within this his realm, in all causes, matters debates, and contentions, happening to occur, insurge or begin within the limits thereof, without restraint, or provocation to any foreign princes or potentates of the world.[30]

One of the great achievements of the Tudors, especially Henry VIII and Elizabeth, was to contain the nation and the community within the terms of this constitutional revolution. However, even Elizabeth's marginally more modest statement of the Royal Supremacy did not remove the serious doubts about the absoluteness of the claims being made in relation to the church. On the other hand, Anglicans were seriously divided on the reform front. Disciplinarians, called by some Puritans, wished to proceed with a Reformation that operated according to a claim for the exclusive authority of the Bible. The point of greatest conflict came when that claim was applied to ecclesiology and the demand that church order must comply with the order which they said was taught in scripture and no other. That conflict became part of the political struggle throughout the sixteenth and seventeenth centuries. In the process it seriously complicated the reform of the church and the clarification of the longer-standing Anglican tradition of church order and authority. As a result of political ambitions in parliament at the time of the 1662 Restoration, episcopacy was thrust into a different location in ecclesiology and had attached to it a series of assumptions from the hinterland of these politics.

One hundred and thirty years of turmoil and civil war had not settled the tensions between power and authority, control and influence. Charles II's declaration from Breda set out in remarkable terms the prospect not only of a general pardon, but also of a general freedom of conscience in religious matters:

And because the passion and uncharitableness of the times have produced several opinions in religion, by which men are engaged in parties and animosities against each other (which, when they shall hereafter unite in a freedom of conversation, will be composed or better understood), we do declare a liberty to tender consciences, and that no man shall be disquieted or called in question for differences of opinion in matters of religion, which do not disturb the peace of the kingdom; and

---

[30] H. Gee and J. Hardy (eds.), *Documents Illustrative of English Church History* (London: Macmillan, 1921), p. 187.

that we shall be ready to consent to such an Act of Parliament, as, upon mature deliberation, shall be offered to us, for the full granting that indulgence.[31]

The progress of the Hampton Court conferences in 1661 seemed to confirm that instinct of the king for some form of toleration. Whether this was a genuine attempt to give some place to Puritans or because he wished beyond this move to see some tolerance for Roman Catholicism is difficult to tell with certainty. What is certain is that the Act of Uniformity which came into force in 1662 hardly breathes the same air as the Breda declaration.

The language of the sixteenth-century Reformation Acts was taken up in theological debate at the time, and afterwards. Richard Hooker found the Royal Supremacy hard to digest. His defence of it is so circumscribed that one has the feeling that given his choice he would rather not have to deal with either the idea or the political reality. Others, particularly in the Caroline period, seemed more open to such configurations of power, though with a preference to see such *dominium* located in the office of the bishop. Given the institutional traditions in England and the configuration of religious and political life, both these claims of imperial power stand out for their oddness. The same could be said for the similar language in the religious realm used by the Puritans. The conflicts of the sixteenth and seventeenth centuries represent the convulsions of imperialisms in both religion and politics.

The birth of the modern nation-state and the convergence of social and political forces in Europe tested the traditions of dispersed authority and power in England and in Anglicanism. The destruction of moderating sources of authority such as the religious orders, and the narrowing of the lines of authority in ecclesiastical affairs, was a substantial challenge to the continuity with the earlier developments in the character of Anglicanism. The residual presence in Anglicanism of the imperialisms of scripture alone and episcopal divine right have been the unhappy legacies of this period.

WALKING APART – ALMOST: THE DISINTEGRATION
OF THE IMPERIAL MODEL

In politics the 1662 Act of Uniformity was secured by the Cavalier parliament. Charles may have wanted something more generous, and some of the bishops seem to have been open to a wider range of possibilities. As an exercise in power the Act failed to strengthen the church or to unify the

---

[31] Declaration of Breda, available at: www.constitution.org/eng/conpur105.htm (accessed 2 July 2006).

religious character of the nation. By 1714, if not by 1689, 'an age of religious pluralism had begun'.[32]

By early in the eighteenth century religious dissent not only existed, it was accepted, but the pathway to religious toleration was not the same for all religions. Full acceptance of Jews did not come until 1858 and of Roman Catholics not until 1829. The dynamic working itself out over two hundred years from the Restoration is not the pulsing energy of an idea of a plural nation striving to come to expression. Rather it is the tale of the responses of national institutions to threats to their position posed by the different forms of dissent.

From medieval times Jews had suffered disadvantages in civil life. The Reformation kindled an interest in the Old Treatment and thus in Hebrew, and this in turn gave Jews some purchase. However, it did not lead to real political or civic relief. Despite severe legal disadvantages, Jews nonetheless gradually gained space to be able to participate in public life. In 1667 the King's Bench ordered that Jews could give evidence in cases, and in 1684 Judge Jeffries ruled that Jewishness was not a bar to bringing an action in the court. A Jewish naturalisation bill was passed by parliament in 1753, but a public outcry forced its repeal shortly afterwards. Nonetheless a Jew was admitted as a solicitor in 1770.

A bill for Jewish emancipation was passed by the Commons in 1830 but failed in the Lords where the opposition was led by the Archbishop of Canterbury on the grounds that the bill implied a demonstrable change in the character of England as a Christian nation. Fourteen times bills were passed by the Commons and various disabilities were removed, except the form of the oath of allegiance for members of parliament. This last change finally occurred in 1858 when each house was empowered to formulate its own oath of allegiance.

The arguments turned on the question of the national self-understanding. England was a Christian country and non-Christians should not have a role in national decision-making. But it had already become apparent in the first quarter of the nineteenth century that England was no longer a Christian nation in that strict institutional sense. Not only had the age of religious pluralism come, but the way of defining the religious character of the nation had long since ceased to be in terms of universal conformity to Anglicanism.

The story of Roman Catholics is different and highlights the essentially political issues that were at stake. In the sixteenth and seventeenth centuries

---

[32] C. Cross, *Church and People 1450–1660. The Triumph of the Laity in the English Church* (London: Collins, Fontana Press, 1976), p. 242.

the issues were clearly political: Roman Catholics were regarded as subversive. After all, in 1570 Pope Pius V had excommunicated Elizabeth I and absolved Roman Catholics of the responsibility to obey her. The last thirty years of Elizabeth's reign were marked by this pseudo-religious terrorist mentality. The Jesuit mission begun in 1574 seemed only to confirm the disloyalty of Roman Catholics, and so a series of laws addressed this threat. In 1581 it became high treason to convert to Roman Catholicism and any Roman Catholic priests found within the queen's realms were automatically guilty of high treason. Guy Fawkes and the Gunpowder Plot of 1605 confirmed yet again that Roman Catholics were traitors, a disposition sustained each year with the burning of effigies of Guy Fawkes on 5 November. But disabilities continued, and the relief given in 1778 to enable Roman Catholics to inherit and to hold land was followed in 1779 by the anti-Roman riots stirred up by Lord George Gordon. There were moves for further change, though their path was opposed by George III and blocked by the Tory government from 1812 until 1827. Roman Catholic emancipation became law in 1829.

The issue with Roman Catholics was much more directly that of political loyalty. They owed allegiance to a foreign power, the Roman Pope. Two things changed this situation. The allegiance to the Pope came to be seen more in religious terms than in political terms. That change in perception implied a dramatic shift in the terms of understanding about both the nature of religion and its political significance. The Pope was not now seen as commanding allegiance of any significant political kind. Clearly gone were the days when English kings corresponded with the Pope in order to refuse his demands of fealty. The great crisis of church and state of the twelfth and thirteenth centuries when Pope and crown claimed jurisdiction over the totality of human life had resulted in a stand-off. Each claimed authority and jurisdiction over their own now-refined notion of realm, and apart from a few brushfires conceived of their relationship in terms of respectful recognition.

However, Methodism was by far the most subversive dissenting movement in the eighteenth century, because it was home-grown and politically loyal. The Wesley brothers claimed to be Anglicans, and to all intents and purposes they were. They experienced and promoted a form of religious life that could conceivably sit alongside the structured life of the national church. It was institutional matters that caused an organisational separation. In 1760 Methodist preachers are recorded as having celebrated communion, and in 1784 John Wesley laid hands on the ordained Anglican priest Thomas Coke as the Superintendent for Methodists in America. Coke immediately changed this title to that of bishop, much against Wesley's wishes.

But Methodism and the religious revival associated with it not only marked out the political problem of a large body of organised but loyal home-grown dissent, it also marked out cultural changes in the way in which people understood the world in which they lived. For a hundred years these changes in the tacit assumptions of life had been percolating down in England and Europe, and in the middle of the eighteenth century Methodism flashed a light of reaction and response. These movements were to transform the living self-understanding of the English as citizens and Anglicans, though the full effect of these forces did not come to political expression until the nineteenth century.

In 1702 John Locke published a book called *The Reasonableness of Christianity: as delivered in the Scriptures*.[33] The book argued that the religion described in the New Testament could be found by the reasonable investigation of the natural world in which we live. This was a cloud the size of a man's hand which would grow to be the storm which brought the divine authority of the Bible into question and eventually disrepute. It was a sign of a great change of thought in European culture which has come to be called the Enlightenment, but which for our purposes can be seen as opening up a distinction between the church and the Bible on the one hand, and the kind of knowledge which can be discerned from the natural order on the other. This knowledge would become the powerful engine of modern science and in turn the Industrial Revolution.

In the broader culture the reaction to these movements took the form of Romanticism with an assertion that true insight and knowledge can be found within the experience of the individual. In Germany the Romantics found expression in theological circles, especially Lutheran, and, in the words of a modern expositor of this tradition, they called not just for salvation by faith alone, but for knowledge by faith alone.[34] These were themes which in time would shake the foundations of western culture and cast Christian faith and theological knowledge into new contexts and challenges.

However, it was a very long century between the publication of Locke's essay and the manifest upheavals in the established position of the church

---

[33] J. Locke, *The Reasonableness of Christianity: as delivered in the Scriptures*, ed. J. C. Higgins-Biddle (Oxford: Clarendon Press, 1998).

[34] See J. Milbank, C. Pickstock and G. Ward (eds.), *Radical Orthodoxy. A New Theology* (London: Routledge, 1999), p. 23.

and the assumptions of political and social life which emerged in the period 1828–33. The long eighteenth century (1689–1833) has only recently begun to be studied in more depth by social and political historians. For a long time church history has simply ignored it; as Mark Pattison recommended in 1860, 'the genuine Anglican omits that period from the history of the church altogether'.[35]

A different picture of the period is now emerging.[36] The older image of a decadent church plagued with deism and dereliction of duty is now giving way to a more variegated picture. Clergy are now seen to be better paid and educated and to be increasingly identified with the gentry. Their pastoral energy and commitment are clear, and in the first half of the century their bishops were more consistently drawn from the ranks of the aristocracy. Certainly there was a church crisis of low attendance and unease in the fifty years following the 1689 Toleration Act, which was seen by many as an Act of indulgence which excused people from serious church attendance. For a fleeting instant clergy and bishops were faced with the question of whether they could work in a church which was essentially a voluntary body. The foundation of the Society for Promoting Christian Knowledge seemed to embrace that possibility and encouraged clergy in the understanding of their role as pastoral educators. A similar crisis of the church in danger in the 1740s brought forth the voluntarist impulse again and saw the formation of Sunday schools and later the Proclamation Society. There were signs of renewed lay piety and the publication of books and tracts to serve that purpose. Alongside this a quiet revolution in diocesan organisation meant that at the end of the century the diocesan system was well placed, with clear roles for rural deans and archdeacons.[37]

The key intellectual force in the century was Latitudinarian. Never an organised party, it rather influenced the way in which the challenges facing the church and the nation were framed. Latitudinarian principles were very influential on generations of clergy trained at Cambridge, and effectively the movement 'ousted the more emotional and affective preaching style of

---

[35] M. Pattison and H. Nettleship, *Essays by the Late Mark Pattison, Sometime Rector of Lincoln College* (Oxford: Clarendon Press, 1889), vol. II, p. 43.

[36] See J. Walsh, C. Haydon and S. Taylor, *The Church of England, c. 1689–c. 1833: From Toleration to Tractarianism* (Cambridge : Cambridge University Press, 1993), p. ix. This set of essays contains an excellent introduction to the new historical work.

[37] See A. Burns, *The Diocesan Revival in the Church of England c. 1800–1870* (Oxford: Clarendon Press, 1999).

Puritanism to become the accepted standard for clerical discourse'.[38]
Popularised as people who believed little and practised less by their
Victorian successors, the eighteenth-century Latitude people saw this appeal
to nature and the new science as a way of supporting orthodoxy rather than
betraying it. However, by the end of the century debate tended to be formed
in terms of the competing claims of the evangelicals and the High Church
group.

The eighteenth century did constitute a pathway into the disruptions of
the nineteenth century, though not quite in the way portrayed in the
rhetoric of the party factions of that century, who had a rhetorical interest
in portraying their own position as a way of dealing with the black
inheritance of the previous century. The aristocratic character of English
political life continued right through the period of the Napoleonic Wars,
and the Anglican character of the nation continued with it.

The Church of England entered the nineteenth century with clergy
broadly speaking committed to the pastoral role implied in the parish
system and united in a commitment to the Book of Common Prayer and
the Thirty-Nine Articles. Because tenure in the parishes was effective, and
appointment was very widely dispersed amongst lay people and clergy, no
centralised action for change was possible. On the contrary, a habit of
moderation had grown up, partly in reaction to the excesses of the post-
revolutionary controversies. Such moderation also influenced episcopal
appointments and there was growing popularity in seeing the Church
of England as representing a middle way, a *via media*. That middle way
was seen through a variety of lenses – Puritan/Papist, Methodist/deist,
Calvinist/Armenian. Such moderation was part of the interaction of the
elements in the Anglican nation. Clergy in this period often became Justices
of the Peace and were committed to the propertied character of the social
structure.

The claim that England was exclusively an Anglican nation was still part
of the argument used by the Archbishop of Canterbury against admitting
Jews to parliament in 1858. The continuing arguments about church and
state in England since that time have been less about what kind of profes-
sion the state should make in regard to Anglican Christianity than about the
kind of adjustments that could be made to the institutional enmeshment of

---

[38] Walsh *et al.*, *The Church of England*, p. 42. See also I. Rivers, *Reason, Grace, and Sentiment: A Study of the Language of Religion and Ethics in England, 1660–1780* (Cambridge: Cambridge University Press, 1991).

the Church of England in the instruments of state. The Church of England has been persistently unwilling to disentangle itself from this relationship.[39]

Where the eighteenth century seemed quiet on the ecclesiological front, the nineteenth century raged with the question. The gradual step-by-step accommodation to religious plurality had to precipitate a crisis sooner or later. That crisis came in 1832, and in the reaction of the Tractarians, who wanted a complete separation from the state on the grounds that the church had an integrity of its own, which often meant that bishops had a vocation to govern the church on the basis of their apostolic office if not their apostolic succession. It was not a point of view that prevailed.

The quest for an Anglican ecclesiology in England has thus been set within frameworks which complicated and constrained the question in a unique way. But that has in fact been the particular heritage of Anglicanism. It has worked with an understanding of itself and its heritage in the context of the social and political situation in which it has been located. That was the case for Bede, Lanfranc and all their successors in England. Anglicanism, shaped in the framework of a Christian nation, could not evolve in any other way. That is why the radical independence of the episcopate and the lay imperialism of Tudor sovereignty were so impossible to digest.

However, that same shaping force of particularity in the tradition was part of the baggage of those Anglicans who took their faith and their church overseas, beyond the territory of the Anglican nation of England. In doing so they encountered similar issues to those in England, but often in different forms and with very different issues for their vocation as Anglicans. It is to that part of the story that we now turn.

---

[39] See the account in W. Sachs, *The Transformation of Anglicanism. From State Church to Global Communion* (Cambridge: Cambridge University Press, 1993), ch. 3.

CHAPTER 3

Forming Anglican churches around the world

We reach a vital point in the narrative of Anglicanism with this theme. The Christianity which had been locally shaped in the English nation and its culture is now transported overseas into many different localities and cultures. The very principle of enculturation which had created a particular form of Anglicanism in England was now to encounter totally new contexts.

HISTORIOGRAPHY

From its Celtic and English formation Anglicanism had emerged with a number of characteristics. It had developed a provincial institutional pattern, with the Archbishop of Canterbury as primate of all England, and regarded this as providing that reasonable extension of the local to sustain workable catholicity. It consolidated its long-standing relationship with other national churches on a basis of friendly conversation. Since the very earliest times it had held the Pope in honour and sought significant connection with the wider Christian world of Europe. Its rulers had regularly, though not always, rejected any notion of fealty to the Pope or any recognised jurisdictional power, especially for the reformed centralised papacy after Gregory VII.

The Reformation and the wars of religion had left European Christianity with a radically altered framework of catholicity. Effective wider fellowship and unity were hindered by the emergence of new tightly determined religiously confessional nations. These nations established high cultural and religious tariff barriers. That was precisely what the Gregory VII reforms of the papacy had done in the eleventh century on a pan-European scale. Those reforms introduced a new idea which saw the church as a tightly controlled international organisation. This meant that the Pope and his church were seen as essentially and dangerously foreign by non-Roman

Catholic nations. The whole process meant a significantly reconfigured context for catholicity in European Christianity.[1]

Within its national borders England had evolved a significantly dispersed concept of authority and institutional arrangements to go with that dispersal. That process also meant that by the eighteenth century the authorities which influenced the life of Anglicans were quite variegated. The laity controlled much of the organisation and fabric of the church. Parish appointments were mostly made by lay patrons. Parliament remained supreme in all church matters. Bishops were the instruments of this structure, and at the local level the clergy mostly came to be identified with the gentry; their education carried none of the professional theological elements which came to mark the late nineteenth-century scene. In all of these respects Anglicanism could hardly have been more of a contrast to the clericalised and centralised new papacy and Roman church.

Within this framework legitimating authority was sought by appeal to apostolic antiquity. This had always been a mark of Anglicanism, as witness the calendar of Bede which led from Jesus and the apostles to the contemporary life of the church whose sense of time was to be defined in terms of its relation to the incarnation of the divine logos in Jesus. The Reformation formularies emphasised the place of scripture in this appeal, but did not remove it from the sequence.[2] The appeal to apostolic antiquity meant that a threefold order of ministry was sustained and also a commitment to sacramental life in the church. The canon of scripture operated as an ultimate restraint, or point of reference, for contemporary experiments. These were positions which set Anglicanism apart not only from the Roman church, but also from the continental Protestant churches whose stricter appeal to scripture took them off on more adventurous paths in regard to the orders of ministry, sacraments and church organisational structures.

The story of the growth of this overseas Anglicanism is the mixed garden out of which present world Anglicanism has emerged. Our interest here is not the general story of the British overseas expansion, but rather the way in which that story impinges upon our narrative of Anglicanism. The British began their overseas endeavours in the late fifteenth century and for over a

---

[1] For its impact on the notion of catholicity in the English reformers see B. Kaye, 'Power, Order and Plurality: Getting Together in the Anglican Communion', *Journal of Anglican Studies* 2.1 (2004), pp. 81–95.

[2] This is especially clear in the structure of the argument of Thomas Cranmer in his *A Defence of the True and Catholic Doctrine of the Sacrament of the Body and Blood of Our Saviour Christ, with a Confutation of Sundry Errors Concerning the Same, Grounded and Stablished Upon God's Holy Word, and Approved by the Consent of the Most Ancient Doctors of the Church*, ed. R. Wolfe (Appleford, Berks: G. Duffield, 1964; first published 1550).

hundred years it was essentially a private enterprise activity. 'Once pirates, then traders, the British were now the rulers of a million people overseas – and not just in India. Thanks to a combination of naval and financial muscle they had become the winners of the European race for empire. What had begun as a business proposition had now become a matter of government.'[3]

The role of the English church in all of this varied and developed. Chartered companies appointed chaplains to minister to their staff in far-flung places. Anglicanism was established in some colonies as the official religion, either by a local legislature or governor, or by the action of an individual who held the charter for the colony personally. Some colonies had official religions which were not Anglican and which saw themselves as beyond the reach of the English government in this and other matters. Some were located in places where non-Christian religions were in the majority and recognised by the colonial power. Some colonies were established on the basis of religious toleration. Diversity and plurality were experienced in the colonies long before such matters were adopted in England.

The growth of worldwide Anglicanism has been portrayed as an aspect of British imperial history, or as simply the result of the nineteenth-century English missionary movement. In the last quarter of the twentieth century a new postcolonial direction has emerged in this general area of history and in recent times this has begun to influence the way Anglican history is presented. There is the beginning of a new historiography which seeks to move the non-metropolitan perspective to the centre of concern.

The writings of Lamin Sanneh have stressed this theme. 'The West still looms so large in the standard accounts of Third World Christianity that there is little room for the men and women on the ground who were responsible for church planting.'[4] As early as 1978 Robert Strayer put the contrast in terms of a metropolitan-ecclesiastical school of mission history written by European missionaries which focused on 'European strategies for the planting of Christianity in Africa, and on the heroic missionary efforts to implement these plans'.[5] The point has been made in relation to a detailed study of the origins and growth of Anglicanism in Kenya by Colin Reed: 'The chief aim of this narrative is to give to the African clergy and others who played such a part in the founding of this church something of the

[3] N. Ferguson, *Empire: The Rise and Demise of the British World Order and the Lessons for Global Power* (New York: Basic Books, 2003), p. 44.
[4] Sanneh, *Whose Religion Is Christianity?*, p. 35.
[5] R. W. Strayer, *The Making of Mission Communities in East Africa: Anglicans and Africans in Colonial Kenya, 1875–1935* (London: Heinemann, 1978), p. 1.

recognition and respect they deserve.'[6] In a general survey of the history of global Anglicanism, Kevin Ward makes the same point and takes it as his interpretative point of view.[7]

Clearly this is an important move in the history of Anglicanism and it has implications for the way we understand contemporary world Anglicanism. It is also important to recognise that English Anglicans were not the only ones who sent missionaries to other places. The missionary outreach of the American church has been very substantial and has legacies which affect contemporary world Anglicanism. Similarly churches in places such as Canada, South Africa, Australia and Japan have established themselves in various locations, and in doing so have had an influence on the character of the churches there. In other words, to imagine world Anglicanism simply in terms of the exportation of English Anglicanism not only fails to represent the history, but also distorts our understanding of contemporary world Anglicanism.

In order to highlight something of this we can take four examples of different patterns. The case of the United States of America is particularly significant for its current influence in worldwide Anglicanism.

THE AMERICAN NATIONAL CHURCH

In 1589 that Anglican and missionary enthusiast Richard Hakluyt, sometime Archdeacon of Westminster, dedicated his account of the exploratory journeys of the English with the hope that these journeys would lead to the sending of the gospel to all corners of the world. Not all those who adventured on the high seas for plunder, exploration or trade shared the full extent of Hakluyt's religious ambitions, but there was always a sense that the Anglican faith was the natural and necessary faith of the English and that wherever they went it went with them. Many ships of war carried a chaplain, and most trading and exploration ships did so. The Revd Francis Fletcher accompanied Sir Francis Drake on his round-the-world voyage from 1577 to 1580. He suffered the indignity of being excommunicated by Drake for a failure of faith, and for having undermined the authority of the captain when the ship ran aground on the coast of Java. He was later restored, and when they landed for repairs on the coast of California he led the company in the prayers of the church in the presence of a group of natives.

---

[6] C. Reed, *Pastors, Partners, and Paternalists: African Church Leaders and Western Missionaries in the Anglican Church in Kenya, 1850–1900* (Leiden: Brill, 1997), p. xii.
[7] Ward, *A History of Global Anglicanism*.

He thus became the first Anglican clergyman to conduct an Anglican service on the territory of the modern United States of America.

Such scant contacts did not lead to an enduring presence. That happened on the Atlantic coast. After two unsuccessful attempts to establish a colony, a charter was granted in 1605 for the London and Plymouth Virginia Company to establish a settlement in Virginia. A further charter in November 1606 provided for commerce, religion and exploration. The religion was to be that of the established church in England: that is, Anglican.

The expedition reached Virginia on 26 April 1606 with the Revd Robert Hunt as chaplain. The colony was to be controlled by a group of councillors and a governor appointed by the Company. The colony survived and local authority was enhanced in 1619 with the provision of twenty-two locally elected settlers to sit in a General Assembly with the six appointed councillors. In 1624 the company collapsed, and although this meant that the status of the colony was uncertain, the settlement prospered. Tobacco was grown and exported, and numbers in the settlement grew; despite recurrent conflicts with the native Americans, the extent of the settlement also expanded.

The colony was generally supportive of the king in the civil war in England and reacted strongly to the execution of Charles I. The English parliament asserted control of the colony with a force sufficient to overwhelm a local militia of a thousand men without any shots being fired. The Book of Common Prayer was formally abolished, but all the liberties and privileges of the colonists were guaranteed by the parliament. The greatest change for Virginia under the Commonwealth was that the House of Burgesses, which was made up of the elected representatives of the settlers, became supreme in legislature, executive and judicial matters. During the eight years of the Commonwealth 'Virginia was an independent commonwealth in everything but name.'[8] In 1658 the General Assembly agreed to a revised law for the colony which contained no commitment to any doctrine or forms of worship, but delegated the whole arrangement of religion to the parishioners. By such a method Anglican services continued to be used in the colony. With the restoration of the monarchy in England a governor was appointed by the crown and the period of the supremacy of the Assembly of Burgesses came to an end. In March 1660 a revised code of law was agreed, which among other things made the Church of England the established church.

---

[8] R. L. Morton, *Colonial Virginia*, 2 vols. (Chapel Hill, NC: University of North Carolina Press, 1960), vol. I, p. 187.

The seventeen colonies which formed the United States of America had different forms of religion and different arrangements for churches. Virginia is a useful example to highlight the beginnings of the American ecclesial experiment because of the great change it experienced. The church in Virginia was steadfastly loyal to the forms of the Church of England. It was parochial in organisation and vestries had considerable authority. For just under two hundred years the colony was entirely without bishops.

The established position of Anglicanism came to an end in a striking and dramatic fashion with the revolution. In 1786, after the War of Independence, James Madison successfully argued for the adoption in the Virginia Assembly of the statute which Thomas Jefferson had drafted, and which prohibited the establishment of religion. The statute came to have wide influence in other states and its terms can be found in the First Amendment to the Constitution of the new United States of America.[9]

After independence the Episcopal Church of the United States of America (ECUSA) came into being with a constitution similar to that of the new republic. Missionary activity became the responsibility of a Missionary Society, but in 1835 at the General Convention the membership of the church and of the Missionary Society was made the same. Mission was to be the responsibility of the whole church. It was also agreed at the convention to appoint bishops to advance the mission in the continental United States. Later, in 1844, missionary bishops were appointed to work outside the United States in China and Liberia. ECUSA was to be a missionary church at home and abroad. The establishment of a missionary episcopate is said to be one of the greatest contributions to the Anglican mission from ECUSA. In fact it was not taken up elsewhere in the world until the end of the twentieth century in Nigeria, where missionary bishops were appointed to evangelise the predominantly Muslim north.[10]

By the end of the nineteenth century ECUSA had grown in strength and increasingly saw itself as a national church. It could not be the church of the nation because the constitution forbade such a move, but it set out to be the de facto national church, taking on the natural leadership of Protestant churches. This national church ideal began to draw the church into closer relation with the government, as the United States became a more powerful country. At the high point of American imperialism at the end of the

[9] M. D. Peterson, R. C. Vaughan and the Virginia Foundation for the Humanities and Public Policy, *The Virginia Statute for Religious Freedom: Its Evolution and Consequences in American History* (Cambridge: Cambridge University Press, 1988).

[10] Samuel Ajayi Crowther was an exception to this in that he was ordained as bishop of the Niger in 1862.

nineteenth century Christian mission became linked with the purpose of the nation. Mission became a matter of bringing the benefits of American civilisation to the rest of the world, and ECUSA saw itself as a national church in doing this. The building of the National Cathedral in the capital, Washington DC, was clearly seen as an expression of this understanding.[11] 'The drive to spread "our religion, our civilisation, our schools" epitomised the national church ideal of episcopal foreign mission, and led to a dramatic increase in the church's missionary activities in the first two decades of the twentieth century.'[12] At just the same time as empire became the name of the game for European nations, in which Britain played a highly successful role, so at the turn of the century America entered into this arena and continued to grow in strength throughout the twentieth century. Americans such as John Mott, imbued with such imperial notions, had a considerable influence on the emerging mission mentality of the ecumenical movement.

The twentieth century also saw the development of a national unified organisational structure for ECUSA. In 1919 the national organisations were consolidated and the General Convention agreed to have a full-time presiding bishop. After the First World War many Protestant missions were re-thinking their strategies to accommodate what they saw as a changed situation. They no longer perceived a manifest Christian destiny for America; on the contrary, their nation seemed to be becoming less Christian. The new challenge which they perceived was secularism. However, ECUSA had been so successful in organising itself for a national mentality that it 'pushed forward with the triumphalism of America culture'.[13]

Indeed, in the middle of the twentieth century ECUSA was a growing force and was pre-eminent in the emerging Anglican Communion. It pressed for the Anglican Congress in 1954 and subsidised it to an overwhelming extent. Max Warren, the general secretary of CMS in London, regarded ECUSA as the senior partner in the Communion at this time. The second Anglican Congress in Toronto in 1963 was also pushed for, planned and carried forward as an American initiative. Out of this Congress came the document 'Mutual Responsibility and Inter-Dependence in the Body of

---

[11] The land for the cathedral was purchased in 1898 and the building took eighty-three years to complete: 29 September 1907 to 29 September 1990.
[12] I. T. Douglas, *Fling out the Banner. The National Church Ideal and the Foreign Mission of the Episcopal Church* (New York: Church Hymnal Corporation, 1996), p. 94. I am indebted to Ian Douglas for his exposition of the story of the national church ideal.
[13] Ibid., p. 161.

Christ' (MRI) which marked a dramatic turning point in the institutional development of the Anglican Communion.

In all of this ECUSA was the very model of a modern superpower like the nation in which it was formed. Its mission activities overseas extended, and increasingly large areas of the Anglican Communion were being under-written by the American church. Throughout there is a persistent theme of catholic Anglican practice and, in the twentieth century, of the social gospel with its emphasis on the welfare of people and the gospel as acted out in life. The tumultuous 1960s and 70s tested this position. Clearly race riots and civil disorder indicated something was very wrong at home. ECUSA responded to this with a Special Programme and sought by every means to address those disadvantaged in American society. The MRI programme, which had set out to provide a framework for mutual exchange in the Anglican Communion, had become little more that a funding arrangement for Americans to provide support for developing countries.

An Overseas Review Committee of the General Convention addressed the question of how to do mission work in a postcolonial age. In a candid review of past policies the committee identified the difficulties these policies presented to growing autonomy in mission churches.[14] In 1973 the General Convention adopted a raft of proposals to move towards autonomy for mission districts and also to begin the task of viewing mission in a global perspective rather than a colonial one. However, the heady days of constant growth and extensive resources for the work of the national church were coming to an end, and major reductions in the size of the national organisation were made. Voluntary initiatives began to appear and so the process of re-conceiving the national church ideal was started.

Ian Douglas concludes his extensive study of this theme by asking 'Can the Episcopal Church participate in God's mission without the national church ideal?'[15] It is a challenging question. The national church ideal had been the central understanding of what it meant to be the Episcopal Church in the United States of America. It is the ideal that has produced architec-tural ecclesiastical dominance in the national capital and enabled vast resources to be raised and expended in extravagant generosity around the globe. But did it create dependence in the receivers and even a form of ecclesiastical imperialism in the benefactors? Douglas responds to his own question by saying that it is difficult, 'but Episcopalians are a resurrection people who believe that in the death of old ways we are always given new

---

[14] Ibid., p. 311.   [15] Ibid., p. 328.

possibilities and opportunities to engage in God's global mission of reconciliation and redemption'.[16]

Clearly a church is called to put its trust in its crucified Lord and not in the temporary exigencies of the nation in which it is located. Seen as an experiment in forming an Anglican Church on the basis of its inherited Anglican tradition and in realistic engagement with its context, the experience of ECUSA is quite startling. It is marked by a range of experimental commitments pursued with vigour and remarkable energy. These experiments show a persistent attempt to engage with the social and cultural context in which God had placed them. That engagement sometimes looked a little like collusion and identification, yet on other occasions it was clearly costly, determined protest. Despite the dominance of the national church ideal for such a long period of its history there is a recurring note in the life of ECUSA of the self-generation of the gospel witnessed by the recurrent interest in the writings of Roland Allen.[17]

Throughout it has tended towards a comprehensive approach to the life of the church community. The history of the membership of the Domestic and Foreign Missionary Society testifies not just to the persistence of the theme of mission, but also to the vision of a unified and comprehensive institutional expression for the church community. This is in some contrast to England, where independent societies have been a much more significant channel for church life. In this respect it is notable that in the nation of private enterprise the voluntarist principle did not lead these Anglicans towards a minimalist church institutionality. Rather the church organisation tended to look more like an American business corporation. A corporation is after all an institution designed to provide representation, which is the underlying social value in a conciliarist ecclesiology. One notices as well the presence in this experimenting of a good deal of theological reflection in a pragmatic environment. The overwhelming impression, however, is of one hundred years of near coalescence with the culture, its institutions, its thinking and sense of its location in the world, through the vehicle of the national church ideal. One cannot but notice that at a time when the USA is the one world superpower, ECUSA is not able to play an analogous role, but on the contrary is facing significant internal division and conflict with some other churches in the Anglican Communion. Perhaps that demonstrates

---

[16] Ibid.

[17] R. Allen, *Missionary Methods: St Paul's or Ours?*, second edn (Grand Rapids, Mich.: W. B. Eerdmans, 1962).

that ECUSA is itself going through a profound transition in its role as a Christian witness in the United States, the outcome of which is as yet unclear.

AUSTRALIA: EMBEDDED REGIONALISM

When the British government decided for whatever complex reasons to establish a colony in Botany Bay, New South Wales, they in fact sent a governor with military powers under the rules of war with 600 convicts and 100 free settlers. The colony was to be run as a military operation and the governor had virtually supreme authority. He was given instructions to treat the natives kindly and to 'enforce a due observance of religion and good order among the inhabitants of the new settlement'.[18] The Revd Richard Johnson had been appointed as chaplain to do this. He was responsible to the governor and was commissioned to work with both the convicts and the settlers. It was not an easy task and eventually he returned to England dispirited.

Nonetheless Anglicans remained in the ascendancy in the colony and clergy of other churches were not permitted to officiate until 1810. In 1822 the Church of England in the colony was made an archdeaconry of the diocese of Madras which had just been constituted in connection with the renewal of the charter of the East India Company. The archdeacon had a monopoly over the official records of marriages and held a place of privilege in the civil ordering of the colony.

In 1836 the second archdeacon, W. G. Broughton, was appointed by Letters Patent of the crown to be bishop of Australia, but in the same year, by an act of the local governor, support for churches, previously restricted to Anglicans, was given to Presbyterians and Roman Catholics. Bishop Broughton objected strenuously but unsuccessfully to this proposal and when the principle was extended to education Broughton appeared before the Legislative Council to claim that the state had a moral and constitutional obligation to support the Church of England because it was the true religion and the best protector of liberty. His argument and the extensive petition he presented delayed but did not stop the process of pluralisation.

As bishop of Australia Broughton was responsible to the Archbishop of Canterbury as his metropolitan. That changed in 1847 when Australia was divided and Broughton was made bishop of Sydney and metropolitan to the

---

[18] Phillip's Instructions, 25 April 1787, in F. Watson and Australia Parliament Library Committee, *Historical Records of Australia* (Sydney: Library Committee of the Commonwealth Parliament, 1914), vol. I, p. 141.

new bishops as well as the bishop of New Zealand. Broughton attached a great deal of significance to this since he regarded the province and the office of metropolitan as marking the completion of the Anglican ecclesiastical system. Once a province had been established it could not be influenced or intruded upon by any other bishop, not even the Archbishop of Canterbury, a point of view taken by Archbishops of Canterbury in relation to the Pope. Within his province, however, he had more difficulty in establishing oversight. The young bishop of Melbourne, Charles Perry, was disposed to go his own way and was more inclined to refer to the Archbishop of Canterbury, with whom he had more theological sympathy, than Broughton.

In line with the development of elected legislatures in the separate colonies, diocesan synods were established in the 1850s along representative lines with strong lay membership. This development was easier in Victoria and South Australia where the diocese was co-terminous with the borders of the colony. The process was delayed in New South Wales because of the complications of having two dioceses, Sydney and Newcastle, in the same jurisdiction and also the interregnum between Broughton's death and the arrival of his successor. The various church constitutions were somewhat different, but in general they were all related for legal purposes to the way in which church trust property was to be used. There was certainly to be no thought of establishment in what was by this time a religiously plural political context.

The separate colonies had begun quite differently: New South Wales as a convict settlement, South Australia as a government-supported free settlement, and Victoria as an extra-legal private enterprise. After they had established responsible government the states continued to develop their own individuality and independence. This strong regionalism was reflected in the church. A General Synod was established in 1872 but its powers were obscure and limited. Nothing of any significance could intrude on diocesan autonomy. These dioceses represented themselves as the Church of England throughout, and this caused later difficulty in securing a constitution since it implied that their property remained in some sense entailed with the English church. Even though the Commonwealth of Australia was established in 1900, a national church constitution was not agreed until 1962, by which time Australia had become a much more obviously self-conscious national entity, while the national character of Anglicanism remained regional and highly pluralised.

This history has left its marks on Australian Anglicanism. It still suffers from the publicly disfavoured baggage of an English and establishment heritage. This image is fading but it still affects those who wish to criticise the church and also some in the church who imagine that they still have privileged positions in society because of their ecclesiastical office. The chaplaincy mentality still resides in the fabric of Australian Anglicanism.

For the first hundred years of European presence in Australia the Anglican Church did little for Australian Aborigines. There were some minor exceptions to this, but a Eurocentric and chaplaincy mindset left a disordered and unattractive record of Anglican activity. That record changed for the better in the second hundred years, though it was not until 2001 that indigenous Anglicans were given reserved places in the General Synod in recognition of their position in the nation and the church. There is now a Torres Straits Islander bishop and an Aboriginal bishop, both of whom have some degree of national responsibility, though technically they remain assistant bishops in the diocese of North Queensland. No indigenous Australian has yet been elected as a diocesan bishop despite the presence of large numbers of indigenous Anglicans in at least three of the twenty-four dioceses.

The priority of the diocesan structure of the church has been strongly entrenched in Australia. The historic regionalism of the colonies laid the foundation for this and then in the late nineteenth and early twentieth centuries church party groups gained ascendancy in particular dioceses. This overlay has consolidated the diocesan priority because the ecclesiastical and dispositional differences were able to entrench their position in the national church constitution which was formulated in the second half of the twentieth century. This has meant that the interest groups tend to be weak and not organised on a national basis. This history has also meant that there has been limited influence on Australian Anglicanism from the English missionary and interest group societies. At the end of the twentieth century the principal nationally cohering institutions were the emerging schools and welfare networks and the Mothers' Union.

Australian Anglicanism has been, and to a large degree remains, a church of the European settlers. It lags behind the developing multicultural diversity of the wider society which so markedly grew in the last quarter of the twentieth century. Its regionalism facilitates diversity between dioceses, though not so much within them. Its history and its loosely federal constitution make it very difficult to require conformity to any national models or decisions and even harder to gain internal agreement to respond to international movements or to react effectively or quickly to international requests.

In these respects it stands in polar contrast to the experience of ECUSA with its national church ideal. The first full-time officer of the General Synod was appointed only in 1972. The general secretary is the principal national executive officer of the church and the primate is one of the diocesan bishops, operating on a part-time basis with minimal constitutional authority. The present national church office is a small affair with a staff of approximately seven people. Even so this office organises the triennial meetings of the General Synod and coordinates the work of half a dozen commissions and a variety of other task forces on particular topics. It also organised two large national Anglican conferences in 1997 and 2002 with around 1,600 participants.

The juridical powers of the General Synod are very limited and any canon of the General Synod which concerns ritual ceremonial or the good order of the church in a diocese does not have force until it has been adopted by that diocese. The synod is essentially an arena of persuasion and a place of debate and argument. In that respect it has the potential to be very influential. It can also give permission for particular things to happen in a diocese, such as the ordination of women as priests, though that 1992 canon has not been adopted by all dioceses. However, the fact remains that Australian Anglicanism exists mainly outside the national synodical structure of the church. Whatever evaluation is made of this, it remains the reality which has come from the vigorous engagement with the social context in the nineteenth century.

The life of the church is focused on the dioceses and most of its assets are held there. There are several large metropolitan dioceses, but by far the largest and wealthiest is the diocese of Sydney. There are a growing number of church schools which are related to the diocese in different ways. Some fall under the control of the diocesan synod, but most are independent institutions with their Anglican identity secured by the terms of their own constitutions. There are many welfare organisations that are similarly structured. These two groups of institutions are currently the fastest-growing parts of the church, in no small measure due to government funding for the operations. They represent a huge investment of resources and energy by Anglicans. Because of their connections with government they sit exactly at the interface between church and state. Unlike in the United States, there is no separation of church and state in Australia. The constitution provides that the Federal government may not establish any particular church and so historically governments from the mid-twentieth century have entered into funding arrangements and tax benefits with churches on an equal non-discriminating basis.

Mission activity is mainly conducted through independent mission agencies in many ways similar to the schools and welfare bodies. From a structural point of view Australian Anglicanism is highly disaggregated. This often means that it is strong locally, but nationally and in the wider international arena it is less strong and less able to take initiatives.

How are we to explain such a different shape to the Anglican experiment in Australia and how does it relate to the host society? In the nineteenth century this loose federated style would have corresponded with the pattern on the continent. The population was small and distances were vast. Even at the beginning of the twenty-first century there were only twenty million people occupying the coastal fringe of an island the same size as the continental United States, or one-third the size of the total land mass of Africa. The British monoculture of nineteenth-century Australia meant that Anglicans could be seen in most places to be the natural form of Christianity and the mainly Irish Roman Catholic Church was something of a dissenting group. In the second half of the twentieth century that situation was reversed, to the confusion of both churches.

The truth is that such experimentation in church formation has been largely local in scope and from a historical point of view easily missed. The culture of the major cities is in large measure reflected in the style of the dioceses in those cities. Given the poor resources and the dispersed character of the church, there has been limited substantial theological work. Universities have almost all been state institutions and determinedly secular, with the result that in general terms theology was not taught in them until the last decades of the twentieth century. Also in the 1990s there was a veritable renaissance in theological activity and that in itself is already showing some signs of significant critical engagement with the host society and the Anglican heritage.

KENYA: INDEPENDENT NATIONAL AGENT

As far as can be discerned, Christians first came to what we know today as Kenya in the sixteenth century. They were mainly European traders on their way to India. Vasco da Gama was amongst these visitors. There was a Christian community of some six hundred near Mombasa. However, Anglican contact with Kenya came first in 1844 in the person of a Swiss-trained German, Johann Krapf, who had been sent to Abyssinia by CMS, was expelled, and arrived in Zanzibar on 7 January 1844 and settled in Mombasa. Two years later he was joined by Johannes Rebmann, and between them they sought to explore the hinterland. In doing so they had to establish relations with the local peoples and in the process discovered the different political structures that pertained. While most tribal groups such as the Nyika had a generally communitarian social structure, some, amongst them the Chagga, had a centralised system and a chief.

Krapf and Rebmann worked on their own and sought to develop local church communities. Krapf envisaged these communities as networked through mission stations with a string of such stations across Africa from east to west. Krapf returned to England in 1850 to gain support from CMS for this vision and to gain recruits for the work. He eventually left Africa in 1853.

From 1847 the British royal navy enforced the Hammerton treaty and stopped slave-trading ships in the Indian Ocean. Some of the African slaves from these ships were taken to Bombay and placed in the care of CMS agents there. Among them were three boys, Ishmael Semler, William Jones and George David. Semler and Jones were educated in India at the CMS Money school, set up to provide an education for future leaders in the church in India, and at what was then called the 'African Asylum' which came in due course to be seen as a place to train future church leaders who could return to Africa. In 1864 all three were sent back to Africa as missionaries. CMS was led at this time by Henry Venn and imbued with his theory of indigenised mission. European missionaries were to start churches, establish indigenous leaders and then move on. The churches were to be grown by locals and develop from the bottom up. The arrival of Semler, Jones and David with their families marked a significant step in this conception of the work of CMS and its success has permanently marked the character of Anglicanism in Kenya. 'It was this group of capable African men and women who provided the consistent leadership in the church and its extended communities . . . It was these African Christians, rather than the missionaries, who were the true "fathers" of the church.'[19]

From 1880 CMS collaborated with the Imperial British East Africa Company (IBEAC) in establishing stations into the interior. The company helped to settle difficulties in Frere Town where slaves who had taken refuge with CMS were claimed by their Arab owners. The company paid the owners compensation on the pretence that the slave had been lost, since it was against British law to purchase slaves. In 1885 the IBEAC was granted a licence for the area and thus Anglican churches found themselves dealing indirectly with British authority through the company. From this period the future of Africa was deeply affected by the failure of the Berlin Congress of 1885 and the subsequent scramble for Africa.

---

[19] Reed, *Pastors, Partners, and Paternalists*, p. 3.

More formal arrangements for British control came in 1895 with the proclamation of a British protectorate, and even more in 1921 when Kenya was made a crown colony. The age of empire, and direct rule and exploitation by expatriates, was set in train.

In 1884 a new bishopric of Eastern Equatorial Africa was established comprising modern Uganda, Tanzania and Kenya. This diocese was divided in 1897 and the diocese of Mombasa established, comprising essentially modern Kenya and central Tanganyika. A further division in 1927 led to the establishment of the diocese of Mombasa. Thus in the forty-year period at the turn of the century Kenya experienced a parallel set of changes in church and state. It moved from open trade to supported trade to exclusively licensed trade, and in turn became first a protectorate and then a directly ruled crown colony. The church felt the impact of wider church structures with the establishment of territorial dioceses and their steady division into more numerous entities.

A remarkable feature of the Kenya scene was that the archdeaconry and diocesan structures served separately the white settlers' chaplaincies and what was called the African Anglican Church. This indigenous/settler divide in church ministry was not changed until 1953. The story of twentieth-century development follows the well-worn path of colonisation and decolonisation. The Church of the Province of Kenya, with Festo Olang as the archbishop and metropolitan, was created in 1970, and it subsequently changed its name to the Anglican Church of Kenya.

Kenya thus represents a remarkably diverse and rich experience of frameworks within which Anglicans have flourished. That experience has left its marks. The long involvement of CMS has meant many things, but two are especially significant. First the evangelical style of Anglicanism represented by CMS remains the dominant strand amongst Anglicans in Kenya. Secondly, the mid-nineteenth-century commitment in CMS to the Henry Venn vision of an indigenous self-supporting church coincided with the emergence of effective African leaders from the very earliest times to create a highly Africanised Anglicanism. In clergy alone the point can be seen. In 1900 there were three African clergy and fourteen European clergy. In 1980 the figures were respectively 390 and 12.

The absence of a history of a quasi-establishment has meant that church–state relations for Kenyan Anglicans have been worked out in the political arena rather than the legal or constitutional one. The predominance of Kikuyu amongst Anglicans inevitably brought them into the political arena. From the beginning there was a strong emphasis on education and schools. These were started and run by the church and in postcolonial politics this investment and resource provided leverage for the involvement of church leaders in political debate.[20]

The public position of the church in Kenya has given church leaders a significant opportunity to engage with public issues. The former arch-bishop, David Gitari, conducted such a ministry over many years. He campaigned on land issues, the rigging of elections and corruption. His style was first expository, and later involved direct treatment of the social or political issue he had in mind. In October 1982 he preached in All Saints Cathedral in Nairobi following a failed coup two months earlier:

> The way of peace in Kenya, like it was in Judah, is justice and righteousness. As part of our self-examination after the sad events of August 1, Kenyans should investigate where there has been injustice and seek to do what is just. The way of peace is for the powerful to beware of temptation of accumulating wealth by unfair means. The way of peace is for justice not only to be done but to be seen to have been done. The way of peace is for Kanu elections to be conducted in a fair manner. It is not justice when only certain people have access to Kanu membership cards which they distribute only to those they are sure will elect them.[21]

This kind of direct preaching occasionally led to trouble, but more often than not it drew attention to public evil and fault very publicly and directly. It is very much in the Kenyan Anglican style to sustain an engagement with the structures of society through political activity.

Such experiments in church formation in Kenya reflect the very particular character of the founding of the church and the impact of African ministry. This form resulted in a much more direct engagement with the society than was even remotely possible for a European. It meant that the style of public engagement in politics displayed by David Gitari was much more possible in the new independent nation. The engagement with education stood as a witness against the failures of public authorities and to the social commitment of the church.

JAPAN: EXPERIMENTING IN NATIONAL CONTEXTUALISATION

It is difficult to know with certainty when the first Christians reached Japan. We know that Portuguese traders arrived in 1543 and a Christian mission followed in 1549 in the person of Francis Xavier. That Christian mission was to last for nearly a hundred years and included missionaries from the Jesuits,

---

[20] See G. Sabar-Friedman, *Church, State and Society in Kenya: From Mediation to Opposition, 1963–1993* (London: Frank Cass, 2002).
[21] D. Gitari, *In Season and out of Season. Sermons to a Nation* (Carlisle: Paternoster, 1996), p. 46.

Franciscans and Dominicans. Dutch traders were in Japan early in the seventeenth century. All that came to an end in 1639, with the Sakoku edict which ended all trade with the Portuguese and all Japanese traffic with Roman Catholic lands. The closure of Japan was complete in 1708 when the last Christian missionary was captured. He died in prison in 1714.

In a combination of military force and trade, Japan was opened to outsiders again after Commodore Perry of the US navy sailed into Tokyo Bay on 8 July 1853 and demanded a trade agreement. A formal treaty was agreed in 1859 which allowed foreigners to practise their own religion and soon afterwards three ECUSA missionaries were moved from China to Japan. They were able to do this because of ECUSA connections with the trading groups. They worked in educational and medical areas because the Japanese government would not allow proselytising, a rule which remained until 1871. English missionaries arrived in 1869 from CMS and in 1873 from SPG.

In 1866 the General Convention of ECUSA appointed Channing Moore as bishop of both China and Japan. The American work grew, especially with renewed resources after the end of the US civil war. An English bishop was sent to Japan in 1887 and found that the American work was much more extensive than the English. In the same year Channing Moore persuaded the two groups to meet and this resulted in the formation of the Nippon Sei Ko Kai (NSKK), the Holy Catholic Church of Japan. In keeping with the predominant position of ECUSA in Japan, the basis for the NSKK included the recent American-promoted Chicago–Lambeth Quadrilateral. Despite the independence of the NSKK the dioceses in the church remained episcopal mission districts of the English and American churches. In terms of superintendence and resources, ECUSA remained in a very influential position.

The mission concentrated on work among the educated middle classes and especially the samurai, who were the traditional warrior class, but more generally intellectuals and administrators. It also established medical and educational institutions. The combination of the ECUSA national church ideal thinking and the tradition of social and national service in the samurai tradition encouraged a sense of the NSKK having a role in the nation. With Japanese imperial expansion into Taiwan, Korea and Manchuria, this sentiment influenced the NSKK to send missionaries to these places, though they mostly directed their attentions to the Japanese expatriates. In 1897 the NSKK sent Minagawa Akio to Taiwan as a missionary priest: 'Anglicans, including leading clergymen like Imai Judo, were deeply committed to the idea that it was the calling of Japan to light up the hope of civilisation in East Asia . . . in which overseas missionary work would play a crucial role.'[22]

Anglicans, along with other Christian groups in Japan, had to come to terms with the tradition of Japanese national identity. The Anglican mission gained momentum and the NSKK came into existence and established itself during the Meiji period (1868–1912). During this period notions of filial piety shaped from a Confucian background, together with a Shinto tradition of loyalty to the emperor, combined in the development of a system of emperor worship: 'In theory the emperor is no more divine than his subjects, but for the people he is the embodiment of the divine, a combination of god, priest and ruler. In the name of the emperor Japan began the period of military adventure in Asia.'[23] The heritage of a national church ideal from ECUSA and the Japanese Anglican desire to play a loyal role in national life provides the basis for a vivid experiment in contextualisation. These commitments were tested when an Imperial Education Rescript in 1890 required that the official cult should be taught in all educational institutions. It is not surprising, therefore, that Japanese Anglicans had to confront not only the theological issue of how their faith related to the religious traditions of Japan, but also the practical and political issues that would arise from the religious character of their country. It has been a journey of much pain.

The twentieth century brought the ultimate test for the NSKK. The issues can be seen in the experience of the bishop of Tokyo, Paul Shinki Sasaki. In 1939 the government brought in a Religious Corporation Law which demanded that all Protestant groups should combine into one church to be called the Koydan (United Church). No account was taken of doctrinal differences or commitments. It was a politically motivated control measure. The NSKK tried unsuccessfully to gain an exemption. The country was at war in 1942 when the government refused to grant it, and as a result about a third of the NSKK joined the Koydan. Bishop Sasaki refused and he was imprisoned as a spy.

At the end of the war, after his release from prison, Sasaki became the rallying point for the restoration of the NSKK which most of the dioceses which had joined Koydan now rejoined. However, the post-war NSKK had within it a most profound division between those who had complied and

[22] A. H. Ion, 'The Cross under an Imperial Sun. Imperialism, Nationalism, and Japanese Christianity, 1895–1945', in M. R. Mullins (ed.), *Handbook of Christianity in Japan* (Leiden: Brill, 2003), p. 78.
[23] E. Tang, 'East Asia', in J. Parratt (ed.), *An Introduction to Third World Theologies* (Cambridge: Cambridge University Press, 2004), p. 94.

those who had not. This is not a new issue in Christian history. The early persecutions in the Roman Empire created exactly this sort of challenge, though here it involved not just individuals but the church itself. In 1946 Bishop Sasaki confessed the guilt of the church and its complicity in the imperial cult which contributed to the horrors of the war but he did so alone. Not until a younger generation began to come forward in the NSKK did a more critical approach to social evils in Japan emerge. It became clear that the more accepting attitude towards the Tenno and Shinto cult was not acceptable and that the church should distance itself from the public veneration of the war dead at the Yasakuni shrine. In 1996 the NSKK solemnly agreed to a public confession for its compromises and its failure to admit its guilt at the end of the war. The document was widely distributed not only in Asia but around the whole of the Anglican Communion.

From the point of view of mission and contextualisation which have been so much part and parcel of the theological tradition of Anglicanism the Japanese experience is striking. Here was a country to which the gospel came through missionaries from two countries, the USA and Great Britain. These Anglican churches each shared a commitment to the idea of a national church, England from the standpoint of a long history of establishment, the USA from a very recent commitment within the church but set within a national identity which was constitutionally diametrically opposed to the English tradition. Japan also had a national religious commitment and so all three national identities were at the formal level similar: they had a religious component. It is not surprising that these different loyalties should eventually come into conflict. The tragedy gradually developed because the Anglicans in Japan took steps to support aspects of the Japanese national idea. They collaborated with the imperial expansion and sought accommodations with the demands of the state which were cast in political contexts but with religious implications. They did all this to promote their faith and witness to the gospel, but they came in the end to regret those actions. The experience in England and the USA has been similar, though not as obviously tragic.

While Japan never became a colony of the USA, it was occupied by American-led forces after the Second World War and the initial entry of American missionaries was on the coat-tails of American trade. Furthermore, the NSKK adopted structures and theological bases which were primarily drawn from the experience of ECUSA. Taiwan remains attached to ECUSA as a constituent part of Province IX and sends delegates to the General Convention. In recent years a theological conversation on contextual theology has begun between Anglicans from Japan and Korea.[24] All of this goes to show that the gospel in its Anglican form will invariably prompt social engagement and the need for contextualisation and experimentation as to how that might work in practice. That experimentation is part of the strength of the tradition.

TIES THAT BIND SUCH DIVERSITY

The nineteenth-century colonial encounter between western countries and their mentalities and the culture and social impulses of those they colonised or conquered has not been either straightforward or easy. By and large initial contact came with a conviction of superiority. The ECUSA commitment to the American ideals of democracy in its Enlightenment formulation is not much different from the British 'civilising' commitment, nor from the attitude of Japanese missionaries during Japan's imperial expansion. However, reflection on the engagement with the religious heritage of new Christians in these lands often led to a greater appreciation of the complexity of this issue, and in numerous contexts notions of fulfilment were used to explain this relationship. This certainly happened in Japan. Hamish Ion refers to a leading Anglican layman, Imai Judo (1863–1919), who 'believed that *yamato damashii* [the spirit of Japan] only needed to be perfected by union with Christianity'. He goes on to say that it 'was a widely held Anglican view there was much good in Japanese culture, but that it needed to be perfected by Christianity'.[25] Similar themes can be found in the development of Australian indigenous rainbow theology which seeks to associate the dreaming of Aborigine cultures with the creation tradition of the Old Testament.

Even the examples just described are enough to show that the diversity in the Anglican Communion arises from attempts to engage with local contexts out of a common tradition. It would be too easy to say that the Americans are too American, the Australians too Australian, the Kenyans too Kenyan and the Japanese too Japanese, though there is probably some truth in this. Certainly the contextualisation of the Anglican tradition of faith creates, by its very commitment to the local and to engagement, a serious issue about the ongoing connection across local differences between Anglicans around the world.

---

[24] The Japan–Korea Association of Anglican Theology held its third assembly in February 2006 in Seoul under the theme of 'To be Anglicans in the Context of East Asia'.
[25] Ion, 'Cross under an Imperial Sun', p. 73.

Unfortunately it is actually more complicated than this. In general the agencies of connection which are discussed in the literature tend to refer to the official ecclesiastical structures of the provinces: synods or general conventions with synod officers such as primates and others. This is true of the four examples above. But within the national churches these arrangements often have quite different roles in comprehending the community of Anglicans in that country. The US example is much more comprehensive in this respect than those of Kenya or Japan which are themselves more comprehensive than that of Australia. In fact there are a myriad ways in which the Anglican community in these nations is held together and it would be a serious distortion to imagine that the ties that bind Anglicans together within the provinces are restricted to the synodical or ministerial structures.

The same is true in relations between Anglicans around the world. The story of the development of the Anglican Consultative Council (ACC) and the meetings of bishops at Lambeth and of the primates has been told elsewhere. But besides these so-called 'Instruments of Unity' there are numerous other connections of which only some are connected with the Anglican Communion organisation. The Inter-Anglican Standing Commission on Mission and Evangelism (IASCOME) included a list of some of these groups in their report to the ACC in 2005.[26] They note the Partners in Mission programme and the Decade of Evangelism as recent projects and also the Companion Dioceses links, whereby dioceses in different parts of the world establish a companion relationship. They then list seven formal networks recognised by the ACC and seven others that have simply come into existence. They also note some other ways by which connection is sustained around the world: day-to-day life, congregation life, movements of people, missionary bishops and new dioceses, responding to social need and injustice, pastoral chaplaincy among peoples who have moved, new mission movements and programmes, projects of sharing, regional and Communion-wide gatherings and mission links resulting from IASCOME meetings.

But this is not even the half of it. There is the vast explosion in communication and information via the worldwide web. The Anglican Communion website, so dramatically improved in recent years, is a fund of information and news, to say nothing of the websites of the provinces, dioceses, parishes and literally thousands of other groups and organisations. There is no

[26] J. Rosenthal and S. Erdey (eds.), *Living Communion. The Official Report of the 13th Meeting of the Anglican Consultative Council, Nottingham 2005* (New York: Church Publishing, 2006), pp. 191–380.

reference to the church media: *Anglican World* from the Anglican Communion Office and hundreds of church newspapers and magazines. To this should be added scores of Anglican book publishers and theological journals such as the *Anglican Theological Review* in North America, the *Journal of South African Theology,* or the international *Journal of Anglican Studies.* Then there are the welfare and support groups such as the Archbishop of Canterbury's Anglican Communion Fund, the inexhaustible generosity of English church societies and American trusts, along with many others from around the world. The list makes no mention of one of the best established and influential organisations in Anglicanism, the international Mothers' Union, which has 3.6 million members around the world, nor of the network and meetings of the provincial secretaries. There are literally thousands of ties that bind.

I do no criticise IASCOME for the scanty character of their list. It is just that the 'official' organisations to which inevitably we give attention do not comprehend all that is going on by any means. Furthermore, because of the character of the communities that Anglicanism creates which are local and relational, the official organisations have a vital but limited role. They exist to sustain a disciplined ministry of word and sacrament in communities which can become the agents of the mission of God, or, in the terms of the first IATDC report, can be witnesses to the kingdom of God. In the present disputes in worldwide Anglicanism it is therefore important to notice that the point at issue is the very specific organisational arrangements of the provinces. What happens in the local communities may turn out to be quite another matter.

PART II

The practices of mission

CHAPTER 4

Changing outlooks

We come now to the central part of this book. What kind of house was built and is being built on the foundations which we have just described? Is it gothic in shape, or perhaps English perpendicular, or, like St Albans Abbey in England, a bit of a mixture, as bits have been added on from time to time? Or is it the case that an architectural image is really not adequate to characterise this religious tradition as it sorties out into the third millennium? The reality is that this is a communion of people who are working out the terms of their Anglicanism in quite different ways.

The practices described here are those of a church tradition committed to the engagement of the faithful with their neighbours. That witness is set in the particular local context, in the concrete activities of living. It is also at the same time a life in the presence of God in Christ. The practices are thus practices of the mission of God.

There is a vast array of particular practices among Anglicans worldwide. The following are chosen because they are generally what are practised by most: they are the public element of the tradition. They are also those which occupy the attentions of worldwide Anglicans and emerge in relations between provinces. Inevitably this means they are more focused on the judicature of the church and the ministerial orders. That focus is unavoidable because of the role they play in the tradition. There is a certain irony in this since the tradition is most centrally about the daily lives of believers. It is about faith and witness. The practices described here serve that purpose. They are not ends, either in themselves or in any sense. They are in every sense penultimate. They are ministries – arrangements for serving others.

We begin with liturgical formation as a central grassroots practice which expresses and forms faith. That formation also leads naturally to a consideration of decision-making and power in the church. Ecclesial formation prompts engagement with the world of politics and with other traditions of faith. The public institutions of decision-making and power in the church precede the practices of the ministerial offices. These take up more space because they are currently the focus of such controversy.

A proper understanding of these practices must take account of the context in which they are pursued. It is also important to remember that the vast majority of Anglicans do not engage with church practices beyond their own parish or local community. The wider the circle, the fewer people are directly involved, and the type of people involved also changes. This can be seen when we open up the character of these horizons: parish/local/ diocese/national/global. We need to set that context out a little more fully as the framework of the practices to be described.

These frameworks draw attention to the particular form of catholicity represented in *world Anglicanism*. Catholicity is the character of a group of Christians or a church connected to something wider and more comprehensive. When Anglicans say in the creed they believe in the 'one holy and catholic church' they generally mean that they identify with the tradition of mainstream orthodox Christianity going back to the apostles and Jesus, and also to the wider spectrum of Christians in their own age who confess Christ. Thus the national constitutions of Anglican churches around the world tend to claim that they are part of this one holy, catholic and apostolic church. Within their own tradition there is a pilot scheme version of this catholicity. It is that comprehension of the differences and commitments of other Anglicans who confess the faith within the framework of this tradition. Any claim that world Anglicanism is the catholic church in any exclusive sense would contain a serious internal contradiction. 'Anglican catholic' in this sense would be an oxymoron, just as would 'Roman catholic'.[1]

There is a further complication about the sources we have for world Anglicanism. Those sources which speak directly about world Anglicanism derive mostly from the various world agencies: the records of the Lambeth Conferences and the Anglican Consultative Council are the most obvious sources. But these sources represent quite particular interests. Until very late in the twentieth century they have flowed from conferences of mainly white bishops with western American or British education and attitudes. At this international level this is what world Anglicanism was like, even though on the ground it was quite different. This only serves to highlight the changing character of world Anglicanism. It invites a question: how Anglican is world Anglicanism? It also highlights the problem in a religious tradition which privileges the local, or rather the region or the province, as the arena of faith.

[1]　See Kaye, 'Power, Order and Plurality'.

Is the very idea of world Anglicanism a mistaken category in this tradition and is the development of global institutions of an Anglican Communion a mistake? Or, in the terms of the current debate, how far should the experiment in global organisations go, and according to what principles? These are questions which can never be far away from our story, but for the moment we turn to the theme of outreach and mission.

EVANGELISM AND OUTREACH

When the preface to the 1662 Book of Common Prayer included a service for the baptism of those of riper years, thought not to have been necessary in the former book, it was justified on the grounds of the influence of Anabaptists, and also that it would 'always be useful for the baptising of natives in our plantations, and others converted to the faith'. Evangelistic outreach was not central in the thinking of either church or state or privateer. Nonetheless the missionary impulse came to the fore amongst Anglicans and it led to a most astonishing commitment to reach out to all corners of the earth with the gospel. That missionary heritage has left its mark on world Anglicanism for both good and ill. For a faith tradition that, in its formative English experience, itself claimed a priority in local enculturation and responsibility over many centuries, it found itself struggling to pursue the same principle in relation to the new local churches which its missionary labours had brought into being. Colonial and imperial ghosts still lurk in the shadows of contemporary world Anglicanism.

For many years there has been a commission or working group of the Anglican Communion concerned with mission and outreach. The evolution of these successive groups itself tells a story of the emergence of a notion of mission and outreach which points to the character of world Anglicanism. The Mission Issues and Strategy Advisory Group (MISAG-I 1981–6, MISAG-II 1987–92) was replaced by a commission called MISSIO (1994–9) and then by an Inter-Anglican Standing Commission on Mission and Evangelism (IASCOME, 2001–5). Their reports, together with the Decade of Evangelism and the South to South movement, provide a window into the key features of mission and outreach in world Anglicanism at the beginning of the twenty-first century.

EMERGING UNDERSTANDINGS OF MISSION

MISAG-II offered its report to the ACC in 1992. It set out a theological reflection on Christ's mission in contemporary contexts. This way of addressing the question already anticipated the theme of incarnation and enculturation which MISAG was commending. A theological pattern of God's creation–incarnation redemption provides the basis for dealing with mission issues. Because the whole world is the work of God's creative activity, there is a continuity between the created order and the redemptive incarnation of God in Jesus Christ. Furthermore, the church belongs to this creative activity as the community of this incarnate Lord. It is a community of redeemed sinners who have haltingly embarked on the adventure of being the agents of God in the world to carry out his creative and redemptive work.

Such a formulation of the situation of the church means that there is immediately present a basis for connection between the different particular conditions in which humans find themselves. There is no culture that can in principle be impervious to another. What is called for here is openness and dialogue in order to hear and understand, to find the attachment points. This applies not just to individuals but to communities and families. Thus the church's model for mission is incarnational and will be marked by self-emptying and humility.

MISAG deplores the way in which Christians have 'consciously or unconsciously, tried to impose their own cultural expressions of Christianity on people of other cultures. When this has happened, the cause of the Gospel has not flourished and Christianity has been "ghettoised", isolating Christians from their cultural roots.'[2] The report does not think Anglicans have taken the enculturation of worship seriously enough, nor given attention to the spiritual traditions within which people live. The report also suggests that the church needs to make more serious efforts to review its structures so that they are mission-productive. This report refers to the formation of the South to South consultation and sees it as the first of a number of such consultations between different groups.

The report offers ten principles of partnership for mission in the Anglican Communion. These are: local initiative, mutuality, responsible stewardship, interdependence, cross-fertilisation, integrity, transparency, solidarity, meeting together and acting ecumenically. These principles were adopted by the ACC. Taken together they represent an attempt to state a postcolonial understanding of the relationships between the various parts of the Anglican Communion. However, it is one thing to state some principles, it

[2] MISAG, *Towards Dynamic Mission: Renewing the Church for Mission. Final Report of Mission Issues and Strategy Advisory Group II (MISAG-II)*, (Anglican Consultative Council, 1992), available at: www.aco. org/mission/resources/documents/towardsdynamicmission.pdf (accessed 10 January 2007).

is quite another to see them actively in place and shaping the relationships between Anglicans and their institutions around the world.

MISSIO was the successor of MISAG. Its mandate contained seven points, of which four were practical, seeking to provide ideas and resources for member churches. Apart from the requirement to report to the ACC, these tasks did not lead very far. MISSIO collected ideas on strategies for mission and made them available through the ACO. The crux of their contribution, however, was to continue the trend in mission understanding which MISAG had begun. The striking development of the MISAG line of thought is the emphasis in MISSIO that mission implies transformation of the church. 'Transforming mission does not just lead people to experience Christ, but to experience him in such a way that their faith communities experience both renewal and transformation.'[3]

This orientation in their thinking moved them to seek a revision of the five marks of mission which had been developed by the ACC between 1984 and 1990. Those five marks were:
• to proclaim the good news of the kingdom
• to teach, baptise and nurture new believers
• to respond to human need by loving service
• to seek to transform unjust structures of society
• to strive to safeguard the integrity of creation and sustain and renew the life of the earth.

MISSIO was understandably concerned about the linear thinking that these points represented. They urged a revision that would incorporate a notion of the transforming mission of God, a sense that mission defines the nature of the church, and the great diversity of models, strategies and practices which such a notion of the universal mission of God in creation will produce. Faithfulness produces diversity. The MISAG/MISSIO approach looks for the transformation of the church: the character of its relationships, the shape and operation of its institutions and the orientation of its whole life. That is why MISSIO expressed concern about church growth which was principally thought of in terms of numbers. MISSIO focused on the quality of church life and it is not surprising that it was concerned that the Partners in Mission programme had somehow turned into simply an exchange of resources between church agencies. The notion of mutual belonging had been lost in this and they wanted to reconfigure the process in terms of companionship.

---

[3] MISSIO, E. Johnson and J. Clark, *Anglicans in Mission: A Transforming Journey* (London: SPCK, 2000), p. 15.

There are crucial issues at stake here which go to the heart of the nature of the Anglican form of Christianity. If it is the case that Anglicanism is about a way of knowing God in Christ which is determinedly incarnational in its redemption of the human condition, then that implies a more open and textured knowledge of God than is expressed in MISAG's five points. If the tradition is about a notion of divine providence in the world then the creative elements in the MISAG/MISSIO conceptions have a lot to do not just with a theology of mission but with the shape of an Anglican understanding of the church. Such a church is more readily seen as a community of people in a particular place and time belonging to a tradition of community stretching over generations to the apostles, and at the same time linked with communities in other places who share that tradition of history and faith.

These themes are continued in the new Inter-Anglican Standing Commission on Mission and Evangelism (IASCOME) which ran from 2001 to 2005. IASCOME saw itself as the 'heir to a distinguished history'.[4] In its report it returned to a number of the themes of MISSIO and MISAG. It continued the quest for more relational images to describe the connections around the Communion and canvassed images such as affection, companionship, brother–sister relationships and friendship. In this context it proposed a covenant in mission for the Anglican Communion. There is a brief note of eschatology in the report with an acknowledgement of the pilgrim character of the church. It strongly brings to the surface the critical issue of the colonial baggage of worldwide Anglicanism: 'There is a need for the communion to address the reality of the colonial and post-colonial past, and the present neo-colonial context, of Anglican mission.'[5]

The report also explores ways in which mission relationships are formed and fostered around the world. The exiting linkages through Partners in Mission and Companion Diocese Links are reviewed, but then it goes on to detail the growing range of networks by which people keep in contact. Not all of these are official networks of the ACC.

These themes of connection and mutuality are continued through the consideration of evangelism, responding to need and theological education. The report claims on two occasions that the Anglican Communion 'grew out of a vision for world mission'.[6] In support they refer to Stephen Neill's work *Anglicanism* One may be forgiven for doubting this claim. English Anglicanism was reluctant in the extreme to envisage such a mission and only late in the empire period did such language come to the fore. Furthermore, it

---

[4] The report of the commission is printed in Rosenthal and Erdey, *Living Communion*, p. 333.
[5] Ibid., p. 230.   [6] Ibid., pp. 224, 323.

overlooks the local mission activities which are often marginalised in the history of the spread of Anglicanism. This historical bias is now gradually being rectified.[7] It is not so much that Anglicanism had some kind of vision of world mission embedded in its pedigree so that it spread throughout the world. Rather it is more the case that the essential dynamic in Anglicanism to live out in the particular the meaning of the catholic faith of Christianity prompted such sharing of the faith in word and deed. That is what English Anglicanism attempted to do throughout its chequered history. That is what others who have come into this tradition have tried to do elsewhere.

The mission commissions of the Anglican Communion have sponsored two initiatives which have shaped contemporary worldwide Anglicanism: the Decade of Evangelism and the South to South encounters. The Decade of Evangelism had a profound effect in some African churches, but in other places it passed by without great impact.[8] The South to South encounters began as mission collaborations and have retained something of that direction, though from 1998 they have taken an active role in the debates in the Anglican Communion about sexuality.

---

[7] See, for example, Reed, *Pastors, Partners, and Paternalists*; and Ward, *A History of Global Anglicanism*.

[8] See C. C. Okorocha, *The Cutting Edge of Mission: The Report of G-Code 2000, Global Conference on Dynamic Evangelism Beyond 2000: Mid-Point Review of the Decade of Evangelism from 4 to 9 September 1995 at the Kanunga Conference Center Hendersonville, North Carolina, USA* (London: Anglican Communion, 1996).

CHAPTER 5

Liturgical formation

From the very earliest times Anglicans have been accustomed to ordered prayer and the reading of scripture as part of the church experience. Even when the liturgy was found only within monasteries and convents, or in the houses of bishops and clergy, or in churches which were not much attended, it was still part of the furniture of the Anglican experience. There is a profound truth at work in this. Prayer, scripture reading and worship both express the faith and devotion of the Anglican believer, and also shape the development and character of that belief. Persistent praying shapes behaviour and nurtures faith. The Latin tag *lex orandi lex credendi* ('law of praying – law of believing') has a long history in Christianity and especially in Anglicanism. The tag can be read both ways: how we pray shapes what we believe, or what we believe shapes how we pray.

Both these senses have been important in the history of the Anglican tradition, and are becoming increasingly crucial in contemporary experience. The Tudor imperial crown in England defined the faith of the nation by means of state-enforced liturgical uniformity. But that was nearly five hundred years ago, and a veritable torrent has flowed under the bridge since then. While there is a great deal of commonality, strict liturgical uniformity no longer exists between Anglican churches around the world. The question that arises in the context of the *lex orandi* principle is whether there is any effective, recognisable commonality in the liturgical experience of Anglicans in different parts of the world.

Anglicans inherited the broad western tradition of liturgy, and for centuries they were shaped by the liturgical practice of western Europe. Within that tradition there was some variety, even given some attempts to regularise it. The cathedral practice tended to set the tone and style of the parishes in a diocese. In England the fifteenth-century pattern of liturgy was varied, and related to the pattern in the diocese and in some cases to the province.

The sixteenth century opened with two large-scale forces of change. First, printing made it possible to reproduce liturgical texts accurately and in great numbers, so that it was possible to have some notion of uniformity over a wider area. Second, the growth of national sentiment and national structures which marked the collapse of the Holy Roman Empire and the decline of feudalism meant that centralising forces on a national scale were propelling England into a modern state.

The reform legislation of Henry VIII in the period 1532–4 repatriated all political authority from the papacy, which included all church matters in England. After Henry died and Edward VI became king at the age of nine, government was effectively in the hands of the Council, especially the Lord Protector, Edward Seymour, and the Archbishop of Canterbury, Thomas Cranmer. These people carried through a major revolution in worship in Anglicanism in an attempt to effect a religious reformation along Protestant lines. Their central ambition was to enable the people to hear and live by the word of God, which meant for them that both the Bible and the liturgy were to be in English.

The Royal Proclamation for the 1548 Order of the Communion made it clear that the issue was not just liturgy and liturgical reform, but also political conformity. As in the Homilies, which were first published in 1547, there is a strong note of conformity and political obedience. Nonetheless, the Act of Uniformity that came with the new liturgy made the programme all the more revolutionary from the standpoint of church practice. The programme required 'high abilities centrally, dumb subservience in the local clergy, and passive receptivity by the consumers'.[1] The 1548 liturgical text was a moderate revision of the old order of the diocese of Salisbury, but that was to change with later prayer books. The programme ran until 1552, perhaps driven by the knowledge that the Roman Catholic Mary would succeed Edward to the throne and the changes had to be well embedded before that happened. In the event Mary reversed all of these changes and they were in due course re-established by Elizabeth in 1559. Elizabeth allowed the modest local element of a song at the beginning and end of morning or evening prayer.

This was the prayer book adopted in the Anglican colonies in North America in the sixteenth and seventeenth centuries. The Commonwealth period in the seventeenth century changed all of this for a short time, but after the Restoration the 1662 Book of Common Prayer maintained the general tightness and is the classic text referred to by Anglicanism around the world. One of the curious legacies of this is the fact that many of the national and provincial church constitutions around the Anglican Communion

---

[1] C. Buchanan, 'Liturgical Uniformity', *Journal of Anglican Studies* 2.2 (2004), pp. 41–57.

commit those churches to the doctrine and principles of the highly political 1662 book.

Compulsory uniformity, however, could not be sustained, in regard to either liturgy or the Anglican monopoly on state religion. The evangelical revival under the Wesleys in the eighteenth century used hymns to create a whole new world of religious experience. The Catholic revival in the nineteenth century introduced styles of dress and choreography borrowed in large measure from the Roman tradition. The various parties in Anglicanism in this period innovated from the Reformation standard by using additional material in the service and by covert use of unauthorised material outside the regular services. Despite court cases, these trends persisted, in large measure because neither the means nor the will existed to contain church liturgy within the sixteenth-century limits. Therefore, while at the height of the extension of imperial Anglicanism strict liturgical uniformity was dissipating for reasons of practicality and religious revival in England, elsewhere other forces were working to make the definition of Anglican identity by conformity to a strict liturgical uniformity unworkable.

The spread of Anglicanism around the world introduced another complicating factor in the shape of Anglican worship. From the very earliest times enculturation was a potent element in Anglicanism. The Celtic mission took on many of the Celtic colourations of the existing religious environment. That is also the style commended to Augustine by Pope Gregory the Great. Bede records a letter sent by Augustine to Gregory in which he reports on the situation in England. This long and detailed letter contains this remarkably practical and catholic passage:

> Augustine's second question: 'Since we hold the same Faith, why do customs vary in different Churches? Why, for instance, does the method of saying the mass differ in the holy Roman church and in the Churches of Gaul?'
>
> Pope Gregory's reply: 'You know, my brother, you are familiar with the usage of the Roman Church, in which you were brought up. But if you have found customs, whether in the Church of Rome or of Gaul or any other that may be more acceptable to God, I wish you to make a careful selection of them, and teach the Church of the English, which is still young in the faith, whatever you have been able to learn with profit from the various Churches. For things should not be loved for the sake of places but places for the sake of good things. Therefore select from each of the Churches whatever things are devout, religious, and right; and when you have bound them, as it were, into a Sheaf, let the English grow accustomed to it.'[2]

---

[2] Bede EH, I,27, p. 73.

Anglicans imbibed this eclectic enculturating habit. Within the Anglican family the Scottish Episcopal Church had developed its own prayer book, and it represented a stream of somewhat more catholic tendencies than those which persisted in the English book. The impulse to enculturation expressed itself also in translation, first of the Bible and then of the prayer book. But the translation of such texts is not entirely straightforward. Translating involves not just the transposition of words from one language to another, but the transformation of the way in which ideas and meanings are expressed. Even the transposition into more modern English in similar societies can be a very ambiguous exercise, as can be seen by the arguments which surrounded the multitude of translations of the Bible in the second half of the twentieth century.

From the very earliest times, when official Anglican prayer books have been produced translations have been made. Even before the beginning of the twentieth century the list of translations was extensive.[3] The English prayer book of 1559 had a Latin translation the following year and a Greek translation in 1569. Early translations were made into the languages of the British Isles – Welsh (1567), Manx (1765), Irish (1608) and Gaelic (1794) – and French was provided in 1553 for the king's subjects in Calais and the Channel Islands. Translations into European languages followed: Spanish (1617), Portuguese (1695), Italian (1685), Dutch (1710), German (1704). A translation was produced in Arabic (1672), and also Turkish, Armenian, Amharic, Persian and Pashtu. In the Indian subcontinent translations appeared in Bengali, Hindi, Marathi and Urdu in the north, and Malayaman, Tamil and Telugu in the south, as well as Sinhalese in Sri Lanka and Burmese and Karen in Burma. In all, up to the end of the nineteenth century, the Book of Common Prayer of the Church of England was translated into 198 different languages.

Different prayer books were in use in China at the commencement of the twentieth century, in large measure because dioceses used the prayer book of the originating country of the missionaries who served there: that is, England, Canada and the United States. In 1921 the General Synod of the Anglican Church in China, the Chung Kua Sheng Kung Hui, adopted a principle of prayer book revision to give local expression, and in 1931 approved the preparation of vernacular versions of morning and evening

---

[3] For details here I am indebted to the survey in W. K. L. Clarke, *Liturgy and Worship: A Companion to the Prayer Books of the Anglican Communion* (London: SPCK, 1932). See also the encyclopedic C. C. Hefling and C. L. Shattuck (eds.), *The Oxford Guide to the Book of Common Prayer: A Worldwide Survey* (Oxford: Oxford University Press, 2006), especially part 3.

prayer. In Japan the Nippon Sei Ko Kai agreed to a prayer book in 1871 which was published in 1891.

In Africa there was considerable diversity in translations from the beginning. This was due not just to differing cultural and linguistic contexts, but also to the different styles and schools from which different parts of Africa were evangelised. Even within the different traditions diversity was to be found. The model of the 1549 prayer book was widely use in Central Africa and in some instances material was borrowed from Roman Catholic sources. The Church Missionary Society produced many translations which in the main followed the 1662 Book of Common Prayer. In the United States a Mohawk Prayer Book was published in 1715 and a Cree version was produced in Canada. In his extensive bibliography covering the period 1549–1999, David Griffiths lists 4,810 editions, of which 1,200 are translations. Of the 3,610 English editions 2,200 were published between 1801 and 1999.[4]

The publication of the Canadian prayer book into Japanese in 1967 reflects a desire seen in the earliest translations of the Book of Common Prayer in England to provide for linguistic minorities within the church. The American prayer book has been much more extensively translated than the Canadian, though nothing like as many times as the English Book of Common Prayer. Of the fifteen languages into which the American prayer book has been translated, nine have also had English Book of Common Prayer translations. Only three appear to have been made for overseas mission work (Grebo in West Africa in 1867, Chinese in 1880 and Vietnamese in 1961). Four appear to have been done for indigenous Native Americans and three for linguistic minority groups, while Spanish and Portuguese served both local linguistic minorities and mission enterprises in Latin America. The Book of Common Prayer had been translated into a number of Native American languages prior to the War of Independence from Britain. The Australian prayer book of 1992 has been translated in part into Creole for indigenous Australians and the 1992 New Zealand prayer book is strikingly set out in both Maori and English.

David Griffiths suggests three reasons for this massive translation enterprise: to meet the needs of linguistic minorities, to commend Anglican worship to other churches and most of all to 'further overseas mission'.[5]

[4] D. N. Griffiths, *The Bibliography of the Book of Common Prayer, 1549–1999* (New Castle, Del.: Oak Knoll Press, 2002).
[5] Ibid., p. 19.

Much of this took place before the great flood of de-colonisation swept across the globe in the second half of the twentieth century. The SPCK had produced something of the order of 150 translations of the prayer book. These publications were all sanctioned by the Archbishop of Canterbury only after a substantial schedule of questions about the publication had been answered. That practice ended in 1920 on the instructions of Archbishop Davidson. The same year the Lambeth Conference resolved:

> While maintaining the authority of the Book of Common Prayer as the Anglican standard of doctrine and practice, we consider that liturgical uniformity should not be regarded as a necessity throughout the Churches of the Anglican Communion. The conditions of the church in many parts of the mission field render inapplicable the retention of that Book as the once fixed liturgical model.[6]

The principle of enculturation, upon which the Anglican tradition had emerged in England, now required, in a new situation, a priority of local over general uniformity. The fate of the prayer book, so firmly insisted on in England in the sixteenth century by a state imposition of complete uniformity, demonstrates that the particularities of that English legislated uniformity were in fact just part of the changing context in which Anglicanism acculturated itself. That process of enculturation has continued with unceasing vigour through the twentieth century, accelerated by the independence movements of the postcolonial era, by the coming of communist governments in China and North Korea, and by the impact of the Second World War on Japan and its empire.

In 1920 the Lambeth Conference asked the Archbishop of Canterbury to appoint a committee of liturgical scholars to advise dioceses about liturgical reform and change, but ten years later the conference saw no need to re-appoint this group. This balance between local option and general pattern continued relatively undiscussed in the Lambeth Conferences throughout the twentieth century. The 1988 conference repeated the same sentiments as the 1920 conference:

> This conference resolves that each province should be free, subject to essential universal Anglican norms of worship, and to a valuing of traditional liturgical materials, to seek that expression of worship which is appropriate to its Christian people in their cultural context.[7]

---

[6] LC.1920,36.   [7] LC.1920,47.

In 1998 the tone had changed. Other issues such as gender relations and the recognition of same-sex unions dominated the discussions and there was thus more interest in keeping things together. That instinct was reflected in the resolutions on liturgy. The conference called for the appointment of a Liturgical Coordinator for the Communion and commended the work of the International Anglican Liturgical Consultations (IALC) in providing liaison and collaboration between provinces in the Communion. The work of those consultations has been a very important aspect of the liturgical life in the Anglican Communion. The IALC was recognised as a network of the Communion by the ACC and now functions as an official liaison group on liturgy for the Communion. The themes of their consultations have been published and they provide a litmus test of the state of Anglican liturgical thinking and development around the world. The consultations have addressed issues such as the participation of children in communion, historically inhibited by rubrics in the 1662 Book of Common Prayer, but now widely practised.

In 1991 the consultation developed a series of recommendations on initiation. Moves to allow children to participate in communion, and the re-casting of the notion of church membership which that entailed, meant that rites of initiation had to bear significant weight in setting out the character of the church and of the Christian way. The recommendations highlight these challenges and point to the direction in which Anglicans were moving as they reached out at the end of colonialism and its establishment memories:

1. that since baptism is the sacramental sign of full incorporation into the church, all baptized persons be admitted to communion;
2. that provincial baptismal rites be reviewed to the end that such texts explicitly affirm the communion of the newly baptized and that only one rite be authorized for the baptism whether of adults or infants so that no essential distinction be made between persons on basis of age;
3. that in the celebration of baptism the vivid use of liturgical signs e.g. the practice of immersion and the copious use of water be encouraged;
4. that the celebration of baptism constitute a normal part of an episcopal visit;
5. that anyone admitted to communion in any part of the Anglican Communion be acknowledged as a communicant in every part of the Anglican Communion and not be denied communion on the basis of age or lack of confirmation;
6. that the Constitution and Canons of each Province be revised in accordance with the above recommendations; and that the constitution and Canons be amended wherever they imply the necessity of confirmation for full church membership;

7. that each Province clearly affirm that confirmation is not a rite of admission to communion, a principle affirmed by the bishops at Lambeth in 1968;
8. that the general communion of all the baptized assume a significant place in all ecumenical dialogues in which Anglicans are engaged.[8]

These recommendations point to a number of changes in community understanding. The baptism of infants was previously undertaken on the basis that they were not able to answer for themselves because they were infants. Baptism thus implied some sense of volitional and articulated response which was yet to come in confirmation, which would mark full incorporation into church membership and participation in Holy Communion. The new model changed this. Baptism was to replace confirmation as the episcopal rite. The role of the bishop in drawing attention to the wider fellowship of the church, its catholicity, is thus attached to baptism, even though baptised infants can have no role in the life of the wider church until they are confirmed.

The work done on church order in liturgy also highlighted the issue of who leads, or who presides. On the one hand, the universal trend for the last fifty years has been for greater participation in the liturgy by lay people. This is in sharp contrast with the 1662 Book of Common Prayer where the lay people are almost entirely passive recipients of the liturgy. If wholesale participation by lay people is a good thing, then what is the role of the clergy, and is there anything the laity may not do? Why in this circumstance should the laity not celebrate, or preside at the Eucharist? That indeed has been a contentious issue in a number of dioceses around the world, most notably in the diocese of Sydney, Australia. The 1995 Liturgical Consultation held in Dublin even went so far as to say that the assembly is the celebrant of the Eucharist:

In, through, and with Christ, the assembly is the celebrant of the Eucharist. Among other tasks it is appropriate for lay persons to play their part in proclaiming the word, leading the prayers of the people, and distributing communion. The liturgical functions of the ordained arise out of pastoral responsibility. Separating liturgical function and pastoral oversight tends to reduce liturgical presidency to an isolated ritual function.[9]

The advocates of lay presidency say much the same thing, but add two other arguments: first that it was a Reformation principle that word and

---

[8] Quoted in P. Gibson, *International Anglican Liturgical Consultations. A Review* (2000), available at: www.aco.org/liturgy/docs/ialcreview.html (accessed 20 January 2006), p. 2.
[9] Ibid., p. 6.

sacrament went together and that therefore if laity are allowed to preach the word they should not be inhibited from celebrating the Eucharist; second, given the structure of parish ministry, the incumbent who has the pastoral responsibility can reasonably delegate the role of celebrating the Eucharist to appropriate people. The other side of the argument is that presiding at the Eucharist is traditionally the responsibility of the bishop and that the ordained are his representatives by ordination and licensing to the parish. In this way catholic order is maintained in two important dimensions. Catholicity is exemplified and promoted by the bishop, and the bishop also, as part of the historic episcopate, represents an institutional connection with the apostolic church. Sydney sought support for lay presidency from evangelical bishops in Asia and Africa without success and has shelved proposals for lay presidency in the light of the need for combined unity in the more heated, and for them more important, arguments about gender roles.

Liturgy has a forming effect which can be seen in the explicitly educational orientation of the catechism. The ordination of a priest in Anglicanism has been shaped by the belief that the congregation of people should be informed, wise and educated in the faith. So the ordinand in the older service books is told to bring the congregation to 'that understanding in the faith and knowledge of God, and to that maturity in Christ, which leaves no place among you for error in religion or viciousness in life'. Modern liturgies have softened the language but not removed the sentiment.

Anglican liturgies have reflected this notion of an educated membership. The liturgies not only enable the worship of God in prayer and singing, but also, as part of that same worship, edify the people. The services must be in the common language and are full of scripture. They contain significant theological material and represent the belief of the church as well as shaping the belief of the participants. Liturgy has thus been at the centre of educational formation in Anglicanism.

At the time of the Reformation this educational aspect of church life was given specific expression in catechisms. In the period from the sixteenth century to the eighteenth a vast array of catechisms were in circulation.[10] Some enjoyed a form of official status, but by its clear official status and availability the prayer book catechism was pre-eminent. Many of the others were elaborations and explanations of this catechism. In 1549 the catechism was in a section entitled 'a Catechism, that is to say, an instruction to be

---

[10] I. M. Green, *The Christian's ABC: Catechism and Catechizing in England c.1530–1740* (Oxford: Clarendon Press, 1996).

learned of every child, before he be brought to be confirmed of the bishop'. That link with confirmation as a rite of entry into full adult membership of the church has been retained in many subsequent prayer book revisions. The 1959 prayer book for Canada places the catechism between baptism and confirmation and retains the same style of rubrics as the 1549 prayer book. The 2002 Modern Services Book of the Anglican Church of Kenya retains the connection, though it has slightly revised the contents. The 1979 prayer book of the USA included an extensive revision of the catechism called an 'Outline of the Faith', though it was related to baptism rather than confirmation.

Confirmation was seldom enforced in the sixteenth and seventeenth centuries in England and was simply not available in the United States until the establishment of an episcopate in 1785 after the War of Independence. In other colonies there was no bishop until later in the nineteenth century. However, in England, the USA and the colonies, catechising still took place and usually in public in the church. In this situation catechising was the process of entering into adult membership in the church.[11] During the course of the eighteenth and nineteenth centuries confirmation became more central in the life of the church.

The degree to which liturgy has become a focus for other broader issues amongst Anglicans worldwide can be seen in discussions of the enculturation of liturgical practice. At one level it would be better to speak of contextualisation of the gospel, since that suggests that the process we are concerned with here is a matter of interaction of the gospel with ordinary human life as experienced within a particular culture. However, that gospel interaction never comes without a history. The third International Anglican Liturgical Consultation in 1989 began its 'York Statement' with some first principles in the following terms: 'The incarnation is God's self-inculturation in this world in a particular cultural context. Jesus' ministry on earth includes both the acceptance of that particular culture, and also a confrontation of elements in that culture.'[12] That interface has proved to be very difficult to negotiate in the history of Christianity, and there have been many blind alleys and self-deceptions scattered along the way.

The Anglican experience is complicated by the fact that its cross-cultural expansion has often been associated with imperial expansion, mostly of

---

[11] See F. Turrell James, 'Catechisms', in Hefling and Shattuck, *The Oxford Guide to the Book of Common Prayer*, p. 503.
[12] D. Holeton, *Liturgical Inculturation in the Anglican Communion: Including the York Statement 'Down to Earth Worship'* (Bramcote, Nottingham: Grove Books, 1990), p. 9.

Great Britain, but also of other nations such as the USA and Japan. In the second half of the twentieth century Anglicans were inevitably caught up in the dynamics of the de-colonisation process and, at the opening of the twenty-first century, the ongoing imperial influence of the western world and the contemporary United States hegemony. A Brazilian theologian who was a consultant at the Lambeth Conferences in 1988 and 1998 highlighted the dilemma when he reviewed the style of worship at the 1998 conference. Each province was invited to take a Eucharist in its own way during the conference. He was overwhelmed by the sameness of it all. The services were all bound by the Book of Common Prayer, they depended on the spoken word and were heavily clerical, and the homilies were 'traditional, and most of the time fundamentalist and moralist'[13] and deeply male-oriented. On the other hand, an English bishop who was responsible for organising aspects of the services saw the variety to be so great as to signify the end of any sense of uniformity or commonality.[14] The different perceptions highlight the challenge of mutuality and commonality across substantial cultural differences.

While these broader questions are crucial to the overall picture of Anglicanism worldwide and to any critical analysis of the present state of Anglicanism, we should not forget that most Anglicans experience liturgy in fairly restricted terms in relation to the ordinary Sunday services and to the pastoral services of baptism, confirmation, marriage and burial. While there is immense variety of style in the presentation of the ordinary Sunday service, some things are fairly common. There is a continuing extensive use of biblical material, not just in the lessons, but also in the canticles and songs used and the set prayers and psalms. Cranmer's ambition for services soaked with the Word no longer survives universally and hardly anywhere in his precise form. But it remains as the general tone and style of Anglicanism. Anglicans in the twenty-first century are accustomed to high levels of participation in the service to a degree which could not have been dreamed of by their predecessors and that dramatic change largely took place in the last half of the twentieth century.

Besides the liturgical texts which are contained in the prayer books, a host of other things influence the character of the experience of worship for Anglicans: architecture, dress, choreography, participation, language and

---

[13] J. Marschin, 'Culture, Spirit and Worship', in I. T. Douglas and K. Pui-Lan (eds.), *Beyond Colonial Anglicanism: The Anglican Communion in the Twenty-First Century* (New York: Church Publishing, 2001), pp. 329f.
[14] Buchanan, 'Liturgical Uniformity'.

music all shape the quality and effect of the worship of Anglicans. It is remarkable how much liturgical dress is a matter of fashion. Dress for celebrants moves with customs, traditions and changing tastes about elaborate or informal styles. It adds to the drama of the liturgy and enables it to be apprehended through a variety of senses. Many of the vestments of the medieval period were discontinued at the time of the English Reformation on the grounds that they signified doctrines that were no longer approved of in the light of Reformation theology. During the twentieth century this approach to liturgical dress was officially abandoned in England, and in general people place on liturgical dress such meaning as they wish.

It is impossible to understand the Anglican habit of life without a central focus on liturgy and liturgical formation. That formation of the faith of Anglicans takes place in order that they will reach 'that understanding in the faith and knowledge of God, and to that maturity in Christ, which leaves no place among you for error in religion or viciousness in life'. The vernacular language of Anglican liturgy, its biblical and theological content and its life and faith-forming purpose make it clear that Anglican liturgy is a practice of mission.

CHAPTER 6

Patterns of engagement – political

Anglicans around the world live in very different political situations. Political engagement for Christians and the institutional church in Japan or Palestine or the Sudan means something very different from political engagement in New Zealand or Canada. How can Christians think they have a natural and accepted place in the world of politics in nations where another religion is either the religion of the state or is the majority and controlling religion in the society? How can a Christian in a committedly secular state sustain an engagement with that secularity in terms of their own religious faith? For the greater part of their history Anglicans have lived in a Christian country where such questions have not arisen and indeed could hardly have been formulated. It was just the most natural thing that the Christian ruler should have had the counsel of church leaders and that they should have exercised some power in the ordering of a Christian society.

Throughout their history Anglicans have experienced a wide variety of church–state relations and hence a variety of ways in which it has been possible to engage with the political process. The privilege of the Anglo-Saxon experience was very different from the experience of Tudor centralism. When Anglicans moved out of England they encountered different patterns of political life. Not surprisingly the republican instincts of the United States of America reacted against many of the monarchical and traditional elements which they had overthrown in their War of Independence. Their constitution provided no authority for the government to establish religion at all. From the beginning this was to be a secular state. Similar reactions can be seen in other colonies in the twentieth century when they obtained their independence from Britain. Within a decade of independence Uganda moved towards a secular state. In the nineteenth century some former colonies took a mediating position, and provided for forms of establishment and entanglement, but not for any particular religion. Anglicans were to be among a number with whom the state would deal.

86

Some Anglicans lived in nations that had never been colonies of the British and where they were inevitably a minority engaging with the political process on terms shaped by another religion.

All of this was complicated by the fact that twentieth-century de-colonisation took place at the same time as the world was divided between the two worlds of communism and capitalism. This was a conflict between a theory of spontaneity and of control, between individualism and communalism, between centralised and decentralised authority. The conflict between the superpowers and their allies left many of the countries coming to independence in a Third World alienated from the economic advances of the second half of the twentieth century and often surrogates in the fight between the two worlds.[1]

This Third World, especially in Africa, was extraordinarily diverse. In speaking of African church–state relations it can be very misleading to generalise beyond one country. Each had it own particular experience of Christian missionary activity, each had its own internal cultural and political traditions and each came to independence in different circumstances and with different resources and possibilities.[2] This varied historical experience of Anglicans is visible in the contemporary experience of world Anglicanism.

Church engagement with the political process is not restricted to church–state relations. Anglicans have engaged with the political process in a variety of ways which have not necessarily involved the institutional church or the official leaders of the church. Many church leaders found that they had a natural role in leadership in their country, not simply because they represented significant communities of people, or substantial institutional resources, but because they fell into that category of educated people who were in demand in the task of nation-forming. The invitation to such a role in some African countries carried with it further ambiguities about the independence of the mission of the church and the forming of the gospel in the life of the church. Deals with Constantine are always ambiguous.

CHURCH–STATE RELATIONS

A survey of the different forms of church–state relations Anglicans experience would require a whole library. However, it is possible with some brief

---

[1] See J. L. Gaddis, *The Cold War: A New History* (New York: Penguin, 2005) especially ch. 4.

[2] M. Twaddle, 'The Character of Politico-Religious Conflict in Eastern Africa', in H. Hansen and M. Twaddle (eds.), *Religion and Politics in East Africa: The Period since Independence* (Athens, Ohio: Ohio University Press, 1995), pp. 1–15.

illustrations to highlight some of the issues for worldwide Anglicanism in the twentieth century. On the continent of Africa Uganda has shown a remarkable transition from an almost established situation to an independent pattern through periods of conflict and persecution. In the second half of the nineteenth century, when the first Anglican missionaries came to Buganda, the area on the northern shores of Lake Victoria, they encountered a social and political structure that was highly centralised and hierarchical. At Rubaga Hill, in modern Kampala, the Kabaka, or king, maintained a huge enclosed area that was occupied by a court, which included many young men who would become leaders in the future. Approaching this court from the wrong direction in 1885 cost the first Anglican bishop (James Hannington) his life.

Earlier CMS missionaries had arrived in Buganda in 1877. This structured society enabled the Christian mission to move out from this point to the rest of the country with great success: 'The British missionaries arrived with a clear idea of the importance of the church–state relationship. They had been drawn to Buganda by Stanley's description of a centralised, hierarchical state commanded by a monarch who desired the Gospels.'[3] The Christian mission was mainly Roman Catholic and Anglican and under the Kabaka Mutesa it encountered significant difficulties in seeking to exploit a relationship with the Kabaka. When Mutesa died from gonorrhoea in 1884 the new Kabaka, Mwanga, was forced from the throne by a coalition of Roman Catholics, Anglicans and Muslims. This followed disruptions and persecutions, during which thirty-two young Christian men, later recognised as the 'Ugandan martyrs', were burned to death at Mamungongo. However, in 1888 Muslims managed to gain control of the country and Christians in Buganda fled to neighbouring Ankole. The Anglicans were restored with the assistance of the Imperial British East Africa Company in 1892, and in 1893 Uganda was declared a British protectorate. By and large the protectorate was administered under the terms of the General Act of the Conference of Berlin, article 6, which provided for religious freedom for all.[4]

At this time Bishop Tucker arrived and began ordaining deacons and priests. The Anglicans enjoyed most of the practical advantages of being an established church without the actual legal status. They had the ear of the new colonial masters and this coincided with growth in religious awareness

---

[3] John Rowe, 'Mutesa and the Missionaries: Church and State in Pre-Colonial Buganda', in H. B. Hansen and M. Twaddle (eds.), *Christian Missionaries and the State in the Third World* (Oxford: James Currey, 2002), p. 62.
[4] See H. R. Hansen, 'The Colonial State's Policy Towards Foreign Missions in Uganda', in Hansen and Twaddle, *Christian Missionaries*, pp. 157–63.

and the vitality of a charismatic revival stimulated by the work of an Irish evangelical layman, George Pilkington. Pilkington was also able to translate the whole Bible into the local Luganda language in five years. Nonetheless, in 1898 the Anglican missionary R. H. Walker wrote that 'Our work here is, on a small scale, so like the work and history of the Church in the 4th and 5th centuries. Many questions are the same as were then settled. The relation of Church and State is continually cropping up.'[5]

With colonial patronage the Anglicans were in the cockpit of the Christian era of Uganda for the next thirty years. The Buganda Agreement of 1900 between the British government and the chiefs recognised the equal status of the Roman Catholic and Anglican missions in grants of land. Under the agreement chiefs were allocated land according to status, and the missions were also given generous grants of land. The infant Kabaka, Daudi Chau, was restricted to a more or less titular role, though he was the first Kabaka to be a baptised Anglican. In the event Anglicans gained from the patronage of the British protectorate, and the 1900 agreement 'enshrined the Protestant favoured status which had emerged from the wars of religion of the early 1890s. For over 50 years this defined the legal status of Buganda within the Uganda Protectorate.'[6] When Leslie Brown arrived to become the Anglican bishop in Kampala in 1953 he found that he was third in order of precedence in the country after the governor and the Kabaka. The 'Anglican establishment' was indeed a long-running affair.

In the first decade of the twentieth century Bishop Tucker developed a church constitution in order to recognise the indigenous church in Uganda as a separate entity from the mission. He did not think the mission as an institution was any longer required, though mission personnel would be needed to work in the church. The constitution built on the 1884 initiative to form a church council, or *Lukiiko*, of twelve young men. Tucker's efforts ran into both racist attitudes amongst missionaries and opposition from the colonial authorities. Nonetheless the constitution for the Native Anglican Church came into existence in 1907, creating a representative and participatory synod structure. By the middle of the twentieth century it was being referred to simply as the Church of Uganda.

Throughout the twentieth century the two-missions policy caused significant difficulties. Both the Roman Catholic and the Anglican missions

---

[5] Archdeacon Walker to his brother, 31 July 1898, Walker Papers, CMS Archives, London and Birmingham, quoted here from Hansen, 'The Colonial State's Policy', p. 157.
[6] K. Ward, 'Eating and Sharing: Church and State in Uganda', *Journal of Anglican Studies* 3.1 (2005), p. 101.

sought to expand, and this led to competition and sometimes conflict. In 1916 and 1934 suggestions were made to divide the country into denominational spheres of influence, but to no avail, even though this arrangement pertained in other African countries. Nor did attempts at interdenominational institutions succeed. The dual mission system was so entrenched that it survived even into the early period of independence.[7]

In the middle of the twentieth century new leaders were emerging and political parties forming. Many of these leaders had been educated in CMS high schools. The Uganda Peoples' Congress (UPC) led by Milton Obote manifested the left-leaning tendencies of the educated Anglican leaders. The mainly Roman Catholic Democratic Party was defeated in the election at the time of independence in 1962. In the post-independence period Obote moved to establish a secular state. He secularised the schools and expelled the Kabaka.

Within the Church of Uganda a revivalist movement stretching back to the 1930s was beginning to have an influence on attitudes to the church's involvement in politics. This Balokole movement moved the church to a more critical engagement with politics. The Amin period (1971–9) sharpened the issues in the face of an increasingly despotic and brutal president. The execution of the Anglican Archbishop Jani Luwum, on the pretext that he was involved in a plot to get rid of Amin, made him at once an international martyr and dramatically symbolised the changed relations of the church to the state.

Since independence the various forms of the constitution of Uganda have guaranteed religious freedom. Furthermore, Section 71(b) of the current constitution, which was introduced in 1995, prohibits a political party from being based on 'sex, ethnicity, religion or other sectional division'.[8] There is thus a legal separation of church and state in modern Uganda. However, the position of the Church of Uganda is still seen to be very close to the government and to enjoy a privileged position in the life of the country.

A curious reversal of the status of the Church of Uganda appeared in November 2003 when the High Court considered a dispute about the election of a new bishop of Muhabura and ordered the archbishop to consecrate the elected candidate. Here was a secular court instructing the church on a point of its internal affairs. It sounds very like other cases in Anglican history. Bishop John William Colenso, first bishop of Natal,

---

[7] Hansen, 'The Colonial State Policy', p. 172.
[8] From the website of the Parliament of Uganda, www.parliament.go.ug/index.php?option=com_wrapper &Itemid=78 (accessed 27 December 2006).

successfully appealed to the Judicial Committee of the Privy Council against his dismissal for heresy by the metropolitan bishop Robert Gray, on the grounds that Gray did not have the authority to depose him. In England the Revd G. C. Gorham was instituted to a parish in the diocese of Exeter against the wishes of the bishop of the diocese Henry Philpotts, on the instruction of the same committee.

The experience of Uganda illustrates the vagaries of church–state relations in the process of missionary and colonial encounter. The pre-existing social and political structure in Uganda aided the expansion of the Christian mission once it was located in the vital centre of the Kabaka court. The coming of colonial rule a generation later consolidated an Anglican pre-eminence and enabled further growth in the church. However, the colonial heritage was itself a burden for the church in the twentieth century and only the sustained efforts of Ugandan Anglicans on behalf of local Ugandan interests mitigated these problems. The political turmoil at the beginning of the twenty-first century complicates and confounds the informal political prestige of the Anglicans. How Uganda fits into the world scene in Anglicanism is inevitably affected by these considerations. On the homosexual issue the close connection with the culture and tradition of the country means that it is unlikely that church–state relations will not be a factor in the formulation of Anglican Ugandan attitudes within world Anglicanism. This historical connection makes it clear that in Uganda the homosexual issue is not simply an extension of the question of the ordination of women. The Church of Uganda ordains women but opposes changes in the public place of homosexuals in the church.

The USA is in some respects a counter-example to Uganda. During the colonial period some colonies in America were deliberately Free Church in tradition. Some had virtual establishment status for traditions other than Anglican, and some, such as Virginia, were very solidly Anglican. However, after the War of Independence any pattern of establishment began to change. Certainly at the federal level the new constitution excluded the establishment of religion: the federal state was to be secular. In the course of time this model also came to be applied at the state level.

In this situation Anglicans began to formulate a constitution for their church which could relate to this reality and enable them to sustain their tradition in the new social and political environment. That church constitution reflected the same political and institutional instincts as the federal constitution. It had a General Convention with two houses which met separately and in which each house had certain powers. One was the House of Bishops and the other a house of deputies made up of elected clergy and laity. The corporate entity was the Domestic and Foreign Mission Society and this body was a registered corporation in New York. The church was to be called the Protestant Episcopal Church of the United States of America. The name itself reflects religious heritage and local ambition. It was to become a national church, even though it would take time for the national church ideal to take full shape.[9]

This church was always a minority church in the USA. Nonetheless it succeeded in creating for itself a role as an elite 'boutique' church with influence in high places in the affairs of the nation. It also came to reflect the culture and social assumptions of the emerging nation. Its strength in the south involved it in slavery, yet during the destructive civil war it was notable amongst national churches in that it did not split. In the second half of the twentieth century it became very active in social justice issues and identified with the civil rights movements and the social aspirations of feminism. As in Uganda it moved easily in the contours of its host culture and found ways of giving voice to what it saw as a gospel witness in that culture. As in the host culture it embraced an individual rights frame of reference and approached the position of women and the place of homosexuals in the public life of society and the church in the same way. Lacking the constraints of an establishment institutionality, American Anglicans more easily divided on issues of authority and power and went their own way.

The pattern of political engagement in the USA thus placed more pressure on finding ways of sustaining dissent within the ranks of the church. The constitution of the church provided for coherence and a jurisdictional authority to sustain that. The political culture encouraged multiplication of individual enterprise. The result has been that political engagement of Anglicans in the USA has led them to more individualist approaches to public practice, and to a consequent heightened tension within the church on some public issues, not least sexuality, that in the wider arena are driven by individual rights values.

There has been a further implication of the political engagement of Anglicans in the rise of the USA as a colonial power. The missionary effort of American Anglicans has naturally proceeded along similar lines to those of the political influence of the nation. That engagement, however, has not meant ecclesiastical withdrawal from overseas locations. On the contrary, these overseas connections have been sustained within the metropolitan structure of the church. Thus the church constitution includes under Province IX the dioceses of Colombia, Central Ecuador, Litoral Ecuador,

[9] See Douglas, *Fling out the Banner.*

Honduras, Puerto Rico, the Dominican Republic and Venezuela and includes Taiwan in Province VIII. The Convocation of American Churches in Europe also operates like a diocese, and is under the jurisdiction of the presiding bishop. In other words ECUSA extends to these overseas dioceses. Indeed, at the 2006 General Convention the church changed its name from ECUSA to the Episcopal Church (TEC) in order to acknowledge the membership of these overseas dioceses. The great exception to this pattern has been China, the largest mission field for Americans. All missionaries were forced to leave after the communist takeover of China in 1949.

RESPONDING TO THE WIDER WORLD OF POLITICS

During the twentieth century Anglicans around the world began to be more critically engaged with social and political issues. This trend is reflected in the kinds of resolutions passed by succeeding Lambeth Conferences. In the nineteenth century the Lambeth Conferences were preoccupied with church matters, ecclesiastical jurisdiction, support for the colonial churches and emigration of members from one church to another. All thirteen resolutions of the first Lambeth Conference were concerned with such matters. In itself that is not surprising, since the conference had been called in order to address church matters. The second conference did not pass any formal resolutions but expressed its views in encyclical letters which included reports that had been received by the conference. In 1888 it passed resolutions on divorce and polygamy, and also the first resolution on a political subject which commended a report on socialism. In 1897 there was a resolution on the evils of alcohol and five political resolutions: three on international arbitration, one on industrial relations and one on justice for native peoples. In the four nineteenth-century conferences a total of 107 resolutions were passed: three on social issues, six on political issues and ninety-eight on church matters.

The situation changed through the twentieth century, during which 756 resolutions were passed at nine conferences, of which 103 were concerned with social matters and 121 with political matters. There have been resolutions on such topics as marriage (35), international relations (30), economic policy (19), the United Nations (17), the arms trade and armaments (17), sexual morality (16), human rights (15), family planning and birth control (12), alcohol (5), polygamy (5), abortion (4), adultery (3), communism (3) and apartheid (2). At the 1998 conference there was a series of resolutions on specific countries and their political and social problems.

The dramatic move towards social and political concerns in the second half of the twentieth century in part reflects the changing character of the world at the time of the conferences and also the evolving character of the conference itself. At Lambeth 1998 there was a majority of non-white bishops. These bishops from Africa, South America and Asia brought different perspectives and agendas from their home countries on social and political matters, and so political perspectives within the conference did not always coincide. The impulse to contextualise the faith and to engage with the political realities has meant that very different conclusions have been reached about how to relate to government on specific issues. No small part of that has been the different opportunities open to Anglicans in different situations. During the period of apartheid in South Africa, English bishops could speak in the House of Lords, but South African bishops could only protest, and often on the streets.

The Lambeth Conferences do not represent a continuous coherent body of opinion. The resolutions represent the views of the particular bishops at the time. Most bishops would attend one or perhaps two such conferences in their lifetime. Each conference therefore has a significant new membership. Furthermore the particular circumstances in world politics at the time of the conferences quite properly affect the issues and the frames of reference within which they were addressed.

In LC.1908,44 the bishops felt constrained to encourage sympathy for the 'democratic movement'. LC.1908,44 recognised 'the ideals of brotherhood which underlie the democratic movement of this century' and called upon the church 'to show sympathy with the movement, insofar as it strives to procure just treatment for all and a real opportunity of living a true human life'. At the same conference, resolution 52 states: 'The conference, while frankly acknowledging the moral gains sometimes won in war, rejoices in the growth of higher ethical perceptions which is evidenced by the increasing willingness to settle difficulties among nations by peaceful methods.' This accommodating view of war was left behind in the light of the experience of the First World War. The 1920 conference was concerned with affirming the formation and work of the League of Nations, but by 1930 the conference declared that settling international disputes by war was 'incompatible with the teaching and example of our Lord Jesus Christ' (LC.1930,9).

In the second half of the twentieth century the conference worked in sections, each addressing a particular aspect of a general theme. In 1948, meeting in the aftermath of the Second World War, the conference devoted a section to the church and the modern world. As in 1920, they were concerned with post-war questions and began by affirming the United Nations and its declaration of human rights. The specific rationale for human rights, however, is that they are necessary in order for people to fulfil their duties to others:

All men are made in his image; for all Christ died; and to all there is made the offer of eternal life. Every individual is therefore bound by duties towards God and towards other men, and has certain rights without the enjoyment of which he cannot freely perform those duties. These rights should be declared by the church, recognised by the state, and safeguarded by international law. (LC.1948,6)

Here rights are not seen as inalienably belonging to all people. They are the necessary precondition to enable all to fulfil their duties to others.

The conference also devoted a series of resolutions to the church and war. They repeated the 1930 statement that war was incompatible with the teaching and example of Jesus as a way of settling disputes. They called for a reduction in arms, international inspection of atomic energy to prevent it being used for war, treaties with Japan and Germany based on principles of justice, care for displaced persons and a settlement of the conflict in Palestine.

The conference then went on to a series of remarkable resolutions on the church and the modern state, directly addressing the issues of the emerging Cold War. The first resolution is doubly remarkable in the context of the Cold War: 'this conference affirms that the doctrine that power is its own justification is a most corrupting influence in political thought and practice today' (LC.1948,17). Against any notion of absolute political claims by the state the conference set the assertion of the sovereignty of God. The state was under the moral law of God and was to be an instrument for human welfare. The conference claimed freedom for the church to practise the faith and that the character of church community life could contribute to containing conflict within states. Furthermore Christians should bring to bear in their secular positions a clear understanding of their faith and its practice.

Communism was singled out for special mention. Resolution 25 of the conference states: 'while recognising that in many lands there are Communists who are practising Christians, [the conference] nevertheless declares that Marxian Communism is contrary to Christian faith and practice, for it denies the existence of God, revelation and a future life' (LC.1948,25). The conference called for the study of communism by Christians in order to know where the points of real conflict lay.

The positive answer to the present world scene was for Christians and the church to be militant – that is, active, informed and committed. We have here the beginnings of a world transformation agenda for Anglicans, but it is formulated in such a way as to sustain a proper role for clergy and laity. They value the witness of those who follow a vocation to keep apart from the life of the world: 'But we believe that Christians generally are called by God to take their part in the life of the world, and through the power of God's grace to transform it' (LC.1948,40). Transformation is here taking place as a result of lay activism in the secular realm, supported and informed by the church community life. With that general principle in mind the resolutions go on to deal with social cohesion, evangelism, racial discrimination, gambling, housing, education, work as vocation, motherhood as vocation, and education.

The 1958 conference returned to many of these issues under the general heading of reconciliation. It restated the earlier view on war and went on to declare, remarkably: 'that nothing less that the abolition of war itself should be the goal of the nations, their leaders, and all citizens' (LC.1958,106). As a first step it called on Anglicans to press their governments to seek the abolition by international agreement of the use of nuclear bombs. It also called for a disarmament treaty and for the United Nations to be strengthened.

Some new themes appeared in the 1968 conference: care of the environment, human unity and interfaith dialogue. Specific mention was made of areas of conflict and suffering in southern Sudan and West Africa and the plight of developing countries. There was a call for recognition of the effects of the responsible and irresponsible use of power at all levels of human society and for the church to address such issues (LC.1968,17). There was also a call for study of the nature of social and political change (LC.1968,18). The 1968 conference breathed some sense that life is a little more complicated and that there are multiple layers of social experience that Anglicans should be engaged with.

In the 1978 conference the bishops said they had found a new level of unity in concern for the future and they 'dare to appeal also to governments' (LC.1978,1). This conference reflected the intensification of the Cold War, the struggles of developing countries and the needs of the environment. The conference addressed systemic issues and called for policy and system changes. There was a sense of urgency in this conference: 'We believe that time is running out. Beneath all the choices lies the ultimate choice of life or death. We join with all men of goodwill in appealing that we shall choose life. We know that tasks and situations which to human view seem hopeless can, with the boundless resources of God's grace, be transformed' (LC.1978,1). These were indeed tense times. Since the last conference a world recession had occurred in 1974 and the oil producing and exporting countries (OPEC) had doubled the price of oil that year. Idi Amin was conducting his terror in Uganda, and the United States was leaving behind a defeated South Vietnam.

In 1988 the bishops were able to glimpse the beginnings of what might turn out to be the end of the Cold War and they welcomed what they saw. Soviet President Gorbachev had just announced a policy of glasnost which looked to an opening-up of the USSR and the lessening of the tensions of the Cold War (LC.1988,32). The conference also focused on the plight of the weak, with statements on human rights, conscientious objection, and poverty and debt. It continued an engagement with the environment, justice and peace, and referred to particular problems in South Africa, Namibia, Latin America and the South Pacific Islands.

This conference repeated a point made in 1978 which in 1998 was to gain a very different emphasis. From the beginning the Lambeth Conferences affirmed the principle of local adaptation of practice and liturgy, though they show an awareness of the tension between local adaptation and wider coherence. In 1897 this took the form of the formation of what was called a native episcopate. On various occasions it related to liturgy and the prayer book. Changing attitudes to marriage and the family illustrate this point very well. There is a long history of the engagement of Anglicans with the institution of marriage, of which the notorious struggle with the problems of Henry VIII of England is but one example.

In world Anglicanism generally similar issues have arisen as those which confronted sixteenth-century English Anglicans. They struggled with how to relate to the state and its laws, which do not always reflect Anglican patterns, together with such issues as divorce and remarriage, polygamy, contraception and the place of the family as a social unit. As external forces have prompted reconsideration of key aspects of traditional teaching, so new ways of thinking about the meaning of marriage have emerged. The character and position of the family in some African nations also gives a particular context for the conflict over homosexuality. It raises for Anglicans in these countries questions about the particular form of traditional hetero-sexual marriage, and also the place of such a family in the wider social structure. The subordinated position of women in some of these countries is an invitation to such a challenge, not always taken up.

The Lambeth Conferences passed only two resolutions on these matters in the nineteenth century and during the twentieth the great majority of the resolutions were passed in the first half of the century. This was a time of great social change, when western states began to change laws governing marriage to allow for more accessible divorce. Nonetheless there is a persistent strand in the Lambeth resolutions in favour of heterosexual monogamous marriage. The first resolution on the subject sets out the basic line, and this resolution is referred to and reaffirmed on subsequent occasions. Lambeth 1888,4 is a fundamental statement: no divorce except for adultery or fornication; no remarriage if divorce has been obtained other than under this principle; no remarriage for the guilty party. There was a diversity of view on whether the innocent party could be remarried in church, but if they had been married under state law they should not be refused the sacraments.

This resolution was reaffirmed in LC.1908,39, while noting the evils that have occurred because of the growth in the facility of divorce. LC.1920,67 repeated the sentiments in different words and recognised the difficulty of formulating laws where many citizens do not accept the Christian standard. Nonetheless, the conference said, in every country the church should bear witness to the Christian standard through its own internal disciplines. LC.1930,11 softened the point. It referred to the earlier LC.1888,4 standard, but then went on to say that 'while passing no judgement on the practice of regional or national Churches within our Communion, [the conference] recommends that the marriage of one, whose former partner is still living, should not be celebrated according to the rites of the Church'. Clearly some provinces were taking a more liberal approach and the stricter language of 1880 had become merely a recommendation.

Lambeth 1948,97 refers explicitly to more lax divorce laws in the USA, Great Britain and other countries, and somewhat quixotically calls for a revision of these laws. In Lambeth 1958,118 these few countries have become 'many lands'. There is nothing in 1968, and in 1978,10 the issue is cast in much more general terms. In LC.1988,34 the bishops note that many outside and inside the church do not live according to Christian teaching, and the bishops urge a caring and pastoral attitude to such people. In LC.1998,3 and 10 the bishops simply encourage the provision of education and support.

The changing tone of these resolutions points to some significant changes on the ground. The social standing of the church, the legal environment, and social standards all changed dramatically during this period. The church no longer had a virtual monopoly on marriage and the assumptions of a Christian society and state in the earlier resolutions are no longer valid. This creates a church problem of discipline which earlier resolutions addressed but later resolutions moved away from. The church as a coherent social entity does not appear to have the capacity to discipline its own members in this area. In many dioceses clergy simply marry whoever seeks a marriage service from them. Cohabitation before marriage is simply assumed in most western societies. While this may not quite indicate what earlier resolutions meant by fornication, it is certainly not the pattern which had been assumed to be correct, and in official terms is still the prevailing canonical teaching in most churches.

During the latter half of the twentieth century the Lambeth resolutions reveal a significant change in the rationale for the Christian standard which points to the changing environment in which Anglicans were living. In LC.1948,92 the bishops addressed the increase in the number of broken marriages and the implications of this for the children involved. It then made a social claim, namely, that the 'stability of home life, the welfare and happiness of children, and the real health of society' depend on the observance of the Christian standard. This is not just a claim about marriage; it is a claim about the nature of human society and well-being. There is a clear continuity between the church and society. There is implied here some kind of natural order which leads to happiness and well-being. Only in this way can the consequential argument in favour of the Christian standard make sense or carry weight. Furthermore it is for the greater good of society that those whose marriages are unhappy should remain steadfastly faithful to their marriage vows.

At the next conference in 1958 the bishops reflected on the eclipse of the assumptions of Christian society. They now argued for the Christian standard, not from consequential grounds but from the divine model. LC.1958,112 says: 'the idea of the human family is rooted in the Godhead. Thus all problems of sex and family life must be related, consciously and directly, to the creative, redemptive, and sanctifying power of God.' This in itself is a reasonably problematic theological claim, but its significance here is that the bishops could no longer assume a social consequentialist argument for their Christian standard. The world had changed, and Anglicans had to find better ways of explaining and defending their positions. In LC.1978,10 the same basic approach was adopted in relation to more general issues of sex and marriage. In LC.1998,34 Anglicans had become advocates within society for a central place for the family in the social structure.

These resolutions reflect an important adjustment to the emerging circumstances of Anglicans worldwide. They have managed to sustain a clear commitment to the general terms of the basic standard enunciated in 1888, but have done so while adjusting to the move from being the church of society to being the church in society. That transition has had very important implications for the nature of the church community. How does it sustain the standard in its community life? Once it could be done through the laws of society. Now it must be done for a discrete community within a broader society. How are lay members to be made subject to any church law? How is it to be enforced? It is easier to see church laws applied to clergy: they can be disciplined in a variety of ways. The effect of this responding to the changing social environment also changes the focus in church discipline and makes clergy a greater litmus test for the maintenance of the church's moral standards.

Polygamy was an issue for the bishops over a long period of time. People in polygamous relationships were converted to Christianity and the question was how to deal with such people and their marital situation. The 1888 conference was divided on the issue, but a majority resolution declared that people in polygamous relations could not be baptised but should remain as catechumens until 'they shall be in a position to accept the law of Christ' (LC.1888,5). The position of the wives of polygamists could be dealt with by local rules. In 1958 and 1968 polygamy was recognised as a problem, but there was no resolution of it. In 1988, however, there is something of a breakthrough. The resolution LC.1988,26 sets out conditions on which a polygamist may be baptised and confirmed with his believing wives. He must not marry again while any of his wives are alive and his reception must be accepted by the local Anglican community. For the sake of the wives he is not to be compelled to put any of them away.

Once again this represents a practical accommodation. This resolution does not address any argument about the social deprivation or subjugation of women that might be implied in polygamy. That is an argument which is still going on in some African countries. The bishops addressed the church question, and the separation of these two aspects of the matter shows again the changing position of the church in contemporary societies. Dealing with the church question did not imply any neglect of the broader social questions. It is not surprising that the bishops welcomed the establishment of the Family Network set up by the ACC. It was a vehicle to sustain the standard so long and persistently held by the Lambeth Conferences in a social environment which could not any longer be relied upon.

Much greater diversity of political and social patterns was represented in the membership of the conference from the middle of the twentieth century. Diversity within the church thus becomes much more explicit in relations between Anglicans around the world. In 1978 the Lambeth Conference encouraged 'every particular Church to strengthen its own identity in Christ and its involvement with the community of which it is part' (LC.1978,36). A decade later the emphasis had changed, and the conference in 1988 urged 'the Church everywhere to work at expressing the unchanging Gospel of Christ in words, actions, names, customs, liturgies, which communicate relevantly in each contemporary society' (LC.1988,22).

In the arena of cultural and political engagement the Lambeth Conferences reflect changes in worldwide Anglicanism which were also apparent on more internal ecclesiastical issues such as the ordination of women. That diversity was beginning to test the sensibilities of coherence. The point is not so much that the Lambeth Conferences were changing their minds on central issues, but rather that they were responding to changing situations in worldwide Anglicanism, and holding the whole tradition together was becoming much more difficult.

At the end of the century this diversity had become the central issue. The sectional organisation of the 1998 Lambeth Conference reflected this challenge. The first section dealt with wider human questions, the second with mission in this wider world. Section 3 was entitled 'Called to be faithful in a plural world'. It was not about being faithful in the wider and increasingly divided world, but rather how to be faithful as a church community which was also increasingly divided. The 'plural world' in the title is the church community.

The structure and content of this report makes manifest the ambiguity of the engagement of Anglicans in the political dynamics of their locations. In the second half of the twentieth century international politics was played out not just in terms of military power, but also in terms of economic power, population strength and traditional patterns of power relationships between states. This was also the period of the pre-eminence of the United States Anglicans in the shaping of the Anglican Communion. The broader political dynamics are reflected within the life of the Anglican Communion. At the 1998 Lambeth Conference the plural world became a way of speaking about the life of the church. Centralised institutions based in the old colonial powers emerged and created disturbing echoes around the globe. The Global South coalition developed during this period. The nuances and locations are different, but the dynamics and the interplay between traditional power represented by Canterbury, economic power located in New York, and the power of numbers represented by Nigeria, echo in a disturbing way the dynamics of the wider secular world.

The extension of Anglicanism has been associated with empire and colonialism – mainly British but also American, Australian and Japanese. That historical heritage has influenced the shape of worldwide Anglicanism and its internal dynamics. It has also given particular shape to the character of the political engagement of Anglicans within nations. We have already seen this in Uganda in relation to church–state relations, but it is also manifest in the political activity of Anglicans in places like Kenya and South Africa. That is not to say that Anglicans in these countries simply extended their colonial heritage into the new circumstances of independence. On the contrary, they often transformed their approach to meet a rapidly changing situation. The struggle against apartheid in South Africa illustrates the way in which aspects of the heritage worked to shape and encourage a social critical approach, as does the public engagement of church leaders in Kenya.

CHAPTER 7

Patterns of engagement – relating to other traditions

For a very long time Anglicans have been engaged in ecumenical dialogue and have repeatedly declared their interest in and commitment to unity between the churches and the ecumenical endeavour. In 1888 the Lambeth Conference passed a sequence of resolutions on this theme. What was then called home reunion was to be sought on the basis of four points: scripture, the creeds, the two sacraments and the historic episcopate locally adapted. This came to be known as the 'Lambeth Quadrilateral' and has sometimes been used to refer to key markers of Anglican identity.[1] This is a slightly odd use of the Quadrilateral in the context of the 1888 conference since the bishops went on to call for the 'dissemination of information respecting the standards of doctrine and formularies in use in the Anglican Church' (LC.1888,13). Clearly the conference did not think that the Quadrilateral contained all that could or should be said about Anglican identity. The conference envisaged ecumenical dialogue with English-speaking churches, though they also refer specifically to Scandinavian churches and the Old Catholics of Holland, Germany and Austria. The wider Communion of Anglican churches is only lightly touched on in these resolutions. Churches are to proceed in concert 'so far as it may be'.

Similar themes returned in 1920, when the bishops issued their Appeal to all Christian People, which in the resolutions of the conference is set out under the heading of 'Reunion of Christendom'. This appeal repeats the first three of the four points of the Quadrilateral, but in place of episcopacy urges an agreed form of authorised ministry. The resolution goes on to commend episcopacy on the basis of history and present experience. The bishops 'believe that it is God's purpose to manifest this fellowship so far as this world is concerned, in an outward, visible, and united society, holding one faith, having its own recognised officers, using God-given means of

---

[1] See J. R. Wright, *Quadrilateral at One Hundred: Essays on the Centenary of the Chicago–Lambeth Quadrilateral 1886/88–1986/88* (Oxford: Mowbray, 1988).

grace, and inspiring all its members to the world wide service of the Kingdom of God' (LC.1920,9). The bishops speak of the sin of disunion. They offer some advice about the process towards reunion which would preserve the integrity of the polity of each church. The task of reunion clearly belongs with the 'various national, regional, or provincial authorities of the Churches within the Anglican Communion' (LC.1920,11).

The whole appeal locates Anglicans between two major groups of churches. 'On the one hand there are other ancient episcopal communions in East and West, to whom ours is bound by many ties of common faith and tradition. On the other hand there are the great non-episcopal Communions, standing for rich elements of truth, liberty and life which might otherwise have been obscured or neglected' (LC.1920,9). It is an interesting balance which has probably been lost sight of in subsequent Anglican ecumenical endeavours, which have ended up being focused on those churches which have an episcopal ministry. Indeed when the Church of South India was formed a number of Anglican provinces would not recognise it because the scheme of union was thought not to encompass adequately an episcopal ministry with a historical pedigree.

The 1920 conference gives thanks for the moves towards unity in the last twelve years. This is a clear allusion to the 1910 Edinburgh Missionary Conference. In 1888 a centenary conference of Protestant missions had been held with the hope that strategic plans could be made to 'divide up the world', so that it could be evangelised in that generation. A second missionary conference in New York in 1900 had been full of optimism about the missionary task in the light of problems of disunity between the churches and especially outside criticism of that disunity. 'Yet not one note of hopelessness was sounded. The mission enterprise is the one surely triumphant movement. Whatever else fails, it will not fail. It can not, for it is an obedience to God.'[2] The time had come, the conference organisers believed, when the world could be evangelised because of the unity brought by that commitment.

In 1910 a further missionary conference was held in Edinburgh which has come to be regarded as the beginning of the ecumenical movement. Two movements grew from it. During the years after the First World War the Life and Work movement began to emerge to deal with issues of war and peace, and the social order. The Edinburgh Conference had brought unity into tandem with mission in a somewhat different way from the earlier mission

---

[2] E. Bless *et al.* (eds.), *Ecumenical Missionary Conference, New York, 1900* (New York: American Tract Society, 1900), p. 62.

conferences. What were seen as the scandalous divisions of the churches hindered mission; therefore the unity of the churches had to be dealt with and this could only happen on the basis of unity of belief. So the Faith and Order movement was born out of Edinburgh in a conference in Lausanne in 1927. These two movements came together in 1948 in Amsterdam, after yet another world war, to form the World Council of Churches (WCC). That merger had been promoted and led by two Anglican bishops, George Bell and William Temple, and the Amsterdam meeting was chaired by Archbishop Geoffrey Fisher. In other words, Anglicans had been in the forefront of this ecumenical endeavour.

There are two notable united churches which emerged as a result of these moves. Discussions between Anglican, Methodist, Congregational, Presbyterian and Reformed churches began in 1919 and a united Church of South India (CSI) was inaugurated in 1947. There are sixteen dioceses in CSI, each with a bishop, and the church overall is governed by a synod. A president is elected every two years. Scripture is the ultimate standard of faith and practice, and the creeds, together with the sacraments of baptism and the Lord's Supper, are accepted.

Consultations for the formation of a Church of North India began in 1929, and serious negotiations were begun in 1951 between the Unwasited Church of Northern India, the Church of India, Pakistan, Burma and Ceylon, the Methodist Church in Southern Asia and the Council of the Baptist Churches in Northern India. Later the Brethren and the Disciples of Christ joined these negotiations, and at the last moment the Methodist Church in South Asia withdrew. The Church of North India was inaugurated in November 1970. There is a basic Faith and Order of the church which accepts two sacraments and the threefold order of ministry of bishops, priests and deacons. Episcopacy is accepted as both historical and constitutional. Representatives from both these united churches are invited to the Lambeth Conference.

The ambitions of Anglicans in the early stages of the ecumenical movement for a united universal church have not come to fruition. Apart from the Church of South India and the Church of North India, no actual reunion with other churches by Anglicans has occurred. As the twentieth century moved on, the talk of mission and evangelism tended to give way to talk about church renewal. The WCC goal has evolved over the years and moved from the promotion of a reunited Christendom to facilitating fellowship and unity between the churches.

As the drive for a united Christendom has faded, bilateral conversations between individual churches have multiplied. There is hardly a province in the Anglican Communion that is not engaged in a variety of dialogues with other churches. In some cases these have led to actual agreements, often expressed in terms of a covenant, or concordat. ECUSA has entered into a concordat with the Evangelical Lutheran Church of America (ELCA). After a failed attempt in 1997 a revised agreement, *Called to Common Mission*, was agreed by the Lutherans at their Church Wide Assembly in 1999 and by ECUSA at its General Convention in 2000. The agreement provides for free exchange of ministries and sacraments and cooperation in mission.

In 1991 the Church of England entered into an agreement with the Evangelische Kirche Deutschland, the German Lutheran Church (EKD). This was the Meissen Agreement which committed the churches to strive for the full visible unity of the body of Christ on earth and to work for the manifestation of unity at every level. A commission was set up under this agreement to foster exchanges and cooperation. The Church of England has entered into two similar agreements with the Baltic churches, mentioned so long ago at the 1888 Lambeth Conference in the resolutions dealing with the Lambeth Quadrilateral.

A more extensive relationship was entered into by the Anglican churches in Ireland, Wales, Scotland and England. In 1994–5 the Porvoo Declaration was approved by the four Anglican churches, four of the Nordic Lutheran churches and two of the Baltic Lutheran churches, and in 1996 it was signed by all the parties. The declaration brought the churches into communion with each other. It committed them to common membership, a single interchangeable ministry, and structures to enable the churches to consult each other on significant matters of faith and order, life and work. It is an interesting question as to how far this agreement by the Church of England implies anything for other Anglican churches, whose constitutions or canons commit them to being in communion with the Church of England, and churches in communion with that church, or alternatively with the Archbishop of Canterbury. A number of churches in the Anglican Communion have considered that question and changed their arrangements in order to reserve a decision on communion to themselves.

Given that the Lambeth Conference correctly reflected the reality that church union was the responsibility of the provinces within the Communion, what was the Anglican Communion to do in this area? Both the Lambeth Conference and the ACC have kept the matter on their agendas and have sponsored world-level conversations with six different church groups; Baptists, Lutherans, Old Catholics, Oriental Orthodox, Orthodox and Roman Catholics.

BAPTISTS

The dialogue partner is the Baptist World Alliance. The dialogue has been conducted on a regional basis, with four members from each party involved in all the regional meetings. The agreed purpose of the dialogue has been:

1. To enable Anglicans and Baptists to learn from each other and to deepen mutual understanding of the relationships between the two Communions in the light of their histories.
2. To share with each other our understandings of the faith and to work towards a common confession of the apostolic faith.
3. To identify issues of doctrine and of the nature of the church to be explored further in possible future conversations.
4. To look for ways to cooperate in mission and community activities and increase our fellowship and common witness to the gospel.

Regional meetings were held in Europe (2000), Asia (2001), Africa (2002), Latin America (2003), the Caribbean (2003) and North America (2003). After these regional meetings a final meeting of the continuing committee (2004) drew up a report entitled *Conversations around the World*, which was presented to the ACC in 2005. The report was commended for study, and the group was thanked for the completion of their work. It was noted that the Baptist World Alliance had experienced some difficulties and the Southern Baptist Convention had withdrawn from the Alliance.

LUTHERANS

The first conversations at a world level began in 1970. After several ad hoc groups a joint Continuation Committee was appointed by the ACC and the Lutheran World Federation to foster dialogue. Between 1986 and 1996 the Anglican–Lutheran International Commission sponsored consultations and published the *Niagara Report* (1988) on episcopacy and the *Hanover Report* (1996) on the diaconate. A new Anglican–Lutheran International Working Group was appointed and met for the first time in 2000. Its terms of reference are:

1. To monitor the developments and progress in Anglican–Lutheran relations in the various regions of the world and, where appropriate, encourage steps toward the goal of visible unity.
2. To review the characteristics and theological rationales of current regional and national dialogues and agreements, particularly with reference to the concept of unity and to the understanding of apostolicity and episcopal ministry. This review would include an evaluation of their

consistency and coherence with each other and with Anglican–Lutheran internationally agreed statements and would take note of issues of wider ecumenical compatibility.

3. To explore the implications of regional developments for deepening and extending the global relationships between the Anglican and Lutheran Communions.

4. To propose forms of closer contact and cooperation between the international instruments of both communions, in specific projects and programmes and in addressing practical issues.

5. To advise whether an Anglican–Lutheran International Commission should be appointed and to recommend the issues that require further dialogue.

The Working Group submitted a long and comprehensive report to the parent bodies entitled *Growth in Communion*,[3] which drew attention to the variety of agreements and the way in which local circumstances and perceptions have shaped these agreements. The report reveals a very extensive list of dialogues and agreements around the world, the most established of which are: *The Meissen Agreement* (Church of England and the German Evangelical churches, 1988), *The Porvoo Common Statement* (the British and Irish Anglican churches and the Nordic and Baltic Lutheran churches in the Nordic and Baltic nations, 1992), *The Reuilly Common Statement* (the British and Irish Anglican churches and the Lutheran and Reformed Church in France, 1997), *Called to Common Mission* (ELCA and ECUSA, 1999), *The Waterloo Declaration* (the Anglican Church of Canada and the Evangelical Lutheran Church in Canada, 1999), and *Covenanting for Mutual Recognition and Reconciliation* (Anglicans and Lutherans in Australia; draft proposal of September 1999). In addition they took note of earlier documentation dealing with Eucharistic sharing in North America, prior to the present agreements (*Agreement on Interim Eucharistic Sharing*, 1982).

The diversity in these reports points to a potential confusion in the overall pattern of relations between Anglicans and Lutherans. The local orientation of the polity of the two traditions contributes to this – indeed makes it more or less inevitable.

Growth in Communion nonetheless is able to point to some general patterns. What is being aimed at in all of this dialogue is portrayed in the report in optimistic terms, and given a theological reading which enhances the status and significance of what is going on.

---

[3] *Growth in Communion* is available on the Anglican Communion website at www.aco.org/ecumenical/dialogues/lutheran/index.cfm.

The goal of unity, for instance, is presently seen not so much as an agenda to be achieved, but as a divine reality to be received, appropriated and exhibited by the churches. This may be taken to be an exegesis of Jesus' prayer. In this case, ecclesial unity is taken to be a deep and continuing sacramental expression of life together in the triune God. Such ecumenism is much more, then, than simply meeting minimum standards for mutuality, the removal of ecclesiastical obstacles, or the overcoming of previous difficulties between traditions.[4]

This could be a description of what it means to be a Christian in the church within a particular tradition. The possibility of such an experience between members of different traditions is not possible without some institutional changes such as inter-communion. If it is intended to suggest that there should be only one tradition, and one church that gives expression to that tradition, then it fails to deal with the reality of the limits of traditions and their institutional arrangements. Lying behind a great deal of the work revealed here are notions of church and traditions which go back to the original vision of the ecumenical movement at the beginning of the twentieth century.

ANGLICAN–OLD CATHOLIC INTERNATIONAL COORDINATING COUNCIL

In 1931 the Church of England and the churches of the Union of Utrecht signed the Bonn Agreement which declared that the churches were in full communion. Most churches in the Anglican Communion also established a similar relationship of full communion. The Old Catholic churches are a group of churches who separated from Rome at various times. The Church of Utrecht separated in 1724. Old Catholic churches in Germany, Switzerland and Austria broke with Rome over the doctrine of the infallibility of the Pope defined at the Vatican Council in 1870. There is a small group of Old Catholics in the USA, mainly of Polish origin.

ANGLICAN–ORIENTAL ORTHODOX INTERNATIONAL COMMISSION

There has been a long history of friendly relations between the Oriental Orthodox churches and Anglicans around the world. The commission met in 2002 and agreed to work on doctrinal matters, and in particular Christology.

[4] Ibid., pp. 39f.

They issued an agreed statement on Christology in 2002 and this has been under consideration by the churches of the Anglican Communion. From a theological point of view it is of some significance since these were the churches which declined to accept the declaration of the Council of Chalcedon in AD 451. The work of the commission was suspended because of the moves in ECUSA on sexuality issues.

INTERNATIONAL COMMISSION OF THE ANGLICAN–ORTHODOX THEOLOGICAL DIALOGUE

This dialogue has been going on since 1973 and has mainly worked on doctrinal differences. It has produced statements on 'The Trinity and the Church', 'Christ, the Spirit and the Church', Christ, Humanity and the Church' (all 1998); 'Episcope, Episcopos, and the Church' (2001); and 'Christ, the Priesthood and the Church' (2002). It has also worked on a statement on the ministries of women and men in the church, and questions of heresy, schism and reception. Like the other Orthodox dialogue, this work focuses on doctrinal areas rather than any plans for union between the churches.

ANGLICAN–ROMAN CATHOLIC INTERNATIONAL COMMISSION (ARCIC)

ARCIC has been the most substantial set of ecumenical conversations Anglicans have been engaged in. They are also the only conversations with a unified global church. All the other conversations have been with churches whose ecclesiological shape, like Anglicanism, has been locally determined. Testing the reports of ARCIC has been relatively simple for the Roman Catholic Church. They have an authoritative structure that can speak and respond globally, even though internally there have clearly been considerable discussions and some consultation. Anglicans, on the other hand, are institutionally ill-equipped to respond authoritatively on a global basis. The real authority for official responses lies with the provinces.

Some of these difficulties are implied in the Common Declaration of Pope Paul VI and the Archbishop of Canterbury, Michael Ramsey, in 1966. They speak of a more friendly spirit in relations between the two traditions and express their desire

that all those Christians who belong to these two Communions may be animated by these same sentiments of respect, esteem and fraternal love, and in order to help these develop to the full, they intend to inaugurate between the Roman Catholic Church and the Anglican Communion a serious dialogue which, founded on the gospels and the ancient common traditions, may lead to that unity in truth, for which Christ prayed.[5]

They recognise that there remain many obstacles to full communion of faith and sacramental life, but wish to press on where they can.

ARCIC has proceeded in two phases which can be seen in the agreed statements which they have issued.

ARCIC I, first phase: 1970–81

1971 *Eucharistic Doctrine*
1973 *Ministry and Ordination*
1976 *Authority in the Church I*
1979 *Elucidation Eucharist – Elucidation Ministry*
1981 *Authority in the Church II*
1981 *Elucidation on Authority in the Church*
1982 *ARCIC I Final Report.*

ARCIC II, second phase: 1983–2005

1986 *Salvation and the Church*
1990 *The Church as Communion*
1993 *Life in Christ, Morals, Communion and the Church*
1999 *The Gift of Authority: Authority in the Church III*
2005 *Mary: Grace and Hope in Christ.*

Some statements claim a higher level of agreement than others. Nonetheless in the introduction to the Final Report the co-chairs are able to make the following astonishing remark:

Controversy between our two communions has centred on the eucharist, on the meaning and function of ordained ministry, and on the nature and exercise of authority in the Church. Although we are not yet in full communion, what the Commission has done has convinced us that substantial agreement on these divisive issues is now possible.[6]

That is not a view that has won support in either communion. What, however, is indisputable is that the work done by both commissions has

---

[5] C. Hill and E. Yarnold SJ (eds.), *Anglicans and Roman Catholics: The Search for Unity* (London: SPCK, 1994), p. 10.
[6] Ibid., p. 15.

introduced into each communion an enormous range and vitality of theological reflection on the nature of each tradition and the character of theological activity itself. This is in part due to the way in which the commissions have approached their work. It has in many respects been a model of conflict-resolving theological work. They have not avoided the key issues of conflict which in general have centred on the understanding and function of the ordained ministry and the nature of authority in the church and how it is exercised. These are very difficult issues and have to do with the long history of institutional practice in each tradition. They also contain issues which are vital in any conflict, such as power, status and prestige. Furthermore, the conflict has been conducted over the centuries with full vigour, and sometimes little restraint of sentiment or language. These were very substantial obstacles to overcome and it is quite remarkable how positive the outcome has been. Nonetheless it should not be imagined that the ARCIC reports have won universal consent in either church. Far from it.

It is clear from the above list of statements that ARCIC I was concerned immediately with ecclesial issues: the Eucharist and ministry. The last two statements deal with the authority in the church and were concerned with the challenge of the primacy of the Pope. The earlier documents were clearly shaped by an approach to the idea of the church as communion – *koinonia*. They argue that their examination of the early traditions of the church provided them with the basic notion of *koinonia* as the key to understanding the various images of the church in the New Testament. Christians are people who have been called to belong to Christ and experience the Holy Spirit. By sharing in the same Spirit by which we belong to Christ, Christians are 'bound to one another in a completely new relationship. *Koinonia* with one another is entailed by our *koinonia* with God in Christ. This is the mystery of the Church.'[7] This becomes the ARCIC way of speaking about the church. It shapes the way they present the Eucharist as a sign of the *koinonia*, bishops as servants of the *koinonia* and the primacy as the connecting point of *koinonia*.

This *koinonia* is not without purpose. 'The Church is the community of those reconciled with God and with each other because it is the community of those who believe in Jesus Christ and are justified through God's grace. It is also the reconciling community, because it has been called to bring to all mankind, through the preaching of the gospel, God's gracious offer of redemption.'[8] It is easy to see why this kind of ecclesiology is foundational

---

[7] Ibid., p. 16.   [8] Ibid., p. 17.

in ARCIC's work. It provides a role for the whole church in the formation of its life, and at the same time invites some form and structure in the life of the community. Thus the themes of authority, ministry and discernment can be worked together in a variety of combinations. It also gives a much more dynamic and open-ended sense to the notion of tradition.

The ARCIC documents also represent a process of dialogue with the two communions. ARCIC has responded to reactions to the statements. This interesting process can be seen in the development on a number of themes in successive statements and in the elucidations that have been published by ARCIC. Not all responses were welcomed. The official Vatican response to the Final Report of ARCIC I, published in 1982, did not come until 1992. Christopher Hill, the Anglican co-secretary of ARCIC I, shows some irritation and frustration at this response. He recounts something of the internal struggles in producing the response in the Vatican, and notes in an earlier piece that the publication of the responses from the regional Roman Catholic bishops' conferences was stopped by Rome.[9] He engages in a careful critique of the response and finally concludes: 'Overall, I have the uneasy feeling that the drafters of much of the response have forgotten the agreed basis for Anglican–Roman Catholic dialogue.'[10] He contrasts the method of the Congregation for the Doctrine of the Faith, then presided over by Cardinal Ratzinger, and the ecumenical method of the Council for Promoting Christian Unity, and suggests that it would be a good idea to have an open discussion about the ecumenical method of going behind definitions before trying to discuss issues like authority.

Yet within the ARCIC I process there are signs of change. In reviewing the range of documents on authority, Mary Tanner concludes that 'an attractive picture emerges of the Church living dynamically from generation to generation, confronting and responding to new situations out of the living Tradition in which Scripture is the normative source of authority for Christian life and witness'.[11] She points out that ARCIC 'came to place more emphasis upon the role of the laity and the vital interconnectedness of lay and ordained in the exercise of authority in the church but it said little about the processes or structures through which this might happen'.[12]

The method set up by ARCIC I was a fairly traditional conflict-resolution process: trying to get behind the words to the issues and interests of the

---

[9] Ibid., p. 4.   [10] Ibid., p. 235.
[11] M. Tanner, 'The ARCIC Dialogue and the Perception of Authority', *Journal of Anglican Studies* 1.2 (2003), pp. 52–3.
[12] Ibid., p. 54.

parties involved. The ARCIC discussions have the same kinds of memory issues as a conflict-resolution process has to deal with, though in this case it is the memory of institutions, which are always vastly more difficult to change. In ARCIC II there seems also to be a development in method. The 1990 agreed statement on *Church as Communion* seemed more like a straightforward exposition. At one level the subject was not a controversial matter. In both communions there had been argument about the nature of the church and especially the relation between the empirical and the spiritual. The hot buttons in the ARCIC programme were 'authority', 'ministerial office', 'the nature of salvation and church membership', 'moral theology' and 'Mary'. The document on 'Life in Christ' is more narrative in style and does not reach the same kind of positive agreement found in other documents.

In this document, and even more so in the document on Mary, there appears to be another approach operating which is familiar in biblical interpretation. Seeking for a spiritual reading of the text of scripture, readers bring all they have to the text and seek in the light of what they bring to it what the text might say in their context. It is a mode of interpretation that moves in almost the opposite direction from an antiquarian or historical critical method, which seeks to understand the text in its own terms and context. The two methods in the Christian reading of scripture are of course more nuanced than this, and they can play an interactive and creative role in attending to God in and through the reading of the scriptures. The Mary document had to encounter more formidable dogmatic differences and many more ancillary issues about institutional authority than the other subjects. The Roman dogmas are read through the lens of some of the letters of Paul.[13] Some of the crucial gospel texts are hardly considered at all. In a theological statement this is an adventurous method, to say the least, and yields a result which fails to convince.

What are we to make of all this dialogue and what does it tell us about the character of worldwide Anglicanism? One response came in 2000 when the Archbishop of Canterbury, George Carey, and Cardinal Cassidy, President of the Pontifical Council for Promoting Christian Unity, called some bishops from each church to a meeting in Canada to discuss how to advance

---

[13] See the essay by Charles Sherlock, in Anglican/Roman Catholic International Commission, *Mary: Grace and Hope in Christ: The Seattle Statement of the Anglican–Roman Catholic International Commission; the Text with Commentaries and Study Guide* (London: Continuum, 2006), pp. 204–18. Sherlock sees the eschatological dimension to this method as helpful for an Anglican approach; see especially pp. 217f.

the progress to unity between the two churches. The following year the International Anglican–Roman Catholic Commission for Unity and Mission (IARCCUM) was established. At the 2000 meeting a vision was agreed: 'We have come to a clear sense that we have moved much closer to the goal of full visible communion than we had at first dared to believe. A sense of mutual interdependence in the Body of Christ has been reached, in which the churches of the Anglican Communion and the Roman Catholic Church are able to bring shared gifts to their joint mission in the world.'[14] They said it was time for the two communions to sign a joint declaration and proceed with an action plan, the first part of which would be to establish a commission to prepare a joint statement and oversee the reception of the work of ARCIC. It is hard to imagine how such a statement of mutual interdependence could truly represent the reality in the churches.

This became clear when the work of IARCCUM had to be suspended because of the conflict over the ECUSA confirmation of the consecration of Gene Robinson. A sub-group of IARCCUM was set up to look at the ecumenical implications of these conflicts. It produced a report which sought to sustain some sense of continuing movement towards union, but it read a little like wishful thinking rather than anything realistic. It recorded the advice from the generally more sympathetic Pontifical Council for Promoting Christian Unity in the following blunt terms:

Clearly the ecclesiological decisions you make will be a decisive factor in determining the shape of our future relations. As we see it, the kind of answer you will give to the current situation will tell us what kind of communion you are.

If you choose to strengthen the authority structures and instruments of unity within the Anglican Communion and find an effective means of addressing the tendency towards divergence on matters of faith and doctrine, we would clearly see this as enhancing the possibility of meaningful and fruitful dialogue in the search for Christian unity, and of an increasing commitment to shared witness and mission.[15]

These are very important issues and they indicate a view which sees the loosely federated character of worldwide Anglicanism as a fundamental obstacle to union between the churches. This is clearly a commitment to a

[14] International Anglican–Roman Catholic Commission for Unity and Mission, *Communion in Mission*, statement from Mississauga Meeting, May 2000, para 6, available at: www.aco.org/ecumenical/dialogues/rc/iarccum/acns2137.cfm (accessed 26 March 2007).
[15] *Ecclesiological Reflections on the Current Situation in the Anglican Communion in the Light of ARCIC . Report of the ad hoc Sub-commission of IARCCUM Presented to the Most Reverend and Right Honourable Archbishop of Canterbury, Dr Rowan Williams and to the President of the Pontifical Council for Promoting Christian Unity, Cardinal Walter Kasper June 8th, 2004*, available at: www.aco.org/ecumenical/documents/pdfs.cfm?fname=200406iarccum (accessed 26 March 2007).

centralised concept of a global church which the 1930 Lambeth Conference had set its face against.

Undaunted by these reactions, a recommenced IARCCUM published its report in February 2007 entitled *Growing Together in Unity and Mission* looking for ways to advance the cause of unity of action between the two traditions, not least in the sharing of resources. Such sharing is more important for declining churches in the west. It is hard to resist the thought that IARCCUM represents a significantly overambitious dream from the bishops. Clearly there is already a lot of interaction and joint activity at the local level and just as clearly these matters are pursued where it is practically called for and possible. IARCCUM also has the effect of being quite misleading in the public arena. It suggests that the two traditions are much closer together than is really the case. The publication of IARCCUM's report in February 2007 led to a rash of media talk about an Anglican minority buyout of the Roman Catholic Church. Both communions instantly distanced themselves from this talk and referred to the report as merely a discussion document.

While IARCCUM is probably a mistaken enterprise at the international level, the same cannot be said for ARCIC. It has contributed immensely to mutual understanding and has facilitated sustained theological engagement on some key issues for more than thirty years. The more relaxed atmosphere referred to in the 1966 joint statement has been significantly extended and informed by the work of ARCIC. It has developed a method of engagement in line with modern conflict-resolution principles and extended mutual understanding about the way theology works in each communion. The method of interpreting the past in the light of the present echoes Rudolf Bultmann's famous axiom, 'no exegesis without presuppositions'. Whether this aspect of the method has adequately represented the inner dynamics of Anglican history and experience is very doubtful. ARCIC has been very good at suggesting new and different ways of framing core theological issues, such as the church as communion, even if the terms in which it was developed echo so powerfully with the declarations of Vatican II. Scripture is a constant problem in ARCIC because of the different modes of defining what is necessary for salvation and how scripture reaches into the ecclesial topics under review. Nor has the understanding of institutionality in ecclesiology been adequately addressed. The Roman Catholic position is reasonably straightforward on this matter because of the way in which authority in theological formulation is shaped; Anglicans have a much more nuanced notion of authority and a more open and dynamic conception which begins with the whole people of God.

These are important matters but should not deflect from the immense contribution that ARCIC has made. The sustained theological engagement, its value for the education of members of each communion, the experience of a cohort of theologians directly involved in the process and the practice of providing for a series of theological inputs into the life of the church, are all matters of great value. However, once these statements begin to be used as planks in a concordat for institutional union they run into difficulties. The approval mechanisms in each communion are so different. The idea of gaining the approval for such statements from every province in the Anglican Communion is beyond the sensible bounds of probability. In any case, as its response to the Robinson/ECUSA conflict demonstrates, the Roman Catholic Church wants the Anglicans to have the same kind of international organisational structure as their own for there to be real union. The early and repeated statements of the Lambeth Conferences referred to earlier in discussing ecclesiology are a plain reminder of a reality which, despite the aspirations of the ecumenical age of the twentieth century, is still part of the Anglican framework. At the global level these two traditions are very different things. But then that only goes to point up the underlying issue of what the nature of unity really is within the broad tradition of Christianity and how far diversities of tradition within that broader tradition are in fact necessary to sustain the overall truth and catholicity of the one Holy and Apostolic Church.

At a practical and more domestic level, the ACC established an Inter-Anglican Standing Commission on Ecumenical Relations with the general brief of monitoring dialogues and proposals on ecumenical relations in the Anglican Communion, and to assist in various ways to enhance the coherence of what was being said and agreed in different places. The commission oversees not only the Communion-level dialogues, but also regional and local ones, and assists in terminology and patterns of agreements. It is a way of facilitating some commonalities in this area.

JUDAISM

Anglican conversations with other Christian traditions have been widely pursued at both the global and regional levels. Conversations with non-Christian religions have not been so vigorously pursued. Judaism presents an immediate and complicated instance of modern attempts to respond to the long history of European anti-Semitism, and in the modern period to the formation of the state of Israel. The Church of England has a long history of work with Jews, and to some extent this work is to be found in some other parts of the Communion.

However, the evidence for conversations with Judaism at the level of world Anglicanism is scant. The Lambeth Conference has passed only six resolutions which refer to Judaism and only LC.1897,16 is devoted to the subject. It calls for more priority to be given to the evangelisation of Jews and for people to be trained for this work. In 1930 Jewish life and thought is identified as the means by which the revelation of Christ was presented to the world and it was then modified by encounters with other cultures. In 1948 there is no reference to the Holocaust from the European theatre of World War II, but an expression of concern for the future of Palestine, a land which is sacred to Christians, Jews and Muslims. In 1978 a resolution which referred to conversation with other faiths asks for support for conversations and contacts with Hinduism, Buddhism, Taoism, Confucianism and Islam, and then adds that the bishops continue to seek opportunities for dialogue with Judaism.

It is thus not until 1988 that Jews figure in an inter-faith dialogue and then only to encourage provinces to engage in such inter-faith conversations. The Lambeth Conference also recommended the establishment of an inter-faith committee by the ACC. This committee was to work in close cooperation with the WCC and to draw up Communion-wide guidelines for a common approach to people of other faiths. In 1998 the resolution dealt with the conflict in Palestine, and Jews are mentioned in this context.

The ACC did establish a Network for Inter-Faith Concerns, NIFCON. This group had begun working in 1992 based in the Church of England. The network operates on the basis of four principles which were identified at the Lambeth Conference of 1988:
1. Dialogue begins when people meet people.
2. Dialogue depends upon mutual understanding, mutual respect and mutual trust.
3. Dialogue makes it possible to share in service to the community.
4. Dialogue becomes a medium of authentic witness.

NIFCON does not actually engage in inter-faith dialogues but rather acts as a clearing house and provides resources for those engaged in such dialogue and others who are interested. World Anglicanism has been more focused on inter-faith matters as they arise in political and social contexts. It is for that reason that there has recently been much more interest in dialogue with Islam.

ISLAM

Modern contact between Anglicans and Muslims goes back to the latter part of the nineteenth century. In 1897 the Lambeth Conference called for people to be trained and supported for mission work among 'Mohommadans' and similar things were resolved in later conferences.[16] With mass migrations creating greater contact with people of different faiths in the second half of the twentieth century, the conference in 1968 called for positive relationships between the faiths, and in 1978 open exchange of thought was sought. In 1988 guidelines for dialogue were set out, and in 1998 the ACC was asked to set up a body to monitor Christian/Muslim and other inter-faith relations.[17]

The defeat of Arab nations in the Six Day War with Israel in 1967 led to an Arab identity crisis. The Islamic summit in 1969 in Rabat, and the formation of an Islamic Secretariat in 1970 and the International Islamic News Agency (IINA) in 1971 all pointed to an international Muslim resurgence. This was made more feasible by the oil 'crisis' in 1972–4 which transformed economic relations between the west and the mainly Muslim nations of OPEC. The 1979 Iranian revolution provided a focus for the imagination of idealistic Muslims around the world.

Besides the more essentially religious divisions within Islam, there are also ways in which the resurgence gained different expression in different nations. Pakistan moved along the lines of an Islamic republic, while Indonesia, with the largest Muslim population in the world, remained a multi-faith state with religious freedom guaranteed in the constitution. In nearby Malaysia serious attempts were made at Islamisation from 1970. In this particular case Muslims were mostly ethnic Malays and constituted just over half of the population. However, Malaysia did not become an Islamic state, to the disappointment of some more radical Muslims. In 1984 the Prime Minister, Dr Mahathir bin Mohamad, put it this way: 'What we mean by Islamization is the inculcation of Islamic values in government administration. Such inculcation is not the same as simple implementation of Islamic laws in the country. Islamic laws are for Muslims and meant to be their personal laws. Islamic laws can only be implemented if all the people agree to them.'[18]

On the other hand, violence and riots were the result in northern Nigeria when local governments sought to impose Shariah law on Christian citizens.

---

[16] LC.1908,26; 1920,32; 1948,36–8; 1958,58.   [17] LC.1998,III,12.
[18] Quoted from S. Batumalai, *Islamic Resurgence and Islamization in Malaysia* (Perak: St John's Church, Jalan, Ipoh, 1996).

The aggressive missionary activity of Anglicans in northern Nigeria from 1990 has created a particular context for that conflict.[19] This engagement with Islam has been an underlying current in the ongoing debates about sexual mores in the Anglican Communion. In the United Kingdom and North America Anglicans are generally able to engage with their Muslim neighbours with reasonable ease and without the risk of violence.[20]

Anglicans encounter Islam in a multitude of different contexts, and Islam itself shows internal differences just as Anglicanism does. In these different contexts Anglicans work for particular goals according to their local perceptions. Comprehending all this diversity at any worldwide level is impossible. What happens in worldwide Anglicanism, however, sets trends and provides models which can be referred to by Anglicans in their local circumstances.

Besides NIFCON, the Archbishop of Canterbury has convened 'Building Bridges' conversations. These have met on three occasions, each with a general theme: Lambeth 2002 on common problems from the past, present and the future; Doha 2003 on the reading of sacred scriptures; and Georgetown in Washington DC 2004 on prophecy in the Bible and the Qur'an. These conversations have involved scholars from each tradition presenting papers for discussion which have been subsequently published.[21] Also in 2002 the Archbishop of Canterbury, George Carey, established an agreement with the Grand Iman of al-Azhar al-Sharif in Cairo, Dr Mohamed Sayed Tantawy, for a Joint Commission of Anglican Christians and Sunni Muslims. This commission is working on ways for religious leaders to use their influence for reconciliation and peace. It is clear that in the world arena Anglicans have tried to play a role in advancing understanding between the two faiths.

---

[19] See J. Idowu-Fearon, 'Anglicans and Islam in Nigeria: Anglicans Encountering Difference', *Journal of Anglican Studies* 2.1 (2004), pp. 40–51.

[20] M. Ipgrave, 'Anglican Approaches to Christian–Muslim Dialogue', *Journal of Anglican Studies* 3.2 (2005), p. 221.

[21] M. Ipgrave, *The Road Ahead: A Christian–Muslim Dialogue: A Record of the Seminar Building Bridges Held at Lambeth Palace, 17–18 January 2002* (London: Church House Publishing, 2002), M. Ipgrave, *Scriptures in Dialogue: Christians and Muslims Studying the Bible and the Qur'an Together: A Record of a Seminar 'Building Bridges' Held at Doha, Qatar, 7–9 April 2003* (London: Church House, 2004), and M. Ipgrave, *Bearing the Word: Prophecy in Biblical and Qur'anic Perspective: A Record of the Third 'Building Bridges' Seminar Held at Georgetown University, Washington DC, 30 March – 1 April 2004* (London: Church House Publishing, 2005).

CHAPTER 8

Influence, organisation and power in the church

World Anglicanism is such a diverse and scattered community that it is often difficult to see how decisions are made and indeed if they are made. The variety of cultural contexts within which such judgements occur makes the task of elucidating the jurisdictional and decision-making fabric of this far-flung community all the more difficult. This is compounded by the fact that the decision-making details actual differ significantly within the various parts of Anglicanism, and those differences often arise out of the different cultural and legal contexts in which Anglicans have had to find their way. However, in general terms Anglicanism has shown a distinct conciliarist tendency in the way in which decisions and jurisdiction have emerged. In many ways we come here to one of the touchstone issues in Anglicanism which marks it out from some other Christian traditions. While holding to a ministerial order of bishops, priests and deacons inherited from early Christianity, Anglicans have fairly consistently developed patterns of decision-making which involve the whole church community. Such a principle obviously implies a notion of representativeness where those decisions are related to more than immediately local matters.

The notion of representation arises because of size and distance. The community cannot all gather together. Furthermore the organisational structures we are concerned with here are not the only ways by which the Anglican community sustains its life. These structures provide for a disciplined ministry of word and sacrament in the church. Served by this ministry, the church community is called to be the agent of the mission of God in the world, to testify to the kingdom of God. There is a multitude of agencies, groups, organisations, networks, programmes and institutions within Anglicanism besides the judicature structures we are about to look at.

FORCES SHAPING CHURCH STRUCTURES

In the development of the organisational arrangements in Anglicanism there have been a number of influences. Those influences have been more manifest at some times and in some places than others, but in general three have shaped the structures of decision-making. First, engagement with the political structures of the context has played an important role. In the longer history of English Anglicanism the partnership between Oswald and Wilfrid in the Celtic north of England shows one aspect of the collaboration between the bishop-evangelist and the king who himself engaged in the ministerial journeys of the bishop. There was a clear, though more structured partnership between William the Conqueror and Archbishop of Canterbury Lanfranc. The king, and sometimes the queen, took a significant role in the early synods Lanfranc held. Indeed, on a number of occasions the king presided. He was after all the Christian king of a Christian nation and he saw himself as a church reformer.

England is not the only place to see the influence of the local political structure on church decision-making. It is often said that when the founding fathers of the American Revolution completed writing the constitution of the new United States of America the leading members walked across the street and put together the constitution of the Protestant Episcopal Church. Certainly the ECUSA constitution mirrors the arrangements in the US constitution. The emergence of parliamentary-style synods in the British colonies in the nineteenth century shows the influence of the political arrangements and ideas at the time the synods were established.[1]

There is a second influence which has shaped the Anglican approach to church governance, namely the notion of 'the whole for the whole'. This is the conciliarist instinct that came to the fore in Europe with the crisis in the papacy of rival popes. The Council of Constance (1414–18), called at the instigation of the emperor, claimed for itself supreme authority directly from God because it represented the whole church. It is not surprising that Anglicans embraced the notions of conciliarism at the time. It accorded with their long-standing social and political traditions. The persistent influence of holistic conciliarist impulses runs through Anglican approaches to governance and decision-making.[2] By way of contrast, the imperial impulse has been generally resisted in Anglican theology, though not always successfully.

The nineteenth-century pattern of synods was followed by new churches, as nations came to independence in the de-colonisation period of the

---

[1] See B. Kaye, 'The Strange Birth of Anglican Synods in Australia and the 1850 Bishops' Conference', *Journal of Religious History* 27.2 (2003), pp. 177–97.

[2] See the older study by R. Albright, 'Conciliarism in Anglicanism', *Church History* 33 (1964), pp. 3–22, and the more recent, P. D. L. Avis, *Beyond the Reformation: Authority, Primacy and Unity in the Conciliar Tradition* (London: T&T Clark, 2006).

twentieth century. In the late twentieth century changes in the pattern of the establishment in England led the Church of England to move to the establishment of a form of synodical governance, perhaps the last of the churches in the developed world to move in this way.

In recent centuries this conciliarist strand has found itself in tension with the jurisdictional authority claimed by bishops. With the episcopal focus of the nineteenth-century Tractarian renewal, tension was inevitable. In recent times it has become popular in some circles to speak of the church as synodically governed and episcopally led.[3] It is hard to see exactly what that might mean in the context of actual decision-making, other than seeking to insert into the synodical pattern of decision-making some vague privileging of the episcopal office. Most synods contain three houses: lay representatives, clergy representatives and the diocesan bishop. Most synods provide for the opportunity of voting by houses. That general arrangement gives the bishop a significant place, though it is usually a responsive role.

The third stream of influence is the instinct to privilege the local. This undoubtedly arises from the commitment in Anglicanism to the local church as the exemplar church. There is a strong tradition of an Anglican Christian nation in the English phase of Anglicanism, but even here the local was privileged. That tendency can be seen in the way that parish officers, magistrates and common law evolved as determinative elements in this national pattern. In South Africa, when organisational arrangements were beginning to be established, a pattern of ordinance churches was established. These were local parish churches which existed under their own ordinance and operated quite independently: so much so that they were accused by some of encouraging congregationalism. At the international level it is noteworthy that the only organisation with a capacity to raise money, indeed the only one with a constitution, is the Anglican Consultative Council, whose constitution was established by a vote of the provinces, and can only be changed by a two-thirds majority of the churches of the Communion.[4]

These influences, engagement with the political context, conciliarism and the privileging of the local can be seen in the actual structures that tend to hold around the world amongst Anglicans.

---

[3] See S. Sykes and S. Gilley, 'No Bishop, No Church: The Tractarian Impact on Anglicanism', in G. Rowell (ed.), *Tradition Renewed* (London: Darton, Longman and Todd, 1986), pp. 120–39.
[4] Clause 10 of the constitution which can be found at www.aco.org/acc/docs/constitution.cfm.

ORGANISATIONAL STRUCTURES

A community as large and dispersed in such different locations and not really having a tradition of precisely uniform structures is likely to display considerable variety in organisational arrangements. The surprising thing is that the differences are not as great as they might be. In general there are parishes, dioceses and provinces embedded into the constitutions of Anglican churches around the world. This is undoubtedly a result of the enormous influence of the experience of English Anglicanism, which in turn shared these elements with western Christianity generally. Both Eastern Orthodox and Roman Catholic traditions have these three forms. However, the particular details of the way they work reflect a distinct Anglican emphasis arising out of the influences we have already noted.

Parish

The term 'parish' designated a Roman administrative unit, and in early Christianity it was used to indicate the natural area where a bishop exercised his responsibilities for the community he served. As congregations multiplied, presbyters were appointed to serve local congregations, and the bishops came to exercise a more general responsibility, now designated in terms of a territory rather than a community. The territorialisation of church organisation was consolidated after Christianity became the religion of the Roman Empire under Constantine. Clergy were often appointed and supported by a large landholder, a practice which created some tensions between the parties involved. At the Third Lateran Council in 1179 it was agreed that clergy should have freehold rights in relation to the lay patron, and the bishop right of appointment. However, once appointed, the clergy had freehold rights in relation to the bishop as well. This pattern was largely followed in England and overseas.

Up until the abolition of church rates in England in 1868 the church parish was also the local civil administrative unit for many purposes. Colonies which adopted the parish structure before this date often took over the pattern of vestries which were the executive bodies of the parish. After the American War of Independence the civil role of vestries was often maintained, though the church functions were designated to church vestries. In modern Anglican practice the annual meeting of the parishioners is usually called the vestry, and the executive body is called a parish council. In general these bodies are elected by the parishioners and have responsibilities for the parish in relation to those of the incumbent. Under this system there may also be church wardens who may have more specific responsibilities for the property. What is remarkable across world Anglicanism is the consistency of the pattern in these arrangements.[5]

This basic system is stretched in many places in order to deal with the local situation. There may be areas of ecumenical collaboration, mission areas, or areas of special need, and these can have a variety of organisational arrangements. Overall there is a balance between the responsibilities of the clergy, or in some places the catechist who is a lay teacher and preacher, the bishop and the diocese, and the parishioners. This pattern assumed that the parish was to some extent responsible for the maintenance of the ministry and the parish – clearly an assumption which could not be sustained in many places.

Diocese

The term came to be used for the area of jurisdiction of a bishop in western Europe only. In the east it marked the wider area of a patriarch. Like a parish it signified an administrative area in the later Roman Empire. The English experience has other important elements. The Celtic church did not adopt such a territorial pattern with a territorial hierarchy, but was monastic in character and had its own distinctive pattern of piety. When Augustine came from Rome in AD 596 at the behest of Pope Gregory the Great he had papal instructions on the organisation of the English church. He was

in several places [to] ordain twelve bishops, who shall be subject to your jurisdiction, so that the bishop of London shall, for the future, be always consecrated by his own synod, and that he receive the honour of the *pallium* from this holy and apostolical see, which I, by the grace of God, now serve. But we will have you send to the city of York such a bishop as you shall think fit to ordain; yet so, if that city, with the places adjoining, shall receive the word of God, that bishop shall also ordain twelve bishops, and enjoy the honour of a metropolitan; for we design, if we live, by the help of God, to bestow on him also the *pallium*; and yet we will have him to be subservient to your authority; but after your decease, he shall so preside over the bishops he shall ordain, as to be in no way subject to the jurisdiction of the bishop of London.[6]

---

[5] See N. Doe, *Canon Law in the Anglican Communion: A Worldwide Perspective* (New York: Oxford University Press, 1998), p. 67.
[6] The letter is preserved in Bede EH, 1,29, p. 85.

Theodore (602–90) used synods to reform the Church of England in his day, and in general dioceses corresponded with units of political authority. Troubles began to emerge when that correspondence began to be compromised. Synods in this context were also used as disciplinary instruments for the bishop. Clergy could be summoned to appear and the synod acted as a court of the bishop for this purpose.[7] Under Tudor church legislation the role of the diocese was diminished, and the idea of diocesan corporate decision-making was simply taken over by the secular arrangements. At the national level the theoretical position was that the parliament stood for the lay involvement in the government of the church. During the nineteenth century diocesan life of the Church of England revived,[8] though by this time Anglicans had spread abroad and diocesan structures had come to the forefront.

During the nineteenth century the ordering of Anglican affairs became a crucial matter. In many British colonies bishops were appointed by the British crown to dioceses, or sees, without any real infrastructure. As colonies developed responsible government, this situation became untenable. Post-revolutionary America had developed a constitution of dioceses and a General Convention which reflected the new republican institutions. Different patterns of synods emerged in the colonial churches in Australia,[9] Canada and Africa, which in the twentieth century became the model for Anglicans generally. The effect of this synodical pattern has been the democratisation of power in the church.

In contemporary Anglicanism the general pattern of a diocese as the area of responsibility of a bishop, and a constitutional area for a diocesan assembly or synod, generally prevails. New dioceses are generally formed by the decision of the provincial authority rather than by a diocese. Bishops are generally appointed by a diocesan assembly or synod. The difference in operation in the diocese of Durham in England, which falls entirely within the bounds of one secular, political and legal authority, is much more straightforward than in the diocese of Cyprus and the Gulf, which includes Cyprus, the Gulf States, Iraq and Yemen.

However, many institutions in Anglicanism had already emerged which expressed this democratic temper. The appearance of independent societies

---

[7] See the very useful description of this process in H. E. J. Cowdrey, *Lanfranc: Scholar, Monk, and Archbishop* (Oxford: Oxford University Press, 2003), ch. 9.
[8] See Burns, *The Diocesan Revival in the Church of England*. He carefully traces the revival of diocesan assemblies in ch. 9.
[9] See Kaye, 'The Strange Birth of Anglican Synods'.

in England in order to prosecute the missionary enterprise is but one large example of this trend. The emergence of religious orders with independent power structures also contributed to the modern Anglican phenomenon of a dominant ecclesial set of structures of parish, diocese and province which is not itself comprehensive of the life of the church. In some respects this phase in Anglican development mirrored the effect of the dissolution of the monasteries in England in the sixteenth century, which had the effect of narrowing the base of power in the church and focusing it on the national power of the crown exercised through the bishop. In the nineteenth and twentieth centuries, that narrow focus was widened and made more complicated by the emergence of dispersed centres of power and influence.

These changes have not, of course, been an unalloyed benefit. The societies were often shaped by dispositional differences made possible by the competing patterns of religious revival. Evangelical and High Church, and later Tractarian, rivers flowed into the Anglican lifeblood and came with their own institutional expressions. These institutions in turn not only served to advance the specific causes for which they had been founded, but also became the institutional focus more generally for those renewal movements. The Church Missionary Society has been a pre-eminent standard bearer for the evangelical cause, just as the Society for the Propagation of the Gospel was for a more catholic stream. The multiplication of these societies and their dispositional character has had the effect of limiting the comprehensive power of the parish/diocese/provincial or synodical structures. It has also had the effect of making Anglican ecclesial life much more complex. It represents one of the interesting contradictions in modern Anglicanism that just as the conciliar and democratic impulses were having their effect on the governance structures of Anglicanism, in making them more inclusive and representative, they became less comprehensive.

Clearly this pattern differs around the world. The Episcopal Church of the United States has had much greater success in sustaining a comprehensive engagement of the synodical structures in the mission and humanitarian work of the church. In part that is because of the coherence of the church nationally from the post-revolutionary period and a stronger centralist – or, in the American political context, we could say a more federalist – conception of the church and its governance. Similar things could be said about the Anglican Church in Kenya. In this case the present province has emerged out of the sub-division of a single diocese of Kenya, and so history has shaped a significant level of provincial coherence and also of provincial activity in key areas, the most significant of which has been education.[10] The trend has been in the opposite direction in the Church of England, in large measure because of the late flowering of synodical governance structures and the continuing remnants of establishment.

These patterns have also affected the relationship between bishops and the governance structures. The idea of Anglicans being episcopally led and synodically governed has its greatest significance in an attempt to define the power relations. Many liturgies of ordination speak of the role of the bishop in terms of government, mostly drawing on the language of the 1662 English Book of Common Prayer, while at the same time having synodical and diocesan structures which give the bishop little significant structural power to govern in any ordinary sense, and certainly not in the sense implied in 1662.

In the post-revolutionary constitution of the diocese of Virginia the parish vestry retained much of its earlier power. The result has been that the bishop is very clearly the constitutional servant of the diocese, whereas in the diocese of Melbourne in Australia the weakness of the early constitutional arrangements has led to a situation where the diocesan council, called in this instance Archbishop in Council, is only a consultative body for the archbishop. It is interesting to note that within the same national constitution the standing committee of the diocese of Sydney has all the powers of the diocesan synod in between meetings of the synod. Creative ways of explaining these differences are found to enable the common traditional liturgical heritage and the modern constitutional and political realities to live together. This is by no means a bad thing. On the contrary, it enables some movement in the balance of power according to changing circumstances.

Province

A province is a group of dioceses joined together to form a constitutional unity. They came to be called a province because they corresponded with the provinces of the Roman Empire. The notion of province came into Anglicanism from this pattern in the letter to Augustine from Pope Gregory quoted above. The province was to be presided over by a metropolitan bishop, later to be called an archbishop, who was to have the responsibility of ordaining other bishops for the dioceses in the province. In general

---

[10] See Sabar-Friedman, *Church, State and Society in Kenya*.

Anglican use, the diocese appoints its own bishop, though that is a trend which only emerged in the later nineteenth century.

In some parts of the world bishops are appointed by others, though this usually involves a different conception of the role of that bishop and the character of the diocese. In Nigeria, as part of the Decade of Evangelism inaugurated at the 1988 Lambeth Conference, a large number of missionary bishops were appointed during the 1990s.[11] Bishops in Nigeria are appointed by the episcopal synod which is made up of all the bishops in the church, though only diocesan bishops and archbishops may vote. The missionary bishops were appointed to evangelise, particularly in the Muslim-dominated northern sections of the country. The bishop had complete authority in the diocese until such time as the organisational arrangements for a synod and diocesan structure were established and approved by the General Synod of the church.

In Anglicanism generally the province represents the wider church in the life of a diocese and provides for the ordination of bishops and their discipline. It is the province that enters into relations with other churches and is also the basic unit of membership of the Anglican Communion, except where a national church structure has been established with more than one province, as in Nigeria or the USA. Nonetheless the province is

---

[11] The full list is given on the Church of Nigeria (Anglican Communion) website, available at: www. anglican-nig.org/history.htm (accessed 20 July 2006). The text on the website is as follows.

Then with unsurpassed missionary zeal, Archbishop Adetiloye initiated deft moves that culminated in the unprecedented consecration of eight missionary Bishops and the Diocesan Bishop of Kano on April 29, 1990 at St. Michael Anglican Cathedral, Kaduna. The missionary Bishops' core remit was the fast evangelism of the predominantly Muslim Northern Nigeria. To the glory of God, the eight missionary Dioceses were inaugurated in September 1990 as follows: Minna (3rd), Kafanchan (5th), Katsina (6th), Sokoto (9th), Makurdi (24th), Yola (26th), Maiduguri (28th), and Bauchi (29th). The Diocese of Egbado (now Yewa) was inaugurated on November 2, 1990 and Ife two days later (4/11/90). Two more missionary Dioceses of Calabar (20/12/90), Uyo (27/11/92), followed. By now the Church of Nigeria (Anglican Communion) had been proclaimed by the Archbishop of Canterbury as 'the fastest growing church in the Anglican Communion'. Living up to its billing, Nigeria under Adetiloye created the Diocese of Oke-Osun (25/1/93), Sabongidda-Ora (27/5/93), Okigwe North (7/1/94), Okigwe South (8/1/94), Ikale-Ilaje (6/2/95), Kabba (12/2/96), Nnewi (14/2/96), Egbu (16/2/96), and Niger Delta North (16/5/96). Then in December 1996, five more missionary Dioceses were inaugurated in the North: Kebbi (4th), Dutse (6th), Damaturu (8th) Jalingo (10th) and Oturkpo (11th). The Diocese of Wusasa and Abakaliki followed on (2/12/97) and (4/12/97) respectively. The autonomous Diocese of Ughelli was inaugurated on January 8, 1998 and Ibadan North (14/12/98). Definitely the golden year which produced the largest number of Dioceses was 1999 when in the month of July four dioceses were inaugurated, namely; Oji River (11th), Ideato (12th), Ibadan south (13th), and Offa (14th), and then November bore eight Dioceses! . . . Lagos West (29th), Ekiti West (22nd), Gusau (24th). Gombe (25th), Niger Delta West (25th), Gwagwalada (26th), Lafia (29th), and Bida (30th). The year ended with Oleh on December 21.

central to Anglican self-understanding and provides sufficient extension of the local to enable reasonable catholicity.

The organisational reforms of Gregory VII in the eleventh century struck at the root of this self-understanding by placing the Pope in the ultimate position as arbiter and sign of catholicity. The English, on the other hand, held to the more traditional understanding of the province as the key to catholicity. It is a point that Anglicans have sustained ever since, with varying degrees of success.[12]

In relation to the diocese there is clearly a disposition in general to respect diocesan responsibility and limit the scope of the province: 'It is a general principle of Anglican canon law that, unless a power is clearly reserved by law, the provincial assembly is not competent to interfere with the internal affairs of a diocese or to usurp the jurisdiction of a diocesan assembly.'[13]

National or supra-provincial units

As Anglican churches expanded and grew, especially during the nineteenth century, it became apparent that there was a need for national bodies that could relate to the form of the political environment in which they were operating. In general this provided for some coherence within the nation and enabled some national expression of unity and national witness to Christian faith. Lying behind this move was also some sense in which provinces could not sensibly become too large. Historical circumstances have dictated the relative power of these national bodies and also the degree of coherence they have sought. For example, the provinces and dioceses in the Anglican Church of Australia were well established with their own character and style, a factor reflecting the socio-political context. The national constitution of Australia was established in 1900. Although there had been an Anglican General Synod meeting since 1872, it was largely a consultative body and had no legal foundation, though it did have a constitution. A national church constitution came into force in 1962, nearly one hundred years after the General Synod had begun meeting. Not surprisingly the dioceses were not disposed to give up well-entrenched powers to the new body. As a consequence the General Synod is empowered to pass canons dealing with ritual, ceremonial and discipline in the church

---

[12] The Anglican Consultative Council in 1979 attempted to define the role of a metropolitan, but without a lot of precision because of the diversity of local constitutional arrangements. See ACC.1979,6B.
[13] Doe, *Canon Law*, p. 55.

under certain procedural requirements, but that canon will not come into force in a diocese unless and until the diocese by ordinance adopts the canon.[14] By way of contrast, the Anglican Church of Kenya has had a different history. Along with Uganda and Tanganyika, Kenya was a part of the diocese of Eastern Equatorial Africa when it was formed in 1884. In 1908 the diocese of Mombasa was formed, comprising the whole of Kenya and Tanganyika, and then in 1926 Tanganyika was separated. By a process of internal sub-division a province of Kenya was established in 1970. As a consequence, the Anglican Church of Kenya has a more coherent character and the General Synod more directly operates a number of national institutions.

These supra-national issues have not played a significant part in the development of Anglican polity around the world except that communion with the Archbishop of Canterbury, or with the Church of England, is a common point.[15]

THE ANGLICAN COMMUNION

The story of the emergence, growth and spread of Anglicanism as a discrete tradition of Christian faith has already been set out above. There is a difference between the spread of this tradition and the emergence of patterns of connection between these local manifestations. The Scottish Episcopal Church has existed since 1690. After the American War of Independence Anglicans in America sought a bishop and went to the independent Scottish Episcopal Church, where Samuel Seabury was consecrated in 1784 on the basis of a formal signed agreement.[16] Seabury was elected as a candidate by a meeting of fourteen clergy in Connecticut, in reaction to the moves towards a General Convention for American Anglicans which had been initiated in the southern colonies. It was hardly a church-to-church agreement and the Scottish bishops refused to ordain a second candidate from the same source in 1787. In 1784 the Archbishop of Canterbury was constrained by English law from consecrating bishops for countries outside the jurisdiction of the English crown. That changed in 1786, when the English parliament amended the law to allow for the consecration of three bishops in America, leading to

---

[14] Constitution of the Anglican Church of Australia, Section 30(a), available at: www.anglican.org.au/docs/ACAConstitution-2003.pdf (accessed 19 July 2006).
[15] See Doe, *Canon Law*, pp. 339–41.
[16] See P. H. E. Thomas, 'Unity and Concord: An Early Anglican "Communion"', *Journal of Anglican Studies* 2.1 (2004), pp. 9–21.

the consecration of White, Provoost and Madison. This English legislation clearly had the purpose of allowing the Americans to establish an 'episcopal line' since, according to ancient tradition, three bishops were needed to consecrate a new bishop. The English parliament thus provided for no continuing legal link between the Church of England and the emerging independent American Anglican Church.[17]

This early excursion into relationships between independent Anglican churches illustrates some of the difficulties. Obviously there was a jurisdictional issue because of the established position of the Church of England. But there were also underlying issues of belief. The agreement between Seabury and the Scottish bishops had significant doctrinal elements. Those elements became important in the negotiations in America about the nature of the doctrinal basis for the new constitution. They recur from time to time in relations between Anglican churches around the world. In 1888 the Lambeth Conference resolved that some doctrinal commitments had to be demonstrated by a church before admission to the conference.[18] These commitments amount to giving central recognition to the elements of Anglicanism as identified in the sixteenth-century English Reformation formularies.

The development of organisational arrangements which enabled the various Anglican churches around the world to remain connected to each other have been both various and multitudinous. Missionary societies, religious orders and voluntary organisations such as the Mothers' Union have all contributed to the connectedness of these churches with each other. The Lambeth Conference itself has consistently rejected any idea of it being a legislative or jurisdictional body. In 1863 the Canadian provincial synod asked the Archbishop of Canterbury 'to establish a General Council of bishops consecrated in England and serving overseas to discuss issues then facing the Canadian church'.[19] There was a good deal of opposition to this proposal and in the end Archbishop Longley invited Anglican bishops to a

---

[17] See R. Prichard, *A History of the Episcopal Church* (Harrisburg, Pa.: Morehouse, 1991), pp. 73–103.
[18] LC.1888,19:

> That, as regards newly constituted Churches, especially in non-Christian lands, it should be a condition of the recognition of them as in complete intercommunion with us, and especially of their receiving from us episcopal succession, that we should first receive from them satisfactory evidence that they hold substantially the same doctrine as our own, and that their clergy subscribe articles in accordance with the express statements of our own standards of doctrine and worship; but that they should not necessarily be bound to accept in their entirety the Thirty-Nine Articles of Religion.

[19] Doe, *Canon Law*, p. 344.

conference to 'meet together for brotherly counsel and encouragement'.[20]
The theme is repeated throughout the nineteenth and twentieth centuries.[21]

The Lambeth Conference has generally portrayed the Anglican Communion as a fellowship of churches in the Anglican tradition. The 1930 conference put it clearly:

> The Anglican Communion is a fellowship, within the one Holy Catholic and Apostolic Church, of those duly constituted dioceses, provinces or regional Churches in communion with the See of Canterbury, which have the following characteristics in common:
> a. they uphold and propagate the Catholic and Apostolic faith and order as they are generally set forth in the Book of Common Prayer as authorised in their several Churches;
> b. they are particular or national Churches, and, as such, promote within each of their territories a national expression of Christian faith, life and worship; and
> c. they are bound together not by a central legislative and executive authority, but by mutual loyalty sustained through the common counsel of the bishops in conference.

The twentieth century witnessed not just a dramatic increase in the number of Anglicans around the world, but also its movement away from the developed north. This trend is reflected in the bishops attending the Lambeth Conference and in the development of regional gatherings of bishops and provinces from the growing south. These changes in the demography of world Anglicanism, which began in the second half of the twentieth century, have occasioned an increasing desire to find ways of holding these increasingly diverse expressions of Anglicanism together. So in the last fifty years new organisational arrangements have been created which have come to be called instruments of unity.

Each step in these developments can be seen as a response to a perceived problem: suspected heresy in response to modern biblical studies, the changing role of women in western countries, turmoil and violence in some parts of the world which have led to the persecution of Anglicans, or manifest failures of leadership in the church in the genocide in Rwanda. The timeline of these developments illustrates how this has emerged and also how it is so concentrated in the late twentieth century.

---

[20] Quoted in R. Coleman (ed.), *Resolutions of the Twelve Lambeth Conferences 1867–1988* (Toronto: Anglican Book Centre, 1992), p. viii.
[21] See, for example, the words of Archbishop Benson in 1888 that he opened the conference as in no sense a synod. Quoted in Doe, *Canon Law*, p. 346, n. 32.

Time line of 'official' organisations of the Anglican Communion

Date	Event	Occasion
1784	Agreement between Seabury and the Episcopal Church of Scotland	Seabury's consecration
1786	English law changed to allow the Archbishop of Canterbury to consecrate three bishops for America thus implying no continuing institutional connection	Requests for American bishops
1787	Scottish bishops decline to consecrate US bishops	
1867	First Lambeth Conference. Subsequently meets every ten years	
1897	Lambeth Conference calls for central body to supply information and advice	Did not happen
1908	Pan-Anglican Congress prior to the Lambeth Conference	
1948	Advisory Council on Mission Strategy on resolution of Lambeth Conference	Fisher initiative
1948	St Augustine's College as an Anglican Communion college	Fisher initiative. Later failed
1948	Regional councils appointed South Pacific Council and Council of the Churches of South-East Asia	
1954	Anglican Congress in Minneapolis, attended by 657	
1958	Lambeth Conference with significant non-European bishops present	
1959	Executive officer of Anglican Communication appointed (Stephen Bayne)	Failure of the Advisory Council accepted at 1958 Lambeth Conference
1963	Anglican Congress, Toronto. *Mutual Responsibility and Interdependence in the Body of Christ* document	
1966	Anglican centre established in Rome	
1968	Anglican Consultative Council with a constitution agreed by the provinces and establishment of the position of secretary-general. Meets every three years.	
1979	Council of Anglican Provinces of Africa established	
1979	Primates' Meeting established to advise the Archbishop of Canterbury between Lambeth Conferences. After 1988 it meets more regularly.	
1981	IATDC established by the ACC	Communication and pluralism in the Communion

Time line of 'official' organisations of the Anglican Communion (cont.)

Date	Event	Occasion
1988	*For the Sake of the Kingdom* (IATDC report)	
1988	Regional conferences called for by Lambeth Conference	Did not happen
1998	Primates decide to meet annually	
1998	*Virginia Report* (IATDC)	
2003	Anglican gathering proposed at request of Lambeth Conference, primates and ACC	Dropped for unspecified financial reasons
2004	Lambeth Commission established October 2003 and presented its conclusions in the *Windsor Report*, October 2004	
2005	Archbishop of Canterbury focus of unity Lambeth Conference, ACC and Primates' Meeting as instruments of unity	

At the time of writing there is a lot of discussion about these institutional arrangements and there is no reason to think that they will necessarily survive or stay the same. But the issue of understanding what is going on in world Anglicanism is more profound than simply these developments.

There are a number of dynamics in the world at large which affect the nature and habit of connectedness in world Anglicanism. It is not surprising that there has been a revival of interest amongst historians in world history. The world itself is getting smaller and the community of humanity is more juxtaposed than it has ever been. More than that, massive movements of people in the late twentieth century have heightened the immediacy of the contact between the great cultural and religious traditions. While the polarities of the Cold War have gone, the dynamics of a global environment in which there is only one superpower for the time being is a new and uncertain thing, both for that superpower and other nations. From another perspective, the demise of Russian and Eastern European communism was really the failure of an experiment in a statist version of the European Enlightenment. The other great Enlightenment experiment, which partnered itself with capitalism, has been the United States of America, and we are yet to see whether it can survive the passing of time and the inner logic of its own radical individualism. The changing relativities of population, economic power, wealth and the advance of technologies all make for a highly condensed and dynamic global environment in which world Anglicanism has to find its way.

UNDERLYING ISSUES IN THE ANGLICAN COMMUNION

Clearly there have been some very controversial issues before Anglicans, and these have produced often heated and sustained argument. The presenting issues have been about the relations between the sexes and the roles that are appropriate for women. The ordination of women came to the fore in the last quarter of the twentieth century, but the general question of the role of women in the church had been running from the beginning of the century. The official acceptance of same-sex relationships, through the recognition of liturgies to bless such relationships, or proposals to ordain people in open same-sex relationships, became a crisis issue at and after the 1998 Lambeth Conference. We will track below this gender-relations issue when discussing ministerial order.

The argument about gender relations has also taken the form of an argument about the nature of the Anglican Communion. One can see this in the claims that are made by some participants that the Archbishop of Canterbury should do something to control particular primates or provinces. That demand expresses a view about the nature of the Anglican Communion and the role of the Archbishop of Canterbury, a role the present incumbent Rowan Williams clearly does not accept.

The very form of this argument points to an underlying change in the patterns of power in world Anglicanism. International influence once lay almost exclusively with the Archbishop of Canterbury as the iconic custodian of the Anglican tradition. Throughout the British colonial period the point of reference was essentially the Church of England, but when it came to the first attempt to deal with an international relations problem it was the Archbishop of Canterbury to whom people looked. Canadians and others were greatly exercised by the matter of church discipline, especially raised by the apparent heresy of Bishop Colenso in South Africa and the difficulties experienced in dealing with that disciplinary question purely through church procedures. As churches emerged within the British Empire they all looked to the Archbishop of Canterbury as the focus and custodian of the essential Anglican tradition. By this I do not mean that the occupant of the office was somehow the specialist in Anglicanism. Rather the office of Archbishop of Canterbury was such that it stood for and provided the focus for the character of Anglicanism. This was not a jurisdictional role, though in some places the local dioceses or provinces did give the archbishop an appellate role in disciplinary matters, or a final appointing role when the locals could not appoint a bishop. But these constitutional roles have mostly died out. The representative role of the position has not. The problem is that the force or power of the role has diminished in the light of changes elsewhere.

During the course of the twentieth century a second power centre emerged located in New York. First it came in the form of the expansion during the time of missionary outreach from ECUSA. A very interesting difference between the British imperial expansion of Anglicanism and that which came from America is that the Americans incorporated many of their missionary churches directly into their own metropolitan constitutional arrangements as Province IX, which sends representatives to the General Convention.

Both the English and American hegemonies in worldwide Anglicanism have left continuing effects on contemporary world Anglicanism, largely through the power of money and resources. Half of the income in the budget for the Anglican Communion is paid by the Church of England and one quarter by ECUSA. But far beyond that is the funding of other Anglican entities and subventions for dioceses and provinces by American Anglicans. That funding comes not just from the central funds of ECUSA but from a score of independent church funds, the most significant of which is the foundation attached to Trinity Church on Wall Street, New York. The power of money continues to be an important element in inter-Anglican relations. From the standpoint of wider political patterns the continuing generosity of these two churches is quite remarkable given the strength of the divisions about moral and theological issues.

Yet a third change in the transactions of international Anglicanism is the power of numbers. As the Anglican churches in the rich and historical 'north' have declined in numbers, those in the 'south' (Africa, Asia and South America) have grown. The website of the Church in Nigeria (Anglican Communion) declares that by 1992 'the Church of Nigeria (Anglican Communion) had been proclaimed by the Archbishop of Canterbury as "the fastest growing church in the Anglican Communion"!'[22] According to Philip Jenkins, this reflects a general pattern in Christianity.[23] It was commonly said in the opening decade of the twenty-first century that there were more people in Anglican churches in Nigeria than in the whole of England, Canada and the United States put together. These changes undoubtedly affect the dynamics of inter-Anglican relations. It would be too cynical to say that they drive them, but clearly international relations in Anglicanism are

[22] See www.anglican-nig.org/history.htm (accessed 24 July 2006).
[23] P. Jenkins, *The Next Christendom: The Rise of Global Christianity* (Oxford: Oxford University Press, 2002).

deeply affected by the differently located powers of history, money and numbers.

Inter-Anglican relations have also been influenced by changing technology. A number of bishops found it difficult to get to the first Lambeth Conference because of the long sea voyage by sailing ship. By the 1968 conference most were able to travel by relatively cheap jet aeroplanes. Now there are the internet, emails and websites which convey instantaneous information. The day after the 2006 General Convention of ECUSA, the Council of Anglican Provinces in Africa was able to issue a comment on the decisions of the General Convention. Of course a long voyage by ship provides plenty of time for reflection and it underlines the distance that exists between the parties. In the twenty-first century these communications are much more immediate and instantaneous, and that very fact actually changes the nature of the conversation. Not only does it take place in public, not only is it immediate, it also lacks the input of actual personal encounter and all the modifiers that creates. Modern technology is not just changing the medium, it is reshaping the character of the conversation. Time will tell whether that is helpful or not.

Since the second half of the twentieth century there has been considerable literature arguing that this was a post-denominational time. This literature grew out of the anti-institutional impulses of the 1960s and 1970s in the west. This social movement looked to a different kind of life understanding in which the felt truths of the human condition could be given fuller recognition. This emergence of romanticism was probably to some degree a reaction to the two world wars of the twentieth century and the institutional rigidities of the Cold War. It bore uncanny similarities to the Pentecostal movement which swept across Christianity in the following decades, a movement which still has manifest power. The effect of these disruptions to the landscape of Anglicanism worldwide has been quite considerable. By and large the Pentecostal, or charismatic, movement has not continued to grow in the western churches of Anglicanism, though it has certainly left its mark. Instead it has become central to the character of the African revival in Anglicanism.[24] In that context it found rich soil in the evangelical tradition of Anglicanism and so the growing edge of Anglicanism in the south has the appearance of a conservative and evangelical movement.

These dynamics have led to some very interesting alliances across the more traditional divides in Anglicanism, and also across some of the political and

[24] See ibid.

national divides. So we find conservative coalitions of American evangelical Anglicans with Africans and others against their non-evangelical American colleagues, thus proving the tradition of territorial dioceses and provinces is not a restraint. The Anglican Mission in America is overseen from Singapore, and it has all the marks of the enthusiastic evangelicalism that is emerging in world Christianity.[25] Its website claims:

The United States is now home to the largest population of un-churched and spiritually disconnected English speaking people in the world, yet also a country where the only religion losing members is Christianity. At the same time, Christianity is experiencing a dynamic renewal and expansion in many other parts of the world, including Africa, South America and Asia. Now is the time. In a groundbreaking response, some leaders of the Anglican Church in Africa and Asia have acted to provide seeds of hope for the dire situation in the United States, by establishing the Anglican Mission in America (AMiA). This new movement, like a wave of the Spirit, is quickly gaining momentum, encouraged by the connection to revivals in other parts of the globe. The Anglican Mission is charged with building an alliance of congregations committed to gathering, planting and serving dynamic congregations in the Anglican tradition.[26]

It is not easy to see which Anglican tradition is referred to here. It is a picture entirely innocent of the Anglican tradition of church polity.

These liaisons operate not just in the United States. At the turn of the century the diocese of Sydney proposed to introduce lay presidency or administration of the Eucharist, despite the strong opposition of most of the other dioceses in Australia. However, Sydney shelved its proposals after consulting with conservative bishops in Asia and Africa who did not want to see lay presidency introduced. The more powerful political constraint on the leaders of the diocese of Sydney came not from the rest of the Australian church, where quite strong institutional ties exist, but from the non-institutional ties to others who shared a particular point of view, and with whom the diocese wished to sustain an alliance in the global arena.

These patterns are not new. The emergence of independent societies to give expression to a particular sub-tradition in Anglicanism can be seen in missionary societies. For example, the evangelical Church Missionary Society has given an evangelical stamp to the character of the church in Nigeria as a result of its missionary activity there. The Anglican Church in

---

[25] See the description on the AMiA website, www.theamia.org/amia/index.cfm?ID=FC74816E-B15F-4E69-BFBE8961A34015FD (accessed 24 July 2006).
[26] Ibid.

Papua New Guinea has a similar catholic tradition to the Australian Board of Mission which has worked there for many years.[27]

There is a clear pattern to Anglican church order – parish, diocese and province, each with conciliar structures of governance with archbishop, bishop and clergy ministering. In this pattern the Anglican Communion is an arena of institutional experimentation to deal with inter-provincial relations in a shrinking world. There are a myriad organisations and entities which contribute to the life of Anglican communities. In such a multi-faceted situation power and influence reside in all sorts of different places.

---

[27] See H. Cnattingius, *Bishops and Societies. A Study of Anglican Colonial and Missionary Expansion 1689–1850* (London: SPCK, 1952).

CHAPTER 9

Ministerial offices – ordination

The position of the ordained ministries in Anglicanism reveals a great deal about the wider dynamics of the community and thus also the issues of identity, power and authority amongst Anglicans. The position of the ministerial offices is often an issue of contention in ecumenical dialogue. The Papal Bull *Apostolic Curae* of 1896, which declared that Anglican orders were null and void, has proved to be a matter of great contention. The Pope's declaration was answered by a joint statement by the archbishops of York and Canterbury, an unusual step in itself. On the other hand, many Anglicans have thought that within the Pope's own framework he had reached a reasonable conclusion, and that what was at stake was not the position of Anglican clerical orders, but the ecclesial framework and its assumptions. The position of the ordained was a matter of deep dispute in the renewal movement of the Wesleys in the eighteenth century, of the Tractarians in the nineteenth century and in the charismatic renewal of the twentieth century.

Despite these conflicts the ministerial orders continue in Anglicanism and in many respects flourish in terms of their place in the ecclesiastical order. They are crucial in missions in the fastest-growing sections of world-wide Anglicanism and retain a central place in the public liturgy of the church.

There are significant local variations in both the style and function of the various orders which in most instances arise from the way in which Anglicans have responded to their local context. This adaptation, as we shall see, has proved to be a very complex matter.

Because the ministerial officers are the public face of Anglicanism they are regularly the focus of conflicts within the church. Revelations of sexual misconduct or abuse by clergy have directly affected the standing and reputation of the church. Issues that are generally contentious amongst Anglicans also find a focus in what is done by and in relation to the ordained. This is true of the two most obvious conflicts in recent times, those related to gender relations: whether women should properly be admitted to the ministerial orders and whether people in same-sex relationships should be admitted to these public orders of the church. These loom so large in contemporary world Anglicanism that they will be dealt with in separate chapters.

NON-CLERICAL MINISTRIES

The idea of people exercising ministries of one kind or another without ordination is relatively recent in Anglicanism. Leaving aside the religious orders, most ministries in Anglicanism were conducted by ordained persons until the modern period. But there have always been volunteers in the work of the church. The church after all is a community of people who profess Christ and seek to serve Him both corporately and in their separate vocations. However, there are a number of classes of people who have performed ministerial functions in the church without ordination. Most have been licensed by the bishop to do this work.

In 1866 the bishop of Gloucester admitted the first reader in the Church of England. The English bishops issued rules to govern the appointment and activities of readers. In 2006 there were over 10,200 lay readers in the Church of England – more than the number of ordained ministers. Catechists are widely used in Africa, though latterly they have often been referred to as evangelists. Youth workers are now employed in large numbers in many churches, and large churches will have paid musical directors, administrators and pastoral care workers. However, it is the ordained who are the designated public face of the ministry of the church.

The Anglican experience of the ordained ministry as bishops, priests and deacons arises out the marrow of their tradition. This is true of the general question of having an ordained ministry in the church as well as the more particular tasks that are envisaged for each of the three orders.

THE TRADITION OF ORDERS

The Anglican approach to orders is essentially historical, and given the nature of the tradition is therefore also theological. Modern Anglicanism has been deeply influenced by the ordinal of the 1662 Book of Common Prayer. This is part of the Reformation settlement which has been embedded in many of the Anglican constitutions around the world. The ordinal sets out not only how people are to be made bishops, priests and deacons, but also the nature of those ministries. The underlying assumptions about the fact of these ministries is set out in the preface to the ordinal, the first section of which traces the Anglican pattern back to early apostolic times. 'It is evident unto all men diligently reading holy Scripture and ancient Authors, that from the Apostles' time there have been these Orders of Ministers in Christ's Church; Bishops, Priests, and Deacons.'

Of course, in the light of subsequent scholarship, it is reasonably certain that these three orders have not existed in the church since the time of the apostles. Debates in the nineteenth century in relation to claims for a more expansive notion of episcopacy by the Tractarians led to renewed interest in the early church sources. It helped that these sources were at that time more readily available through the discoveries and earlier critical work of German scholars, together the conclusive work of J. B. Lightfoot. Despite the most rigorous efforts the claim in the preface to the ordinal could not be confirmed in its literal sense. That, however, only serves to highlight the general disposition in Anglicanism to appeal to antiquity to validate such institutional arrangements and to justify innovations.

The 1662 settlement expressed in this ordinal was a decisive moment in the emergence of modern Anglicanism. After the English civil wars and the Commonwealth period the restoration of the monarchy was accompanied by a rigorous return of a form of Anglicanism which deliberately excluded any sense of the religious patterns of the Commonwealth or variations from a strict episcopal ministry. The Restoration was in many respects vindictive and narrowing. Despite the limitations created by its historical particulars, the 1662 ordinal has been fundamentally influential in modern Anglican ordinals and also in the conception of ordained ministries in worldwide Anglicanism.

This 1662 decision led Anglicans into two dynamic forces which have dogged the tradition ever since. On the one hand, the exclusive and monopoly role of the Church of England in the life of the nation established by the Act of Uniformity, of which the 1662 prayer book was part, could not and did not last even in England. The assumptions behind the role and authority of the clergy, and especially the bishops, which were assumed in the 1662 Act therefore have had to contend with changed political and social realities in England and dramatically different circumstances and assumptions in other parts of the world.

Secondly the conciliar element in the Anglican tradition has been expressed in different ways. In England the lay element in the church was made up of parliament and crown, later in the twentieth century in the Church Assembly, and most recently in the general, diocesan and deanery synods. In the eighteenth century in the USA it was incorporated into the

General Convention and in other parts of the world in synods. Phrases such as 'episcopally led and synodically governed' point to a potential tension in these arrangements between perceptions of the traditional authority of bishops and the role of the synod. The balance has been struck in different ways. Similarly, when Anglicans insisted on episcopacy in ecumenical relations they had to admit that such episcopacy would and should be 'locally adapted'.[1] That local adaptation has not been easy, and we shall see that the models of episcopacy in worldwide Anglicanism have been adapted in very ambiguous and contested ways.

Even with these adapting issues, the 1662 ordinal nonetheless provides a useful starting point for the characterisation of the situation in worldwide Anglicanism.

THE ROLE OF DEACONS

Most ordinals around the world provide for deacons principally in the terms of the 1662 Book of Common Prayer, though there has been a notable move in the late twentieth century towards a pattern of permanent deacons. The ordinal provides that deacons should be properly tested and examined as to their spiritual and moral fitness and that they are convinced that they have been called to the office and ministry of a deacon. The bishop outlines the terms of that office in some detail. The deacon is to assist the priest in divine service and especially in the administration of Holy Communion, to read the scriptures and homilies of the church and instruct the youth in the catechism, to baptise infants when the priest is not available, and to visit the sick, poor and impotent in the parish in order that they might be relieved with the alms of the parishioners.

---

[1] This is the phrase used in the Lambeth Quadrilateral which is the name given to the four items in the resolution of the 1888 Lambeth Conference; LC.1888,11.

That, in the opinion of this Conference, the following articles supply a basis on which approach may be by God's blessing made towards home reunion:
a. The Holy Scriptures of the Old and New Testaments, as 'containing all things necessary to salvation', and as being the rule and ultimate standard of faith.
b. The Apostles' Creed, as the baptismal symbol; and the Nicene Creed, as the sufficient statement of the Christian faith.
c. The two sacraments ordained by Christ himself – Baptism and the Supper of the Lord – ministered with unfailing use of Christ's words of institution, and of the elements ordained by him.
d. The historic episcopate, locally adapted in the methods of its administration to the varying needs of the nations and peoples called of God into the unity of his Church.

See the discussion of the resolution in Wright, *Quadrilateral at One Hundred*.

These welfare provisions reflect the coalescence of church and society assumed in the 1662 book, and so in more recent times the welfare emphasis of the deacon's role has been supplanted by general social provisions, and deacons have become more like assistants to the parish priest.

THE ROLE OF PRIESTS

The priest is an altogether different category. Here the office carries much greater responsibility and the exhortations and warnings are profound and deeply challenging.

And now again we exhort you, in the Name of our Lord Jesus Christ, that ye have in remembrance, into how high a Dignity, and to how weighty an Office and Charge ye are called: that is to say, to be Messengers, Watchmen, and Stewards of the Lord; to teach, and to premonish, to feed and provide for the Lord's family; to seek for Christ's sheep that are dispersed abroad, and for his children who are in the midst of this naughty world, that they may be saved through Christ for ever.

Have always therefore printed in your remembrance, how great a treasure is committed to your charge. For they are the sheep of Christ, which he bought with his death, and for whom he shed his blood. The Church and Congregation whom you must serve, is his Spouse, and his Body. And if it shall happen that the same Church, or any Member thereof, do take any hurt or hindrance by reason of your negligence, ye know the greatness of the fault, and also the horrible punishment that will ensue. Wherefore consider with yourselves the end of the Ministry towards the children of God, towards the Spouse and Body of Christ; and see that ye never cease your labour, your care and diligence, until ye have done all that lieth in you, according to your bounden duty, to bring all such as are or shall be committed to your charge, unto that agreement in the faith and knowledge of God, Wherefore consider with yourselves the end of the Ministry towards the children of God, towards the Spouse and Body of Christ; and see that ye never cease your labour, your care and diligence, until ye have done all that lieth in you, according to your bounden duty, to bring all such as are or shall be committed to your charge, unto that agreement in the faith and knowledge of God, and to that ripeness and perfectness of age in Christ, that there be no place left among you, either for error in religion, or for viciousness in life.

WILL you then give your faithful diligence
- always so to minister the Doctrine and Sacraments, and the Discipline of Christ, as the Lord hath commanded, and as this Church hath received the same, according to the Commandments of God; so that you may teach the people committed to your Cure and Charge with all diligence to keep and observe the same?
- to banish and drive away from the Church all erroneous and strange doctrines contrary to God's Word; and to use both public and private monitions and exhortations, as well to the sick as to the whole, within your Cures, as need shall require, and occasion shall be given?

- be diligent in Prayers, and in reading the Holy Scriptures, and in such studies as help to the knowledge of the same, laying aside the study of the world and the flesh?
- to frame and fashion your own selves, and your families, according to the Doctrine of Christ; and to make both yourselves and them, as much as in you lieth, wholesome examples and patterns to the flock of Christ?
- maintain and set forwards, as much as lieth in you, quietness, peace, and love, among all Christian people, and especially among them that are or shall be committed to your charge?
- reverently obey your Ordinary, and other chief Ministers, unto whom is committed the charge and government over you; following with a glad mind and with their godly admonitions, and submitting yourselves to their godly judgments?

The bishop then goes on to examine the candidate as to their orthodoxy and manner of life. It is clear that this is the central order for giving effect to the ministry of the church. It is the priest who is charged with the essential tasks of creating and sustaining a Christian community by their actions, teaching and exhortation. There is an astonishing level of coherence between the tasks and preaching of the priest and their conduct and life as a priest. Everything hangs on the way the priest lives and conducts their ministry for the effective life of the church. Yet in all this priests are not just the servants of the church, and thus enrolled in the authority structure of the church; they are also, indeed primarily, the agent of God. They are servants and cooperative workers with God in the execution of the mission of God in the church and the world. For this reason the bishop charges the priest to a life of prayer and the study of scripture.

THE ROLE OF BISHOPS

In the tradition of the 1662 prayer book the bishop is essentially a priest with certain other wider responsibilities. They are asked if they will:

- maintain and set forward, as much as shall lie in you, quietness, love, and peace among all men; and such as be unquiet, disobedient, and criminous, within your Diocese, correct and punish, according to such authority as you have by God's Word, and as to you shall be committed by the Ordinance of this Realm?
- and to be faithful in Ordaining, sending, or laying hands upon others?

It is clear that the precise roles and duties of a bishop in 1662 were further detailed in the 'ordinances of this realm', and similarly it is the case that the roles of bishops in modern Anglicanism are set out in canons and constitutions in somewhat more detail in relation to the practicalities of the life of the church. However, in the broader tradition of Anglicanism the essential role of the bishop remains that of oversight and ordination in a diocese.

LOCAL ADAPTATION AND CURRENT PRACTICE

Some of the key adaptations in the role of bishops in worldwide Anglicanism can be seen in the different ways they are appointed, the roles they are given and the leadership styles which they adopt.

The most common method of appointing bishops in Anglicanism is by popular election. This pattern emerged in the eighteenth century in the independent United States under the inspiration of the democratic temper of the new nation. They could very properly claim that this was the way in which bishops were appointed in the early church. However, the manner of the election and the checks and balances which developed in the USA were undoubtedly influenced by local political practices. With some variations an election is held in the diocese in which the person is to be bishop. That election is usually through a synod made up of representatives of the parishes in the diocese. Some dioceses have nominating boards that screen candidates and present nominations. Once elected by a diocesan synod the election must be confirmed by the General Convention, the national representative gathering of dioceses. In between meetings of the General Convention such confirmations can be given by the National Executive Council.

A similar pattern of local election and wider provincial confirmation occurs in many other parts of the world. Sometimes, such as in Australia, the confirmation is simply of the canonical fitness of the candidate rather than a confirmation of the election itself. Some dioceses appoint through a board which has been elected by the synod.

This balance of local election and wider confirmation embodies two principles which have been prominent in Anglicanism: on the one hand, the priority of acting locally and corporately, a conciliarist pattern; on the other hand, a sense of catholicity, which is expressed through the structure of the province. In some cases the national body performs this task, as in the USA, even though there are provinces within the national church. There are also provinces within the national church in other countries and the confirmation happens at the provincial level. Where the confirmation is simply about canonical fitness this confirmation is usually done by the other bishops of the province. Throughout most of Africa and South America this pattern pertains. Sometimes these elections are difficult and captured by local politics within the church. Sometimes candidates openly campaign for election and even contest the result through the civil courts.

A significantly different approach is followed in England, and with some differences in Nigeria. In England bishops are appointed by the crown. For this purpose there is a Crown Appointments Officer in the Prime Minister's office who maintains a system of consultation through a committee with state and church representatives on it. The diocese and others are consulted and three names are given to the Prime Minister, who in turn recommends one of them to the Queen for appointment. Sometimes the Prime Minister declines the advice and asks for more names, or declines the priority of the names given to him.

In Nigeria there is similar consultation in the case of diocesan bishops, but appointments are made by the synod of bishops. Within the Nigerian church constitution there is a national synod and a primate. There is also a synod of bishops who meet regularly and who have specific constitutional responsibilities, one of which is the appointment of bishops. In Nigeria there is an added and very distinctive element in the whole process because the bishops' synod can and does appoint missionary bishops whose task is to establish a church and a new diocese. While they are appointed to dioceses they are in effect putative dioceses, and building the community and structures of those dioceses is the responsibility of the missionary bishops.

Each of these methods of appointing bishops in worldwide Anglicanism reflects different ideas about the precise role of bishops. At the same time they show a similar disposition to adapt to the local social and cultural patterns. The English system reflects a residual establishment pattern with a state role in the life of the church. The democratic model of election is usually shaped by the democratic practices of the political environment, though this is by no means always the case and certainly not in countries where there is not a democratic political system. Nonetheless the election pattern proceeds on the assumption that the bishop is being appointed to an existing operating diocese. The Nigerian model is much more decisively missionary in orientation, and at the same time arises from a constitution which is more episcopally dominated than most other arrangements. The appointments process bears the marks of elders selecting fellow elders in a traditional style.

It is clear that the role of bishops differs greatly around the world, not least because of the different circumstances in which they operate. A bishop in the highlands of Papua New Guinea has different challenges from the bishop of New York. The bishop in PNG directly faces fundamental issues of ministerial oversight, of preaching and evangelism. The bishop is more central to the teaching of the faith in the diocese. The bishop of New York has theologians at hand and theological institutions which are able to engage with the teaching of the faith. The resources of the diocese are more extensive and different in character. Money to employ people is readily available, whereas the bishop in PNG will need to seek volunteers to sustain the work of the diocese.

Bishops in large western dioceses inevitably become managers in a way that does not happen in smaller dioceses, especially in developing countries. The actual size of dioceses differs greatly even within countries. The diocese of Los Angeles has 147 parishes in one metropolitan city, whereas within the same church and polity the diocese of Hawaii has 41 parishes scattered on five islands. The smallest diocese in the Church of England is Sodor and Man with 30 parishes. The largest is London with 500 parishes. Canada has a total of 1,500 parishes with an average diocese consisting of 200 parishes. The comparable figure in Kenya is 68 and in Brazil 24. There is nothing comparable to the situation in the Church of England where a number of bishops are members of the House of Lords. This residue of a direct political role for the church in the affairs of state stands out as entirely unique in worldwide Anglicanism, and in the context of other continuing elements of establishment affects the expectations laid upon bishops in the Church of England as well as the aspirations.

Ordination services in different parts of the world have reflected the changes of emphasis in the role of bishops. In the Episcopal Church in the USA changes in the ordinal have given more specific place to the role of clergy and bishops in the administrative affairs of the church. It has been suggested by a leading liturgy scholar that the development of the ordinal in the USA has also tended in the direction of a managerial bishop.[2] The focus on the nature of the church in the ordinal of the 1662 Book of Common Prayer which was quoted above has changed in some liturgies to a focus on the responsibilities of the priest or bishop. The 1995 prayer book of the Anglican Church of Australia points to the role of the candidate without the church-defining elements in the older book. The prayer book of the Anglican Church of Canada, on the other hand, gives special attention to the role of the bishop in working with other bishops to maintain and further the unity of the church. Unlike an English bishop, the Kenyan bishop is not told by the archbishop in the ordinal to 'govern the church', a phrase which goes back to the earlier English prayer books and their establishment assumptions. It appears in the Australian prayer book and some others. The Canadian ordinal omits the detailed description of the role of the

---

[2] See B. Spinks, 'An Unfortunate Lex Orandi? Some Comments on Episcopacy Envisioned in the 1979 ECUSA Ordinal', *Journal of Anglican Studies* 2.2 (2004), pp. 58–69.

bishop. These differences may in part be explained in terms of degrees of liturgical conservatism, but the language of government holds its position in the ordinals for mainly historical and traditional reasons. To some extent its use can be seen as transference to the bishop in a more thoroughly ecclesial context attributes and authority which in early modern England had obvious political connotations.

There are other liturgical variations in ordination services around the world. Most contain the elements of presentation of the candidate, scripture reading, examination of candidates, prayer and laying-on of hands, and rites of vesting or the presentation of the instruments of office. It is also increasingly thought that ordination is conducted by the bishop on behalf of the whole church, and this is reflected in people participating in the presentation of candidates. The variations in ordinals, as with other services, reflect also the theological emphases of the province. The Nigerian ordinal includes an anointing, and bishops are identified as being 'hallowed for the work of the Pontifical Order by this anointing with the Holy Chrism of Sanctification'. This emphasis is in line with the high place given to bishops in the church constitution in Nigeria. These ordinals reflect 'the spectrum of theological opinion within the Communion as to whether ordination confers a function, empowers existing charisms, accomplishes an ontological change, or has some combination of these effects'.[3]

The way in which individual bishops carry out their responsibilities undoubtedly reflects the personalities and gifts of each person, though that is clearly set within the cultural styles and customs of their context. Those customs may derive from what are thought to be the natural tendencies of a particular class of people – men, for example. This has been one of the elements in the arguments about women bishops to which we shall return later. However, it is not easy to be precise about cultural styles and customs.

The point is well illustrated by Simon Chiwanga, a bishop in Tanzania. In 2001 he published an article on episcopacy in which he pleaded for a change from an authoritarian and hierarchical style of leadership to a more collaborative and servant style of leadership. The title of his article, 'Beyond the Monarch/Chief', illustrates the ambiguity of the issue. He saw this as 'a call from the foreign monarchical influences and the negative aspects of traditional African chieftainship in our leadership style'.[4] He argued that the

---

[3] R. G. Leggett, 'Anglican Ordinals', in Hefling and Shattuck, *Oxford Guide to the Book of Common Prayer*, p. 535.
[4] S. Chiwanga, 'Beyond the Monarch/Chief: Reconsidering Episcopacy in Africa', in Douglas and K. Pui-Lan, *Beyond Colonial Anglicanism*, p. 300.

hierarchical style arises where there is a culture of dependency in the community in which leadership is being exercised. He claimed that this dependency mentality results 'from the fear and inferiority complex created during the colonial period'.[5] He also alluded to the hierarchical aspects of the traditional African chiefdom model of leadership. What is essentially at issue for Chiwanga is the nature of the community within which the ministry is to be conducted. It is not just that the leadership should suit the existing community, but also that the leadership should contribute to the creation of a mature Christian community.

Simon Chiwanga is widely travelled and very experienced in the international Anglican scene. He was the chair of the ACC and is well aware of the styles and movements in western churches. However, when dealing with this issue he focuses his attack on the negative aspects of both the western colonial style and the traditional chieftain style. He deploys scriptural examples and teaching from Jesus in order to argue for a style of leadership which is collaborative and humble, marked by service – *mhudumu* in Swahili. He sees this operating within a church which is more mutual, a 'familyhood' ecclesiology – *ujamaa* in Swahili. He is critical of the 1978 Lambeth statement on the function of a bishop as being clearly hierarchical.

The nature of the argument illustrates the ambiguity of the notion of cultural adaptation. There are in fact negative aspects in most cultural styles. The issue is therefore not simply to enculturate, but rather to do so appropriately in terms of the religious impulses and values in the tradition of faith. Judging what is appropriate enculturation, in this case for the work of a bishop, calls for a critical analysis in the light of the theological tradition of Anglicanism, and that analysis will in itself involve some critical appraisal of elements of that tradition. That very fact raises to the surface the necessity for an awareness of the general character of the tradition simply to enable local adaptations to be carried forward. It is an issue Anglicans have been somewhat slow to engage with.

Many conversations in worldwide Anglicanism are complicated by the desire to keep out of the conversation differences of legitimation for aspects of the institutionality of ministerial orders. There is a very significant range of views as to the theological character and significance of these ministerial orders. On the one hand, there are those who place high esteem on the apostolic and divine character of episcopacy. This ensures a more exact and emphatic doctrine of the sacraments, and of the Eucharist in particular. Here the authority and power of the Eucharist, or indeed what is said to be

[5] Ibid., pp. 297f.

its validity, essentially depends on the divine office of the bishop. On the other hand, a different view of the special divine character of episcopacy places more emphasis on the function of the bishop and regards its divine character more in the divine immanence of the activities of the bishop than in the office. A different emphasis in Eucharistic theology sits with this estimation. In present-day worldwide Anglicanism these differences are virtually intractable, yet they lie hidden behind debates about other issues which appear more immediate and seem to call for some resolution and action. Matters such as emerging patterns of governance in the church between the various parts of worldwide Anglicanism are fraught with this problem. The episcopal character of the new 'instruments of unity' in the current ecclesial experiment worries some people, in part because of these 'under-the-table' issues.

Some distinction needs to be made between the offices of bishop, priest and deacon and the positions which people in these orders hold in the church. Many parts of worldwide Anglicanism provide for assistant bishops who may simply assist a diocesan bishop, or may be delegated a region within a diocese. This model is extensively used in England and Australia especially in the larger dioceses. Some churches, such as the Episcopal Church in the USA, provide for coadjutor bishops to be elected. Such bishops often have a right of succession to the diocesan bishop. Each province will have a bishop who is designated archbishop, or metropolitan. These are positions, not orders, and the titles lapse when the office has been relinquished. The same is true of the title of primate, which is usually used for the prime bishop of a province or a national church. The American Episcopal Church uses the title 'presiding bishop' rather than primate, perhaps reflecting the republican sentiments of the American culture.

RELIGIOUS ORDERS

There is another group of people who are not all ordained, but nonetheless are recognised as being in a limited sense part of the ordered ministry of the church. These are members of religious orders. It is a limited sense because not all by any means are ordained, and for the most part the members of religious orders are not as such subject to the same jurisdiction as other clergy. They fall in the first instance under the authority of the order itself. Nonetheless the religious orders have an important place in the Anglican tradition.

The perception of religious orders in modern Anglicanism is directly affected by the place assigned to the English Reformation in Anglican memory. The Protestant Briton who emerged in the eighteenth century remembered the monastic houses dissolved in the sixteenth century as centres of medieval corruption, and successor post-Trent Roman Catholic religious orders as politically subversive and religiously unscrupulous.[6] This disposition was reinforced for some in the ritualist controversies of the nineteenth century, when the Tractarian renewal also prompted the formation of religious orders in England. Any serious attempt to understand the Anglican tradition will need to go beyond this limited image. The reality is that from the earliest times religious orders were part of English Christianity and thus of the tradition which constitutes the foundations of Anglicanism. They were vital elements in sustaining the faith in troubled times and played some very characteristically Anglican roles. They have not been without blemish, but at times they have represented the utmost commitment and Christian faith. Throughout they have been in their particular and changing way a crucial part of the church and its mission.

In the earliest period of English Christianity monasticism had played a vital role. Monastic houses provided crucial resources of learning and pastoral care. Monastic houses were established in the houses of kings and bishops. Attaching such a monastic house to the bishopric was unusual in western Christianity at the time, and it reflected the location of the bishoprics in the countryside rather than in the towns. Double houses were established, with men and women members unusually presided over by an abbess. Hilda presided over such a house at Whitby where the great synod of AD 664 was held. The monasteries provided the backbone of pastoral care and teaching for the church and were the seedbeds of the growth of a English Christian culture. The essential structure of the church was diocesan and monastic, with the development of parishes coming somewhat later.

There was a revival in monastic life in the second half of the tenth century which led to the formulation of the *Regularis Concordia* under the guidance of Dunstan (909–88). It was an English amalgamation of Benedictine and Cluniac rules. The rule was applied throughout England. After the Norman Conquest there was more regularising under the influence of Lanfranc. In the following centuries the religious houses continued this varied experience. It was inevitable that privileges in a social institution should from time to time attract unworthy people, or that the vows and ideals would be forgotten. That was not a peculiarity of the early sixteenth century, just as the condition of the religious houses was not as notorious as the propaganda which sought to justify their dissolution claimed – an early modern case of 'spin'.

---

[6] On the emergence of the Protestant Briton see L. Colley, *Britons: Forging the Nation, 1707–1837* (New Haven, Conn.: Yale University Press, 1992).

There were undoubtedly other social and political forces at work. Certainly John Bramhall in 1654 stated the case generously when he said 'We fear that covetousness had a great oar in the boat, and that sundry of the principal actors had a greater aim at the goods of the church, than at the good of the church.'[7] The dissolution also had the effect of removing from the political power structure a source of independent authority in religion which the monasteries had represented.

The point I wish to underline here is that this political act and the religious language of its justification should not have the effect of causing us to imagine that religious orders have never been part of the Anglican tradition, and that they are somehow foreign to its instincts. Such a view is in almost every respect inaccurate and misleading. Although the dissolution of the monasteries and the consequent removal of religious orders was very thorough under Henry VIII, the sentiment for religious life did not disappear, and it came to expression from time to time virtually from the time of the Restoration until its more overt revival in the nineteenth century. The material is summarised by Peter Ansom, who draws attention to the Royal Foundation of St Katharine which had continuously existed in London since 1273.[8]

It is all the more a pity that when religious orders were revived in the nineteenth century they copied the patterns of the then current Roman Catholic religious orders and did not go back to their own Anglican foundations. What happened was probably inevitable given the Tractarian inspiration for renewal and the ritualist context in which it took place. Nonetheless, once revived as part of the life of the church, the orders steadily flourished and are a significant part of the worldwide history and experience of Anglicanism.[9]

On the international scene the orders took on a wide variety of roles including evangelism, church planting and building, education and pastoral work. The resolutions of the Lambeth Conference reflect some aspects of the way in which the religious orders were regarded in this period. In 1897

---

[7] J. Bramhall, *A Just Vindication of the Church of England from the Unjust Aspersion of Criminal Schisme, Etc* (London: John Crook, 1654), quoted here in A. M. Allchin, *The Theology of the Religious Life: An Anglican Approach* (Oxford: SLG Press, 1971), p. 2.

[8] See P. Ansom, *The Call of the Cloister. Religious Communities and Kindred Bodies in the Anglican Communion* (London: SPCK, 1964), pp. 1–28. Ansom provides a comprehensive overview of Anglican religious orders.

[9] For an overview of orders see Anglican Religious Communities, *Anglican Religious Communities Year Book. Fifth International Edition 2006–7* (Norwich: Canterbury Press, 2005). Material on Anglican orders is given in P. D. Day, *Dictionary of Religious Orders* (Tunbridge Wells: Burns and Oates, 2001). I am indebted to Tom Campbell for access to his database of Religious Communities of the Anglican Communion in Australia, New Zealand and the South Pacific.

the conference recognised with thankfulness the revival of the brotherhoods and sisterhoods and of the office of deaconesses and commended a report on the subject. In 1908 the conference focused on problems of the relationship of the orders to the episcopate. In 1920 vows of celibacy were said not to be appropriate for deaconesses. In 1930 the conference is concerned about closer cooperation between the episcopate and the communities. In 1948 the bishops value the witness of the communities, but believe Christians are generally called to take their place in the life of the world. In 1958 they hope that the religious life will find expression in a wide range of ecclesiastical traditions and look for closer cooperation with bishops.

The high point of numbers in religious orders came in the early twentieth century, though later in the century there were increasing trends for orders to have other members, called, variously, tertiaries, oblates or associates. These people were not full-time in the community but fulfilled their vocation under a form of the vows of the order while pursuing their other occupations. This tendency sat well with the blossoming interest in spirituality in the western world in the last twenty years of the twentieth century.

From the beginning of the revival of the nineteenth century there was a commitment to the ordered life of prayer. Many orders also engaged in charitable works – often what others were not willing to do. Religious orders were to be found in the down-and-out sections of society. They ran rescue homes for street women, schools, hospitals and nursing homes, and undertook a vast array of pastoral work. Sometimes religious orders in one country established houses in other countries, and often there were local initiatives in response to a perceived need or to a felt calling on the part of individuals or groups. Religious orders have houses in twenty-one of the thirty-eight provinces and Uniate churches and in one extra provincial diocese. There are 102 orders working in 312 locations in thirty-one countries.[10]

In 1865 the Community of the Holy Name had begun in the parish of Vauxhall, London, as a community of women to do parish work. The life of prayer in the community house was the inspiration for the work which was done by the sisters outside the house. In 1943 the community of St Michael and All Angels opened a house in Leribe, Basutoland. The order had been founded earlier by the bishop of Bloemfontein as a community which would give itself to prayer and mission work in South Africa. The sisters engaged in education and nursing as well as maintaining a mother house of prayer.

[10] These figures are derived from the listing on the Anglican Communion website, available at: www.anglicancommunion.org/communities/index.cfm (accessed 16 January 2007).

In 1959, at a time when racial tensions were mounting in South Africa, the bishop of Basutoland asked the Sisters of the Holy Name in England to assist in establishing a multiracial community house in Leribe. Three African sisters from the Leribe community were trained in the novitiate in the English mother house and they returned with five English sisters to establish the multiracial house in Leribe which was called the Convent of the Holy Name. The vows and order of the Community of the Holy Name were maintained, and the central activity of the house became the basis for work in prisons and amongst youth. The daily routine of the house follows matins, Eucharist (several times a week when a priest is available), terce, midday office, evening prayer and compline.

On the basis of their own multiracial character the Community of the Holy Name in Leribe was active in the anti-apartheid movement. In 1969 three sisters from this community moved to Melmoth and established another house. Further houses were established in Kwazulu-Natal (Durban and Nongoma), Transkei (Umtata) and Swaziland (Luyengo). Maintaining a multiracial religious community in apartheid South Africa provided a powerful testimony to the transcultural vocation of the gospel. To engage at the same time in pastoral and social work with some of those most affected by the evils of the apartheid regime gave that witness edge and power. This was an African creation aided in a modest way by English co-religionists, developed in an African context with stunning effect in the political and social situation. It also testified to the socially subversive role of a monastic vocation.

Religious communities do not flourish everywhere but they persist in portraying something of the otherness of faith. They provide a focus for the generalised spirituality of modern societies whether that spirituality is quietist or enthusiastic. They have a long history in Anglicanism and retain a crucial part in the pattern of the worldwide Anglican faith in the twenty-first century. Speaking of the Society of the Sacred Mission, Adrian Hastings said: 'The history of SSM across a hundred years is fascinating, diverse and often sad. It throws a great deal of light upon twentieth-century Anglicanism, both its glories and its failings.'[11]

Within the general pattern of ordained ministry two issues of adaptation have convulsed Anglicans worldwide during the last quarter of the twentieth century: the place of women in the ministerial offices and the issue of same-sex relationships for those in ministerial orders. To these we must now turn.

---

[11] A. Mason, *History of the Society of the Sacred Mission* (Norwich: Canterbury Press, 1993), p. iv.

CHAPTER 10

Ministerial offices – ordination of women

The place of women in the ordained orders of Anglicanism is of course part of a history of the place of women in Anglican institutions generally. For the modern twenty-first-century person it is surprising to find that Anglicans debated with some heat whether or not women could serve as church wardens in local parishes, or on parish councils, or on diocesan synods or on national General Synods. But they did, and those debates reached a sufficient level of general concern to attract the attention of the Lambeth Conference of bishops. In 1920 the Lambeth Conference resolved that 'Women should be admitted to those councils of the Church to which laymen are admitted, and on equal terms. Diocesan, provincial, or national synods may decide when or how this principle is to be brought into effect.'[1] This enlightened approach did not bring about widespread change in the dioceses and provinces for another fifty years. Not until 1970 did the General Convention of ECUSA resolve to admit women as members of the Convention.

Given that the ordained ministries were amongst the most traditional of the church's institutions, and that they directly affected issues of power and authority in the church, it is not surprising that there was considerable disagreement about the inclusion of women in those orders. There were also very important theological arguments which were brought to bear and to which we shall return shortly. The spirit of the early twentieth century can be seen in a 1921 resolution of the London Diocesan Conference that 'It is generally inexpedient and contrary to the interests of the church that women should publicly minister in consecrated buildings.'[2]

---

[1] LC.1920,46.
[2] Quoted from M. Porter, *Women in the Church: The Great Ordination Debate in Australia* (Ringwood, Vic.: Penguin, 1989), p. 20.

THE STORY OF CHANGES

First, however, we set out in brief compass the story of the changes in Anglicanism. The modern story begins in 1944 in the middle of the Second World War when Japanese troops were overrunning China. Florence Tim Oi Li was a deaconess with responsibility for a large parish in Macao which was flooded with refugees from the war. The bishop of Hong Kong, R. O. Hall, ordained her to be a priest so that she could properly care for the parish in its isolation. His action caused a tremendous furore. He was subjected to intense pressure, not least from the Archbishop of Canterbury, and effectively told to reverse his actions. In a situation where it seemed that the bishop would have to resign or accede, Florence took it into her own hands and withdrew from priestly ministry.[3]

The 1948 Lambeth Conference condemned the ordination and refused a request from the Chinese bishops for approval for them to have a trial period of twenty-five years of women's ordinations. It is interesting that this same Lambeth Conference is recalled for its famous resolution on dispersed authority. It did not seem to want the Chinese bishops to have too much dispersed authority. David Paton records a letter from Bishop Hall in which he declares that Lambeth was not the right place to argue this matter. It should be dealt with in the national churches. Following the 1948 Lambeth Conference the debate did indeed go to the national churches especially in North America and England.

In 1968 it came back to the Lambeth Conference and the bishops resolved to encourage the member churches to study the issues and report to the meeting of the newly established Anglican Consultative Council which was to meet in 1971 in Limuru, Kenya. The ACC debated the matter but there was little information from the provinces. The record of the meeting notes that the bishop of Hong Kong had sought advice because his diocesan synod had approved in principle the ordination of women as priests. It was noted that the issue was under discussion in other places, and in the USA 'more than one woman feels called to priesthood'.[4]

After a close debate the ACC resolution 28 noted that 'Many of the churches of the Anglican Communion regard the question of ordination of women to the priesthood as an urgent matter.'[5] The Council asked churches

---

[3] The story is told in D. M. Paton, *The Life and Times of Bishop Ronald Hall of Hong Kong* (Hong Kong: Diocese of Hong Kong and Macao and the Hong Kong Diocesan Association, 1985).

[4] Anglican Consultative Council, *The Time Is Now*, First Meeting, Limuru, Kenya, 23 February – 5 March 1971 (London: SPCK, 1971), p. 34.

[5] Ibid., p. 38.

in the Communion to express their views in time for the next meeting of the ACC in 1973. The bishop of Hong Kong was not present at the 1971 meeting, and the language of the second section of the resolution suggests that the actual request for advice came through the Council of the Churches of East Asia (CCEA). The CCEA was a consultative body for those dioceses in East Asia which were not part of a province and which were 'extra-provincial'. By implication this meant that they fell under the general over-sight of the Archbishop of Canterbury (Michael Ramsey), who was also the chair of the ACC and present at the debate. No mention of his role in relation to the diocese of Hong Kong is made in the records of the ACC meeting. The Council resolved to advise the bishop of Hong Kong:

acting with the approval of his Synod, and any other bishop of the Anglican Communion acting with the approval of his Province, that, if he decides to ordain women to the priesthood, his action will be acceptable to this Council; and that this Council will use its good offices to encourage all Provinces of the Anglican Communion to continue in communion with these dioceses.[6]

This is a quite remarkable resolution for a number of reasons. First it offers its advice not just to the bishop of Hong Kong but to all bishops of the Anglican Communion. Where such bishops are part of a province, which Hong Kong was not, they are urged to act only with the agreement of the province. Second, the resolution shows the ACC willing to make the running on the issue, both with its positive advice and also in its decision to continue with the question at its next meeting. It is not surprising that the resolution was carried by a small margin of twenty-four to twenty-two. Fifty-six members are recorded as present at the meeting, so not all voted.

In 1971 the bishop of Hong Kong, Gilbert Baker, ordained Jane Hwang and Joyce Bennett. The diocese of Hong Kong was not a large entity, though its actions had important flow-on effects. The Episcopal Church of the United States of America was a large church, and in the post-war period was increasingly influential. Despite the US Bill of Rights, women had long struggled in ECUSA for access to governance structures. Only in 1970 did the General Convention have women represented in its membership. At the same General Convention the ordination of women as deacons was approved, but the ordination of women as priests was defeated by a large majority in the midst of noisy opposition to any such move. The first deacons were ordained in 1971.

---

[6] Ibid., p. 39.

In 1973 the ACC began its report by stating that 'there is no more pressing and perplexing problem than that of the ordination of women to the priest-hood'.[7] It underlined that the Council was not a legislative body for the dioceses and provinces, but a consultative one. Even so the Council records that it feels some responsibility for leadership and therefore it proposes to consider the matter[8] and in doing so reaffirmed its previous advice by a large majority. The ACC 1973 report contains a summary of action on this question since the Limuru meeting. It noted that 'no church or province has ceased to be in communion with the diocese of Hong Kong'.[9]

The Anglican Consultative Council had thus not only drawn attention to the constitutional reality of local option at the international level; it had created an environment in which that was an accepted and supported option. In ECUSA independent local action was pursued as a political strategy to secure official agreement at the General Convention. Under the constitution of ECUSA retired bishops retain a role in the Convention and are members of the House of Bishops. One of the new deacons, Suzanne Hiatt, initiated a plan which led to three retired bishops ordaining eleven of the new deacons as priests in 1971. The women were in one sense canonically ordained, though not entirely, since they lacked a licence or a place in the diocesan framework of ECUSA. For this reason their position was described as irregular. They were not allowed to function as priests in their dioceses, and clergy who allowed them to do so were disciplined. There were more such ordinations openly planned in the run-up to the 1976 General Convention. Four more women were ordained in Washington in 1975. The General Convention thus met in a very dynamic and powerful political situation; they voted in favour of the ordination of women as priests and to regularise the ordinations that had already taken place. Other national churches authorised the ordination of women as priests: Canada in 1976 and New Zealand in 1977.

Thus when the Lambeth Conference met in 1978 it was able to note that four churches had ordained women (Hong Kong, Canada, the USA and New Zealand) and that a further eight churches had agreed in principle, or had no objection to such ordinations. That means that twelve of the

---

[7] Anglican Consultative Council, *Partners in Mission*, Second Meeting, Dublin, Ireland, 17–27 July 1973 (London: SPCK, 1973), p. 37.

[8] Ibid., p. 41.

[9] Ibid., p. 39. Only Hong Kong had ordained any women. Eight churches had approved in principle (Canada, England, Scotland, Wales, Indian Ocean, New Zealand, USA and Ireland) and preliminary action had been taken in three (South Africa, Central Africa and West Indies). Singapore had voted against it and Sri Lanka had put it aside as not urgent.

possible thirty-six decision-makers (twenty-four provinces and twelve extra-provincial dioceses) were in favour of the ordination of women to the priesthood. The thrust of the 1978 Lambeth Conference was on maintaining relationships both within the Anglican Communion and with other churches in the light of what was acknowledged as a 'variety of doctrine and practice'.[10] The conference report notes that the focus was on fellowship amongst the bishops, that fewer resolutions were considered and also that this was the first residential conference and was held in Canterbury.

It affirmed the right of churches and provinces to make their own decisions and called on them to maintain communion with each other.[11] There is no suggestion in the report of this conference of acting to sustain communion between those who had gone ahead, and no sense of the conference taking any action other than to call for respect and to urge some constraints on the deployment of women clergy. Rather the conference calls on the ACC to 'use its good offices to promote dialogue' between those dioceses that differ on this point. In relation to bishops the conference acknowledged the constitutional right of provinces to decide to ordain women as bishops. However, before such action was taken the conference called for consultation with the episcopate through the primates, and the presence of overwhelming support in the member church concerned, 'lest the bishop's office should become a cause of disunity instead of a focus of unity'.[12] There appears here a small crack between the bishops and the ACC on what should be done to maintain unity in the Communion. The conference recommends that no consecrations take place 'without consultation with the episcopate through the primates'. This conference looked to a primates' committee meeting during the conference, which appears to be something of an innovation. We see here the beginnings of an extension of the responsibility of the Lambeth Conference in the form of a Primates' Meeting which was to take on an increasing role in public debate as this and the sexuality issue emerged.

When the ACC met the next year, 1979, not much had been done. The ACC asked the secretary general to facilitate a dialogue and urged the primates who were to meet later that year to develop guidelines for exchanges of clergy between provinces. This was a little odd since the Primates' Meeting

---

[10] LC.1978,21. Resolution 21 is set entirely in the context of accepting the fact and legitimacy of the ordinations.
[11] Secretary General of the Anglican Consultative Council, *The Report of the Lambeth Conference 1978* (London: Church Information Office, 1978), pp. 80–2.
[12] The full text of the resolutions is available on the Lambeth Conference website at www.lambethconference.org/.

An Introduction to World Anglicanism

was set up in 1978 by the archbishop, Donald Coggan, for 'leisurely thought and prayer and deep consultation'. Three years later, in 1981, the ordination of women had virtually dropped off the agenda of the ACC when it met in Newcastle upon Tyne in England. The proposed dialogue was reduced to a reflective question in a section report, and a note that the dialogue with the Orthodox churches had resumed after being broken off because some Anglican churches had ordained women. In terms of the engagement of the ACC with the question it seems a very long way from the acceptance of leadership in Limuru to a virtual disengagement in Newcastle. It is perhaps not surprising that questions arose in Newcastle about the role and effectiveness of the ACC.[13] It certainly seemed to have been sidelined.

By 1984, when the ACC met in Nigeria, the question had clearly become the nature of full communion between the Anglican provinces.[14] Three years later in Singapore it had become clear that the dialogue which was previously in the hands of the secretary general was now being conducted by the Archbishop of Canterbury, and the ACC was again in the business of encouraging people to get on with each other.[15] The report on the state of play previously asked for was again requested. The situation was much the same in 1990, though by now the game had moved from the ACO office at Waterloo up the Thames to Lambeth.[16]

The 1988 Lambeth Conference was a watershed in a number of ways. It had before it a report of a working party established by the Primates' Meeting[17] and also the report of ACC-7. The Mission and Ministry section report claims, surprisingly, that 'the threefold order of ministry is instituted

[13] Secretary General of the Anglican Consultative Council, *ACC-5*, Fifth Meeting, Newcastle upon Tyne, England, 8–18 September 1981 (London: ACC, 1981), pp. 74–7. Discussion about the role of the ACC was related to a more prominent role for the Archbishop of Canterbury and more things being asked of primates.

[14] ACC.1984,23 on full communion asked for acceptance of women priests in provinces which did not ordain women and asked the secretary general to distribute a list of the situation in each province.

[15] ACC.1984,4, on the ordination of women to the priesthood and the episcopate, commended a report it had received and generally called for sensitivity. It again asked the secretary general for the report sought at the previous meeting. This would have been an extremely difficult report to produce since not all dioceses within a province necessarily followed a provincial decision. Even in ECUSA, whose General Convention has the capacity to require compliance to its canons, there were dioceses that had not acted, and declared they would not act, on a canon on this matter.

[16] ACC.1987,27: The Archbishop of Canterbury's Commission on Communion and Women in the Episcopate. 'This Council welcomes the Report of the Archbishop of Canterbury's Commission on Communion and Women in the Episcopate [Parts One and Two; popularly known as the Eames Report], and commends it to all member Churches for their study. It urges member Churches whose policies in this regard differ to strive to maintain as high a degree of communion as possible.'

[17] Primates' Working Group on the Ordination of Women to the Episcopate, *Report of the Working Party Appointed by the Primates of the Anglican Communion on Women and the Episcopate: To Aid Discussion in Preparation for the Lambeth Conference 1988* (London: ACC, 1987).

and established by Holy Writ and Sacred Tradition"[18] and draws attention
to the Lambeth Quadrilateral which had referred to episcopacy 'locally
adapted'. How far would the ordination of a woman bishop be an example
of such local adaptation?

The report also draws from the discussion in world Anglicanism several
ideas which had become critical in the ongoing debates about women clergy
and change in general. First the concept of 'reception' had been revealed in
the debates. Reception is a term used in Roman Catholicism to describe the
process by which the teachings of the church, and particularly the *magisterium*, are received by the people of God. In this context in Anglicanism it
has a different orientation which can be quite confusing. Because of the
conciliar character of Anglicanism and the absence of a *magisterium*, change
is a matter which comes about as a result of consensus-building in dioceses
and provinces, and in this instance in the Anglican Communion. The
Anglican form of reception looks a lot more like trial and error than the
Roman Catholic form. The decisive role of lay members in provincial
constitutions and the passing of canons and formularies makes for a much
messier process of reception. In the Roman Catholic model reception refers
to the acceptance in the church of the authoritative teaching of the *magisterium*. In the Anglican model reception refers to the establishment of
teaching that has been offered to the church for consideration.

The 1988 Lambeth Conference faced the fact that the issue before worldwide Anglicanism, with this proposed change to the traditional pattern of
ministerial order, had to have some kind of theological rationale. Reception
was the doctrinal category which they chose. Given the background to that
doctrine in Roman Catholicism, and its very different ecclesial framework,
it was an adventurous choice. Such a concept had the great advantage of
bringing the issue of change within the reach of theological argument. It is
not surprising that in both the report and the resolution of this conference
the bishops recognised that managing the change was going to be difficult
and would involve a lot of pain. For many this change was a matter of
conscience and affected how they understood the presence of God in their
lives and in the life of the church. Robert Runcie had alluded to these issues
in his presidential address and related them to the Anglican tradition of
'dispersed authority' as contrasted with a centralised authority in Roman
Catholicism.[19]

---

[18] Secretary General of the Anglican Consultative Council, *The Truth Shall Make You Free. The Lambeth
Conference 1988* (London: Church House Publishing, 1998), p. 59.
[19] Ibid., pp. 13–17.

This line of argument raised the question of ecumenical relations, and especially relations with the Orthodox and the Roman Catholic churches. Runcie confronted these matters head-on. Anglicans had a clear tradition and it was their contribution to the wider Christian community. This was what they brought to the ecumenical table. A key element in that tradition was the conciliar character of Anglican ecclesiology and that meant the place of the laity in church governance, principally expressed in synodical forms of decision-making. 'If we still have some things to learn about synodical government, I also believe we have something to give to the Church of Rome. For me the major criticism of ARCIC must be its lack of emphasis on the role of the laity in the decision-making of the church.'[20] Runcie was far-sighted in giving this lead. It has become clear in the twenty years since that winning consensus, and developing institutions to facilitate such a process, have been central in the Anglican response to change.

The third element which the 1988 Lambeth Conference brought to the growing conflict was a question about mission. Would the change enhance the mission of the church?[21] This had become a crucial issue in places as different as Nigeria and the USA. Mission drives the church in its local context to seek engagements with the terms and character of the culture in which it evangelises. That means that the contextual engagement with vastly different situations is very likely to produce different patterns of working. This would apply to the mode by which the church shapes its own ecclesial existence, since that is itself a mode of mission. Lying behind the 1988 bishops' inclusion of mission in the questions before Anglicans is the deeply difficult and potentially fragmenting dynamic of local engagement. The use made of the 'locally adapted' language of the Lambeth Quadrilateral moves in the same arena of thought and action. Faithful adaptation in one context may look very different from what appears in another context. That may not cause too much difficulty if the differences are about style or mode of operating. But they become more difficult when they are differences about cultural norms and patterns, about the place of women in society and in the church, or the pattern of personal relations between the sexes.

The 1988 Lambeth Conference also asked the Archbishop of Canterbury to establish a Commission on Communion and Women in the Episcopate. This commission met in November 1988 with the Archbishop of Armagh, Robin Eames, as chair. This group has become known as the Eames Commission and the commission's report as the Eames Report. The

[20] Ibid., p. 20.   [21] Ibid., p. 60.

nomenclature is testimony to the negotiating and facilitating skills of the chair. The commission published three brief reports on the basis of five meetings between November 1988 and December 1993. Subsequently a sub-group of the commission met as a monitoring group and published a report in 1998 which included the earlier reports.[22] While the Eames Commission was meeting, a consultation was held in 1991 to consider the request of the 1988 Lambeth Conference for a 'further exploration of the meaning and nature of communion with particular reference to the doctrine of the Trinity, the unity and order of the church, and the unity of the community of humanity'.[23] This consultation led on to the formation of a new Inter-Anglican Theological and Doctrinal Commission (IATDC), which in due course produced the *Virginia Report*. This report was received at Lambeth 1998 and set the tone of the debate, as well as the language used to describe the Communion-wide organisational arrangements as 'instruments of unity'. There was considerable overlap between these two commissions, and not only in their concerns. Both were chaired by Robin Eames, and Archbishop Peter Carnley (Australia) and Bishop Mark Dyer (USA) were members of both groups.

The Eames Commission saw its task as trying to 'discover the language and context in which Anglicans can continue to live together'.[24] They did so by setting up a framework in terms of fellowship, or *koinonia* (the Greek word used in the New Testament for fellowship). They saw this as deriving from a particular construal of the doctrine of the Trinity, though the elaboration of this was left to the IATDC. They set out the elements of fellowship in the Anglican Communion and the way in which decisions are made. They underlined the role of synods as gatherings of bishops, clergy and laity, though they noted that there were no synods above provinces or national churches in worldwide Anglicanism. Thus a juridical notion of communion could not be appropriate, though they believed there must be some limits to diversity at the global level.

The commission developed the use of the category of reception used in the 1988 Lambeth report and elaborated the open-ended and provisional character of any decisions in this framework. Furthermore open reception must entail ambiguities as different parts of the Communion move in different ways. While strongly encouraging this open-ended approach the

---

[22] The Secretary General of the Anglican Consultative Council, *Women in the Anglican Episcopate: Theology Guidelines and Practice. The Eames Commission and the Monitoring Group Reports* (Toronto: Anglican Book Centre, 1998).
[23] LC.1998,18.   [24] ACC , *Women in the Anglican Episcopate*, p. 14.

commission nonetheless would not entertain the notion that the Anglican Communion was merely a federation of churches. It was indeed a communion. The commission gives no clear reasons to show why it is so definite on this point, which is distinctly odd since the much-quoted definition of the Anglican Communion from the 1948 Lambeth Conference as a fellowship of dioceses and provinces would most naturally be read as referring to a federation of churches.

The commission also set out some guidelines for action in the increasingly mixed situation. They favoured episcopal visitations for minorities, are against parallel jurisdictions, and non-recognition of confirmations by women bishops. They also floated the idea of male bishops performing joint ordinations with female bishops, but the Primates' Meeting responded negatively to this idea as bringing into question the orders of a woman bishop.

Essentially the Eames Commission set out some commonsense advice on how to sustain a reasonable level of communion in the midst of increasingly complicated differences. They underlined again and again the importance of courtesy and respect which had been called for at the 1988 Lambeth Conference. They might also have appealed to Jesus' exhortation to his disciples to love one another. The third and final report of the Eames Commission set out a review of the Anglican institutions for authority, and drew attention to the problems where dissent continues and hardens over time so that openness appears less available. The commission was beginning to encounter the ambiguities and limitations of the notion of reception in an Anglican context.

The *Virginia Report* set out the theological issues which the work of the 1988 Lambeth Conference and the Eames Commission had identified. They grounded their consideration of communion in a doctrine of the Trinity. The very nature of God is the basis and character of the communion in the church. New Testament images of the church 'speak of a communion with God: Father, Son, and Holy Spirit; Christians are participants in the divine nature'.[25] The diversity which is apparent in the church finds its centre in the mission and love of Christ. On this theological foundation the *Virginia Report* develops an argument for belonging together in the Anglican Communion on the basis of elements of the Anglican Way; scripture, tradition and reason, sacrament and worship, interdependence of charisms, ministry of oversight. These themes lead to an argument for certain kinds of

---

[25] *The Virginia Report*, in M. E. Dyer *et al.* (eds.), *The Official Report of the Lambeth Conference 1998* (Harrisburg, Pa.: Morehouse Publishing, 1999), p. 27.

structures of interdependence. The notion of structures and organisation immediately leads to a discussion of decision-making power and thus what power belongs at what level, which in turn leads to the purposes and principles for developing structures for the Anglican Communion.

To this point the report presents a coherent argument deploying theological material with a certain deftness of touch. The final chapter arrives with a surprising degree of particularity in the way in which it puts forward what it calls the instruments of unity: i.e. the Archbishop of Canterbury, the Lambeth Conference, the Anglican Consultative Council and the Primates' Meeting. There is some discussion of the interrelationship of these organisational arrangements and some sense in which these and these alone are the ways in which the unity of the Communion is to be sustained.

The *Virginia Report* has been subjected to a good deal of criticism, not least of the processes of the last stages of the commission's work.[26] It puts forward a very narrow horizon for the Anglican tradition in the English Reformation. Its use of the doctrine of the Trinity seems a little too convenient for the organisational conclusions reached. The notion of metropolitan and primacy are not widely grounded by the report in Anglican history, and the notion of subsidiarity is used in a direction quite different in effect from its more common usage in Roman Catholicism. For a report concerned with unity in the Anglican Communion it remarkably makes no use of the experience of Anglican Congresses, ACC Networks or any of the regional gatherings within the Anglican Communion, to say nothing of the myriad Communion-wide organisations that hold people together. In part this reflects the top-down notion of the church implicit in the report and the consequent invisibility of the laity. This very narrow scope implies a highly clerical ecclesiology and an approach to church unity from a compliance perspective.

Nonetheless the recommendations of the *Virginia Report* have reappeared in subsequent reports and documents as generally accepted conclusions. Whether they will prove to be adequate to the task, and whether they will stand the test of time in theological terms, is yet to be seen. The later crisis over sexuality has in some measure moved around them.

The struggle throughout the last twenty years of the twentieth century was to sustain some kind of communion and unity in world Anglicanism. That struggle was precipitated by the moves to ordain women, first as priests and then as bishops. This meant that the focus was a sense of unity in relation to ministerial orders. Thus the ideal of a complete interchangeability of orders

---

[26] See, for example, B. Kaye, 'Unity in the Anglican Communion: A Critique of the "Virginia Report"', *St Mark's Review* 184 (2001), pp. 24–32.

was and is a central concern, and this has often been the defining element in the debates of whether different parts were in communion or not. It is a peculiarly clerical focus.

THE SUBSTANTIVE ISSUES

The differences on the substantive issue of whether women can or should be ordained have not been the subject of intense argument at the worldwide level. That argument has taken place at the level where the actual decisions whether or not to ordain were being taken, namely in the provinces and national churches and in the dioceses. In those arenas a mountain of literature has been produced and vast resources of time and energy have been deployed.

In 1987 the ACC met at a time when women had been ordained as priests in various parts of the Communion for some time, while in many other parts of the Communion the argument was still going on in. The ACC was concerned with unity within the Communion, and in pursuit of this gaol offered to identify what they saw as the three key issues in the debate: headship, representation of Christ in the church and development in faith and order.[27]

The ACC report drew attention to a Doctrine Commission report from the diocese of Sydney which argued that male headship is part of the order of creation and is taught in scripture. The argument in this report has been repeated and developed in a number of subsequent reports and publications, and has been hotly debated in Australia, where the Sydney diocese is a significant presence. The diocese remains opposed to the ordination of women to any position which implies a teaching authority of a woman in relation to men. Since the frame of reference in Sydney is that of a rector in a parish, whose role is understood primarily in teaching terms, it becomes impossible to breach this biblical principle by allowing a woman to be a parish rector, or to hold an office which carries any implied challenge to male headship.[28] When Harry Goodhew was archbishop of Sydney (1993–2001) attempts were made to create some kind of dialogue within the diocese on this issue, but these disappeared after his retirement and the diocesan synod placed a moratorium on the subject. In 2006 the synod dismissed any further debate on the subject again.

[27] Secretary General of the Anglican Consultative Council, *Many Gifts, One Spirit: Report of ACC-7 Singapore 1987* (London: ACC, 1987), pp. 42–9.
[28] A selection of the main reports in Sydney is available at www.sds.asn.au/site/102969.asp?ph=cl.

This restriction applies to women generally, ordained or otherwise, since it is built primarily on a view about gender relations, and ordination is but one example of the application of the principle of male leadership. More recent argument from this tradition makes use of a notion of hierarchy in a Trinitarian description of God. A particular presentation of the subordination of the Son to the Father is related to some biblical material in order to establish a subordination of women to men on the basis of a doctrine of God.[29] We have encountered the strategy of playing the God card in the form of a particular formulation of the doctrine of the Trinity in the *Virginia Report*, though there it is a different formulation of the doctrine and it is deployed to a different end.

Clearly this Sydney line of argument appeals in the first instance to scripture. The creedal tradition of the doctrine of God and the text of scripture also figures prominently in the form of this argument. The strong appeal to scripture is aligned with the particular evangelical background of those who put this point of view. That other scripturally committed evangelicals treat the texts differently and come to different conclusions suggests that there is more going on here than simply different readings of the texts of scripture. This touches on an important part of the rhetoric of this debate. In its early stages commitment to the authority of the Bible was claimed as the deciding issue. However, it then became a matter of differences of interpretation. Clearly it is not a matter of simply a literal use of texts against a more historically conditioned approach to them. The question has become much more a matter of how an interpretative approach can be defended in relation to the ascription of authority to scripture.

However, even that does not deal adequately with the basis of the differences. At stake here is more than interpretative approach. The argument is influenced further back in terms of the nature of the authority of scripture and the way in which scripture exercises its authority. Sometimes

---

[29] This was clearly expressed in a 1999 report of the Doctrine Commission of the diocese of Sydney. This report, and the point of view, have been the subject of intense debate and disagreement. In Australia it was something of a cause célèbre because of criticism in 2004 of the Sydney Doctrine Commission report from the then primate Peter Carnley in a book *Reflections in Glass: Trends and Tensions in the Contemporary Anglican Church* (Pymble, NSW: HarperCollins, 2004). On p. 235 he declared that the members of the Sydney Doctrine Commission seemed prepared openly to embrace heretical Arianism. This created a storm of protest and a significant public falling-out between the primate and the archbishop of Sydney, Peter Jensen. The issues have been canvassed at length and in great detail in two books: K. Giles, *The Trinity and Subordination: The Doctrine of God and the Contemporary Gender Debate* (Downers Grove, Ill.: InterVarsity Press, 2002), and K. Giles, *Jesus and the Father: Modern Evangelicals Reinvent the Doctrine of the Trinity* (Grand Rapids, Mich.: Zondervan, 2006). Giles is an evangelical graduate of Moore College in Sydney and a long-time advocate of the ordination of women.

this is defended by opponents to the ordination of women as a commitment to scripture alone – *sola scriptura*. The difficulty with this line of argument is that the doctrine of 'scripture alone' has virtually no serious standing in the Anglican theological tradition. It was explicitly rejected at the time of the English Reformation in the sixteenth century and has never really gained much purchase in theological argument even in the twentieth century. It is certainly not represented in the classic formularies of the 1662 Book of Common Prayer, and most of the provincial constitutions follow something like the formulation of the Book of Common Prayer and the Thirty-Nine Articles. The chief article on this subject states the matter more indirectly and in a more restricted form: 'Holy Scripture containeth all things necessary to salvation: so that whatsoever is not read therein, nor may be proved thereby, is not to be required of any man, that it should be believed as an article of the Faith, or be thought requisite or necessary to salvation.' At one level it is easy to understand how an appeal to 'scripture alone' might be attractive in this debate because it provides a clear line in the sand against more liberally inclined opponents. The difficulty is that it lacks any Anglican credibility.

The second line of argument reported in the ACC account of the issues in the debate is described under the heading of 'Representation of Christ in the Church'. There is a formal similarity between this point of view and the preceding one in that both are appealing to a unique and definitive locus for settling the question. Here appeal is to the uniqueness of the incarnation in Jesus of Nazareth. This is not just a question of Jesus' maleness, but rather an appeal to the overarching sovereign plan of salvation implied in the doctrine of the incarnation. The sovereign providence of God in choosing this time and this place for the incarnation must be taken to be in itself important and to reveal something fundamental about the nature of God. Thus the social structures implied in Jesus' maleness, and that of the disciples as leaders in the early church, implies something essential to the revealing intentions of divine providence rather than something simply incidental. 'Thus faith – acceptance of a fact of revealed truth – and order – the structuring of a representative ministry – are seen to be inextricably related.'[30] Jesus confirmed this divinely chosen order by selecting only male apostles. Furthermore the priest, especially in the Eucharist, is a representative symbolic presence of Christ and must therefore be male. This position is confirmed by a particular reading of scripture.

---

[30] Secretary General of the ACC, *Many Gifts One Spirit*, p. 44.

These two views have a good deal in common, though their central interest is quite different. Both look for a unique and compelling consideration for a male priesthood. Both read scripture in a way that seems to support their position. Both are committed to an element in the argument which is of fundamental significance: female subordination in one case and priestly representation in the other. In the first case a particular construal of the doctrine of the Trinity has been deployed in support of female subordination. In the main this has been done by evangelicals, probably taking up a tendency developed in the 1970s in North American evangelicalism to use the doctrine of the Trinity to sustain female subordination in general.[31]

However the two views are quite different in what is of central interest. In the first case it is female subordination, and the ordered ministry of the church just happens to be the particular example in which that general principle has arisen. It is an acute example because the subordination relates especially to authority, and the ordained ministry is construed in the kind of authority terms which suggest power and jurisdiction. That is why the consistent application of the principle leads such people to oppose women teaching men in any situation. The other point of view is focused on the nature of the ordered ministry, especially in relation to the celebration of the sacrament of the Holy Communion.

The third line of argument reported by the ACC report of 1998 highlights the question of whether the ordination of women can be seen as an appropriate development in faith and order in the church. Clearly developments have taken place in Christianity in both faith and order. The doctrine of the Trinity is one such and the threefold ordered ministry is another. Are these uncoverings of what was latent from the beginning, or are they developments prompted by the guidance of the Holy Spirit? Clearly human history testifies to change, not only in the physical circumstances of life but also in the way we think and understand. In Christianity the history of the interpretation of scripture is a well-developed sub-discipline in theology and reflects changes in perception over the course of time.

In the light of these arguments the ACC report suggests two criteria for approaching the ordination of women to the priesthood: the testimony of scripture and what God reveals providentially through human history and in the church. Undoubtedly the immense changes in the place of women in western societies during the twentieth century have had a very considerable influence on this whole issue. Those changes have not occurred in all parts

---

[31] See Giles, *Jesus and the Father*, and W. A. Grudem, *Biblical Foundations for Manhood and Womanhood* (Wheaton, Ill.: Crossway Books, 2002).

of the world and that difference in context greatly affects the kind of response available to Anglicans around the world. It does not explain opposition to the ordination of women in western countries and that distinction highlights that there is more at issue here.

What is fundamentally at issue is the way in which Anglicans respond to different cultural and social contexts. It is the perennial question of how the church and the Christian can be in the world but not of the world. What differentiates western-located Anglicans on this question is not really whether they accept the authority of the Bible. Rather it is a broader theological tendency which shapes how they respond to their culture and handle scripture. The use and interpretation of scripture is clearly contested, but it is remarkable how the particularities of interpretation are resolved by broader principles about the way scripture is relevant to the question, and how it exercises its authority in the life of the church. The issue is not whether scripture has authority, but what kind of authority it has.

The ACC report does not enlarge on the arguments in favour of the ordination of women, and in that respect it mirrors something of the character of the arguments which have taken place in the provinces and dioceses. Those arguments appear in two forms. The first is a passive argument: there is no good reason not to ordain women. This form of the argument arises because of changed cultural circumstances and because what is being sought is simply a change in long-accepted practice. The contest over the interpretation of scripture is set in this context. Appeal is made to those arguments in scripture which point to the removal of the significance of social distinction in the new order of the kingdom of God which Jesus announced. This is such an overwhelming theme in the New Testament and in Christian theology that the question inevitably turned on whether in the apostolic church any distinctions were retained in practice, and whether any significance was or should be attached to them now. This kind of question naturally came to embrace a variety of texts of scripture concerned with social practice – matters such as slavery. For a long time slavery was justified on the basis of such scripture texts, but these arguments did not carry much weight in the late twentieth century.

There is also a range of positive arguments which call upon re-readings of the tradition, the current actual experience of women in leadership responsibilities and the personal testimony of individuals to a calling from God. There is also in some quarters a claim of social rights, though this tends to be deployed mainly in the USA where the local political tradition gives rights language greater rhetorical force.

Many question how such decisions are actually to be made. Does a change in the way in which the ordered ministry is structured call for a precise and specific theological rationale? Is it not the case that many of the decisions about how the church orders its life are made on the basis of sensible use of what is understood as Christianly informed common sense? People are able to have such an opinion if they hold a less exalted view of the precise theological significance of the pattern of ministry in the church, and also of the particular ordering of the pattern of relationships between men and women in human society generally and thus in the church. Much of the disposition in favour of the ordination of women as priests and bishops among Anglicans around the world is of this variety. Such a 'commonsense' view is, of course, itself a theological position with a considerable historical pedigree in Anglicanism.

There are other forces at work in this debate. The cultural context in which different Anglicans encounter this question affects the way in which they are predisposed to think about it. In the USA, for example, the rights of women to equal treatment and opportunity grew in public opinion and practice in the second half of the twentieth century. That feminist move corresponded in time with the civil rights movement. The Episcopal Church had taken an emphatic role in supporting civil rights, including rights for women. How could the church not then be in the vanguard of moves to ordain women? On the other hand, in many African countries the public roles of women were and still are very restricted, and patterns of dependency of women on men were widespread and powerful. That was a very different context in which Anglicans considered whether or not to ordain women as priests, let alone bishops. The interplay between cultural attitudes and more conservative theological arguments is an important underlying dynamic in this whole debate. This dynamic has an extra overlay where Anglicans are confronted near at hand with growing Islam and its conservative social programmes.

LOCATION OF THE DEBATE

The debate over the ordination of women as priests and bishops has essentially taken place at the local or provincial level. The international institutions of the Anglican Communion did not return to the substantive issues after the ACC report of 1987. From the Lambeth Conference of 1988 the energy was in terms of maintaining some kind of peace between provinces. The strategy was to encourage acceptance of plurality on the issue and to foster some sense of testing or reception for the whole idea. In general terms that strategy has worked well. There are still difficulties between and within provinces on this issue but they are not proving to be earth-shattering. The fact that nearly half the provinces in the Anglican Communion allow the ordination of women as priests indicates a significant level of development of the practice.

This international policy in the Anglican Communion is about as much as could realistically be pursued. After all the Anglican Communion has no capacity to make jurisdictional decisions which could carry any force. There have been some moves towards more hegemonic thinking in regard to some of the new organisational arrangements such as the Primates' Meeting and even the Lambeth Conference, but they can only seriously be regarded as tentative experiments.

In the journey from 1944, when Bishop Hall of Hong Kong ordained Florence Tim Oi Li, up to the final report of the Eames Commission Monitoring Group in 1997, the path taken by the Anglican Communion could be regarded as reasonably successful in handling the storm of this change. However, between the creative and consultative approach of the 1988 Lambeth Conference and the embarrassing aggression and hostility on display at the Lambeth Conference of 1998 a moral tsunami struck worldwide Anglicanism: should Anglicans approve of the blessing of same-sex unions, and should people in same-sex relationships be ordained as priests or consecrated as bishops?

CHAPTER 11

Ministerial offices – homosexuality and the public life of the church

As the bishops went home from the 1988 Lambeth Conference they could have been forgiven for thinking that it had all gone fairly well. New steps had been initiated to approach the crisis over the ordination of women in a way that could avoid serious division. The general tone of the conference was positive and friendly, and it seemed to finish on a high note. But the ordination of women was being overtaken by another divisive question: how do homosexuals fit into the public life of the church? Even before the conference there had been stirrings on this issue. The section of the conference concerned with Christianity and Social Order produced a report of 195 paragraphs, of which three were devoted to homosexuality.[1] The conference passed one resolution on the subject calling for more study. In fact the conference was preoccupied with other things, not least the international political tensions associated with the death throes of the Cold War. The Berlin Wall came down the year following the conference, precipitating the biggest international reconfiguration in fifty years. The conference also called for a Decade of Evangelism in the 1990s and for the church to move from maintenance to mission. This Decade of Evangelism was to become a central theme of the work of George Carey, the new Archbishop of Canterbury.

THE ISSUES

If the 1988 Lambeth Conference marked a stage on the way to mechanisms for differences to be tolerated on the ordination of women, the 1998 conference marked the full maturing of open conflict over homosexuality. In many respects the issues were similar to those involved in the ordination-of-women debates. The course of the debate was led by actions taken in the USA, often outside, and contrary to, the decisions of official governing

[1] The Secretary General of the ACC, *The Truth Shall Make You Free*, p. 187.

bodies – in the USA the General Convention. The same had been true of the ordination of women. The cultural contexts and different patterns of enculturation shaped and sharpened the differences. In both the theological arguments focused on the use and interpretation of scripture and the evaluation of change and development. Both issues also raised the question of the interpretation of the place of women and of homosexuals in broader human history. In the ordination question the nature and status of minister-ial orders was central to the debates, though different conceptions of the ministry were at stake. With the homosexuality question an aspect of the ordained ministry was involved, but much more central was a view about human identity. The greater range of this question in the life of the church and in human society inevitably meant that difference on this point would be more contentious.

The debates have led to a more extensive history of homosexuality being studied both generally and in the church. In the second half of the twentieth century social changes in western countries, especially in the USA, contrib-uted to a much more public recognition of homosexual people, and steps were being made to remove their civil disadvantages. It was in this respect that the matter first came to the attention of the General Convention of ECUSA. In the UK the decriminalisation of homosexual acts in private came through the Sexual Offences Act 1967, and little by little other civil disadvantages have been diminished in most western countries. But that has not been the pattern in countries in Africa or Asia. Homosexuality is illegal in many African countries and in 2006 stronger laws against homosexual acts were proposed in Nigeria. The matter is politically complicated where there is a strong Muslim influence.

The matter is therefore very important for the church's engagement with public policy. The church has regularly been involved in public policy for marriage, and in most countries Anglicans work in tandem with civil authorities in the solemnisation of marriages. Throughout the twentieth century there was an ongoing debate about how Anglicans should respond to polygamy. The question arose at meetings of the ACC and the Lambeth Conference from churches in Polynesia and Africa. Successive resolutions of the ACC and the Lambeth Conference have tended to be reasonably accommodating, in that people in polygamous relationships were not required to give up those relationships as a condition of baptism, and in some instances there were even suggestions that it might be possible for Christians to move into polygamous relationships. The church thus faced a significant challenge as to how it should respond to changing social attitudes and legal possibilities in relation to marriage.

When changes to the law affecting homosexuals emerged, the church was immediately confronted with the question of how to view such relationships. It did not take long for the question to appear within the church. In the first instance the issue was raised in the church's response to changing legal arrangements. This inevitably involved a public response and thus a public formulation of the issues within the church. In relation to the church's own community life this focused on the public life of the church as seen in those who were ordained. These were the institutional, recognised officers of the church and the ordinals made it clear that clergy were to be models for the rest of the church. To allow practising homosexuals to be ordained would thus imply something about the character of the model that was expected in the church. The precise meaning and significance of the 'model' role of the clergy, and in what sense a higher standard of personal behaviour was required for clergy, became a tributary theme in the subsequent debate.

Most provinces around the world have a canon to define the standard of behaviour of clergy and have tribunals to enforce those standards. The 'offences' canons generally refer to such things as criminal conviction, drunkenness, adultery, and a number of other things.[2] Changes in many provinces in the early years of the twenty-first century have included child abuse amongst such lists.[3] Most also include conduct unbecoming a minister in holy orders, often with the gloss to include what would be a cause for scandal in the church were it to become public. This very long-standing approach to the personal lives of clergy highlights both that they are regarded as having a higher standard and also that the standard contains some fairly obvious elements, together with a requirement that their behaviour should not be scandalous in the Christian community. Whether homosexual acts in clergy were scandalous is thus a critical issue in relation to the long-standing approach to clerical offences. What is seen as scandalous clearly can and has changed over time and can be different in different cultures.

The church's marriage practice is also another aspect of the conflict. How far can an Anglican province go in authorising liturgical blessings or 'marriage services' for homosexual couples? The issue is not just that such liturgies imply a view about marriage. Such a liturgy is a public statement of the church's belief and life commitments. Because clergy are the authorised

---

[2] See Doe, *Canon Law in the Anglican Communion*, pp. 83–5.
[3] See G. Blake, 'Child Protection and the Anglican Church of Australia', *Journal of Anglican Studies* 4.1 (2006), pp. 81–106, and the resolution ACC.2005,50, Protection of Children and Vulnerable Adults.

officiants at such liturgies the question once again comes back to the ordained ministers of the church.

While there are some similarities between the issues of the ordination of women and the place of homosexuals in the public life of the church, and also in the demography of the crisis, there are also some important differences. A different aspect of the position of the clergy as public figures in the church is involved. What is done liturgically for the recognition and blessing of same-sex relationships for lay people engages laity in the issue in a way which was not so for the ordination of women. Nor does this issue directly affect the understanding of the central rite of the Eucharist as the ordination of women did. On the other hand, the place of homosexuals in the public life of the church goes to a central issue in the Christian understanding of human identity. In a polarity between ecclesiastical and moral we could reasonably say that homosexuality is more of a moral question and the ordination of women more of an ecclesiastical question.

The theological arguments have naturally focused on the three presenting questions: the position of the clergy in the public life of the church, the place of liturgy in the public life of the church, and the public policy of the church in relation to the civil order. The consecration of a bishop is an amplified version of the ordination of clergy in this issue.[4] As with the ordination of women, theological arguments about the use and interpretation of scripture and the nature of change and development play an important role in this argument. The character of human identity takes a clear role rather than the nature of ministerial office and sacrament. Throughout there is the continuing issue of the nature of the connection between provinces within worldwide Anglicanism and the nature of authority and jurisdiction within the provinces.

THE STORY OF DEBATE IN THE ANGLICAN COMMUNION

The encounter with the issue of homosexuals in the public life of the churches in the Anglican Communion began slowly in the USA, but gathered momentum as the twentieth century came to an end. In western

---

[4] The report of the Church of England House of Bishops, *Some Issues in Human Sexuality: A Guide to the Debate* (London: Church House Publishing, 2003), pp. 32f., identifies five issues: should homosexual people change their orientation? should they abstain from sexual conduct? should permanent relationships be encouraged? is it right for people in same-sex relationships to be ordained? and how should the church respond to the needs of homosexual people? This is a statement of the issues from a more determinedly pastoral perspective, but it does not capture the essential matters of the conflict and its institutional character. It overlooks the political issue which came upon the Church of England in 2005 with new government legislation for civil unions.

countries changing cultural attitudes and legal practices prompted much of the debate. The USA was itself an influential force in shaping western cultural changes. It is not surprising therefore that many observers in Anglican churches outside the west perceived the homosexual agenda as American in origin and character.

In the heady days of social agitation in many western countries during the 1960s a cloud the size of a man's hand appeared in the sky of the General Convention of ECUSA. A report from the Human Affairs Commission drew attention to the unusual cultural stresses upon the family. Marriage breakdown, divorce and remarriage were the presenting symptoms of this stress. The all-male convention asked for a report on the Christian understanding of sexual behaviour. The 1967 convention received the report, which declared that the 'traditional and often stereotyped attitudes of the Churches may no longer provide adequate guidance'.[5] The convention asked for studies to express Christian attitudes to a list of things in this area, including homosexuality. This was the first use of the term homosexuality in the *Convention Journal*. The 1970 and 1973 General Conventions did not resolve anything on the subject, though in 1974 a support group named Integrity was formed for homosexuals in ECUSA. The House of Bishops had a subcommittee on 'homophiles' and initiated a dialogue with the 'homophile community'. The thrust of this dialogue involved the public disadvantages for homosexuals and the fact that the church was acting out of concern for the social justice issues involved.

In the 1976 General Convention the issues came clearly to the fore in three resolutions. The first called for study at the diocesan level of issues of sexuality, including homosexuality. The second declared that 'homosexual persons are children of God who have a full and equal claim with all other persons upon the love, acceptance, and pastoral concern and care of the *Church*' and that 'homosexual persons are entitled to equal protection of the laws with other citizens'. The resolution also called upon the wider society to see that such protection was in fact provided. A third resolution called on the Human Affairs Commission to study in depth 'the matter of the ordination of homosexual persons'.[6] In January the next year the bishop of New York ordained a woman who openly acknowledged her homosexual orientation. The Executive Council of the General Convention expressed the hope that no bishop would ordain or license 'any professing and

---

[5] Quoted from Office of Communication, Episcopal Church Centre, *To Set Our Hope on Christ: A Response to the Invitation of Windsor Report Para 135* (New York: The Episcopal Church, 2005), p. 67.
[6] Ibid., pp. 72f.

practicing homosexual until the issue be resolved by General Convention'. The House of Bishops underlined the distinction implied in this resolution between orientation and practice.

What had been a side eddy in 1976 to the larger and more fiercely contested debate over the ordination of women became a storm in the 1979 General Convention. A long report from the Human Affairs Commission could offer no agreement to bring to the convention. After long debate, much committee work and a series of amendments the convention agreed to a set of three points in relation to ordination: first, that many areas including sexuality bear upon a candidate's suitability and, second, there should be no barrier 'to the ordination of qualified persons of either heterosexual or homosexual orientation whose behaviour the church considers wholesome'. The third statement reaffirmed traditional teaching and declared that 'it is not appropriate for this Church to ordain a practicing homosexual, or any person who is engaged in heterosexual relations outside of marriage'. Twenty-one bishops publicly dissented from this resolution and declared they would not be bound by it.

Curiously the General Conventions of 1982 and 1985 did not deal with homosexuality directly. The 1985 convention called for educational material to foster better understanding 'to provide pastoral support, and to give life to the claim of homosexual persons'.[7] The year 1987 saw the publication of a study guide entitled *Sexuality – A Divine Gift*, produced by a working group established by church office staff. It made assumptions and promoted views strongly supportive of homosexuality and quite different from those of the General Convention. It caused a furore and a supplementary book was quickly produced. The executive council distanced itself from the book and the legislative committee of the convention changed the commission's resolution to remove any commendation of the book. At the convention itself various resolutions indirectly kept a more traditional view in the records of the convention, but there were no formal resolutions on the key issues.

In this context the Lambeth Conference met in 1988 and a number of American bishops sought unsuccessfully to win support from the conference for the recognition of same-sex relationships. But the conference was more concerned with other political matters that were disrupting the world, and the place of homosexuals was given only slight attention.

The following year, Jack Spong, the bishop of Newark, ordained a gay man who was living with another man. This created a constitutional crisis at

[7] Ibid, pp. 82f.

the 1990 bishops' conference which, in the face of opposition from Ed Browning, the presiding bishop, voted to restate the 1979 resolution of the General Convention which had been similarly reasserted by the executive council. The issue was now raised to the level of the canonical status of General Convention resolutions and the collegial responsibility of bishops. This collegiality had been exposed as very limited at the 1979 General Convention when twenty-one bishops said they would not be bound by a resolution passed in the House of Bishops.

The 1991 General Convention made four significant decisions. It declined local option by refusing to accept a motion affirming that each diocese was competent to decide who could be ordained. It reaffirmed heterosexual monogamy as being the only appropriate context for physical sexual expression, while noting the discontinuity between this and many members. Thirdly, and for the future most significantly, it took the responsibility for this question away from the Human Affairs Commission and asked the House of Bishops to prepare a 'Pastoral Teaching' on this subject to be brought back to the next convention. Fourthly, it asked the presiding bishop to propose a broad-based consultation on this issue within the Anglican Communion and with ecumenical partners.

The bishops' 'Pastoral Teaching' was significantly sympathetic to accommodating homosexuality. The draft title was changed from 'teaching' to 'study' and two affirmations were circulated stating divergent views. The study reaffirmed traditional teaching but said that discontinuities in the church 'did not interrupt the communion we share'. In the end, at the 1994 General Convention, the House of Bishops reaffirmed the teaching of the church and 'offered' the study to the church as a way of continuing the dialogue. The study was not considered by the convention as a whole, which did, however, call for a report on 'rites honoring love and commitment between persons of the same sex'.[8]

Clearly the General Convention was giving this issue a lot of time. While there were discernible changes in the balance of sentiment on the issue amongst the bishops, and probably among clergy and laity, the actual decisions of the General Convention had not changed significantly since 1979, fifteen years and six conventions before. The matter now came before the ecclesiastical courts. In 1995 Walter Righter was charged with teaching a doctrine contrary to that of the church by ordaining a practising homosexual in 1990. The issue was fought before the court on the question of the 'doctrine of the episcopal church'. The tribunal based its judgment on a

---

[8] Ibid., p. 101.

notion of 'core doctrine': 'It is this Core Doctrine, and not the broad definition urged by dissent, which is protected by the canons of the church.' 'The court finds that there is no Core Doctrine prohibiting the ordination of a non-celibate homosexual person living in a faithful and committed relationship with a person of the same sex.'[9]

For many this was a turning point. It appeared from this that an American bishop could ordain such people with impunity. If that was the case then the whole argument had been turned around. The obligation to prove what was the traditional teaching of the church for this purpose now lay with those who had up until this point thought they were defending the status quo, a perception that was, in fact, embodied in the terms of the various resolutions of the General Convention. Furthermore it suggested that in all probability this was an issue that fell outside the range of things for which a canon of the General Convention could properly be passed in order to make it something that bound bishops in ECUSA. It gave every appearance that it was now legal within ECUSA to ordain people in openly homosexual relationships, a situation which had been arrived at without any resolution or canon of the General Convention.

It is not surprising that the 1997 General Convention focused on the issue of rites for blessing same-sex relationships. Proposals to ask for the preparation of such rites failed. The convention received a report entitled *Continuing the Dialogue*, which revealed a growing disenchantment with continuing requests for dialogue. The report was sent to all provinces in the Anglican Communion but only six responded.

Other parts of the Anglican Communion were turning their attention to this issue. The House of Bishops of the Church of England had produced a discussion document[10] and the second Call to the South gathering of primates of African and Asian provinces in 1997 at Kuala Lumpur issued a statement vigorously addressing this matter. The Kuala Lumpur statement set out the issues which were to be central to the ensuing conflict:

It is, therefore, with an awareness of our own vulnerability to sexual sin that we express our profound concern about recent developments relating to Church discipline and moral teaching in some provinces in the North – specifically, the ordination of practicing homosexuals and the blessing of same-sex unions ...

---

[9] Ibid., p. 103.
[10] Church of England House of Bishops, *Issues in Human Sexuality* (London: Church House Publishing, 1991). This was followed up by Church of England House of Bishops, *Some Issues in Human Sexuality: A Guide to the Debate*. See also, from an English evangelical position, A. Goddard, *Homosexuality and the Church of England: The Position Following 'Some Issues in Human Sexuality'* (Cambridge: Grove Books, 2004).

The Scripture bears witness to God's will regarding human sexuality which is to be expressed only within the life long union of a man and a woman in (holy) matrimony ...

The Holy Scriptures are clear in teaching that all sexual promiscuity is sin. We are convinced that this includes homosexual practices between men or women, as well as heterosexual relationships outside marriage ...

We are deeply concerned that the setting aside of biblical teaching in such actions as the ordination of practicing homosexuals and the blessing of same-sex unions calls into question the authority of the Holy Scriptures. This is totally unacceptable to us ...

This leads us to express concern about mutual accountability and interdependence within our Anglican Communion. As provinces and dioceses, we need to learn how to seek each other's counsel and wisdom in a spirit of true unity, and to reach a common mind before embarking on radical changes to Church discipline and moral teaching.

We live in a global village and must be more aware that the way we act in one part of the world can radically affect the mission and witness of the Church in another.[11]

The essential objection is to changes in church discipline and moral teaching in regard to the blessing of same-sex unions and to the ordination of practising homosexuals. The grounds for the objections were the clear teaching of scripture and thus it is claimed the authority of scripture is at stake. Also at stake is the failure of the 'northern' provinces to act with any mutual accountability.

Clearly the 1998 Lambeth Conference was not going to be easy. The Kuala Lumpur statement was widely distributed and numerous groups and individuals were asked to support it. On the other hand, Jack Spong, the bishop of Newark in the US, sent a White Paper to all the bishops of the Anglican Communion in which he declared that 'The *Kuala Lumpur Statement* is ill-informed and filled with the prejudice of propaganda.' The White Paper attacked statements by the Archbishop of Canterbury, George Carey, and his letter set the scene for increasing ferocity in the debate:

My fears have been enhanced by recent statements issued by Lambeth Palace, the General Synod of the Church of England, the incredible and ill-informed diatribe that came this past year from the Archbishop of the Southern Cone [South America] and the much publicized, hostile and threatening Kuala Lumpur

[11] *The Kuala Lumpur Statement on Human Sexuality – 2nd Encounter in the South, 10 to 15 Feb 1997*, quoted from the Anglican Global South website: www.globalsouthanglican.org/index.php/weblog/comments/the_kuala_lumpur_statement_on_human_sexuality_2nd_encounter_in_the_south_10/ (accessed 15 December 2006).

statement, signed by certain bishops of Southeast Asia. All of these negative messages were widely disseminated through the press.[12]

Carey had been using some of the language of the St Andrew's Day statement issued on 30 November 1995 by a group of English evangelical theologians, which in fact ended up in the Lambeth Conference Section I Report. The St Andrews statement put a view diametrically opposed to Spong.

In addressing those who understand themselves as homosexual, the church does not cease to speak as the bearer of this good news. It assists all its members to a life of faithful witness in chastity and holiness, recognising two forms or vocations in which that life can be lived: marriage and singleness (Gen. 2.24; Matt. 19.4–6; 1 Cor. 7 passim). There is no place for the church to confer legitimacy upon alternatives to these.[13]

Section I of the 1998 Lambeth Conference was concerned with the theme Called to Full Humanity. The report covered thirty-five pages and dealt with six themes. The Human Sexuality theme was dealt with in two pages and noted wide disagreement, though observing that it appeared that a majority of bishops were not prepared to bless same-sex unions or ordain homosexuals.[14]

In the plenary session of the conference, when resolutions from the sections were being considered, the Section I proposal was overwhelmed by acrimonious debate, a motion which rejected homosexual practices, and a refusal to advise rites of blessing or ordination of homosexuals. The resolution has become the point to which later debate has referred and has begun to be referred to by some as the current standard:

Resolution 1.10 Human Sexuality
  This Conference:
  a. commends to the Church the subsection report on human sexuality;
  b. in view of the teaching of Scripture, upholds faithfulness in marriage between a man and a woman in lifelong union, and believes that abstinence is right for those who are not called to marriage;
  c. recognises that there are among us persons who experience themselves as having a homosexual orientation. Many of these are members of the Church and are seeking the pastoral care, moral direction of the Church, and God's transforming power for the living of their lives and the ordering of relationships. We commit ourselves to listen to the experience of homosexual

[12] Bishop Spong's letter to the primates of the Anglican Communion, 12 November 1997, available at: http://newark.rutgers.edu/~lcrew/spng2prim.html (accessed 14 December 2006).
[13] St Andrew's Day statement, available at: www.episcopalian.org/cclec/paper-st-andrews-day.htm (accessed 14 December 2006).
[14] Dyer et al., *The Official Report of the Lambeth Conference*, p. 94.

persons and we wish to assure them that they are loved by God and that all baptised, believing and faithful persons, regardless of sexual orientation, are full members of the Body of Christ;

d. while rejecting homosexual practice as incompatible with Scripture, calls on all our people to minister pastorally and sensitively to all irrespective of sexual orientation and to condemn irrational fear of homosexuals, violence within marriage and any trivialization and commercialisation of sex;

e. cannot advise the legitimizing or blessing of same sex unions nor ordaining those involved in same gender unions;

f. requests the Primates and the ACC to establish a means of monitoring the work done on the subject of human sexuality in the Communion and to share statements and resources among us;

g. notes the significance of the Kuala Lumpur Statement on Human Sexuality and the concerns expressed in resolutions IV.26, V.1, V.10, V.23 and V.35 on the authority of Scripture in matters of marriage and sexuality and asks the Primates and the ACC to include them in their monitoring process.[15]

[The motion was passed by 526 to 70 with 45 abstentions.]

The conference ended in considerable turmoil with one African bishop declaring some western bishops needed to be exorcised and a well-known American bishop accusing an African bishop of being half-civilised. It was not a pretty picture – indeed it was a thoroughly shameful one – and did not augur well for the future. If relationships were going to count in sustaining the institutions of the Anglican Communion this was not a good start to what has proved to be a ballooning crisis.

As the new century began, increasing strain was placed on the international organisation of the Anglican Communion. Anglicanism has always had a 'bottom-up' community tradition and its history is full of local initiatives. Each renewal movement has created its own societies and networks which often live on after the initial impulse has passed into the mainstream. The Tractarian revival, and the evangelical revival in the nineteenth and again in the twentieth century, are good examples of this process. From the nineteenth century the missionary societies have left a considerable heritage of such dispositional networks. It ought not to be seen as surprising that new networks and alliances began to form in the last decades of the twentieth century around the homosexuality issue.

In 1994 a new network was formed called the Global South. This gathering in Limuru, Kenya, grew out of a meeting of the network of Anglican Mission Agencies in Brisbane in 1986. Representatives from twenty-three provinces met to share what they were doing, principally in the area of mission. They

---

[15] LC.1998,I.10.

confronted the central question of how to be Anglican and true to their own cultural contexts. Sexuality issues were hardly touched on. The thrust of the meeting was mission. All of this was in line with the call for a Decade of Evangelism from Lambeth in 1988. However, as we have already noted, the second Global South gathering in Kuala Lumpur produced a document directly concerned with issues of sexuality. That concern has remained central to the Global South network, which has met on three subsequent occasions when issues of sexuality have always been centre stage.

ECUSA, AN INTERNATIONAL FOCUS

At the international level the conflict has been seen as largely between most of the rest of the Anglican Communion and ECUSA. But ECUSA itself is internally divided and one of the emerging features in the progress of the crisis has been the interplay between dissenting groups within ECUSA and bishops, dioceses and provinces outside the USA. In August 1996 the American Anglican Council was formed in the USA. It described itself as:

a network of individuals (laity, deacons, priests and bishops), parishes and special-ized ministries who affirm Biblical authority and Christian orthodoxy within the Anglican Communion. In response to the Lord's calling and by His grace, we commit ourselves to proclaim the Good News to every person and to reform and renew the Church of Jesus Christ. We are uniting in order to fulfill our apostolic mission and ministry, working to build a faithful Anglican witness in America.[16]

The American Anglican Council has provided a network of connections with other groupings in the USA.

The interplay between dissidents in ECUSA and Anglican bishops and provinces took a leap forward in January 2000 with Chuck Murphy and John Rodgers being consecrated by Bishops Colini (Ruanda) and Yong (South-East Asia) as missionary bishops to the United States. Here was an international version of the strategy used in the USA with regard to the ordination of women in Philadelphia in 1971 and the ordination by Bishop Righter of a publicly homosexual man in 1990. The General Convention of ECUSA was bypassed in order to advance a development. Now in 2000 the jurisdictional institutions of ECUSA, and the generally accepted jurisdic-tional integrity of dioceses and provinces, were ignored in order to respond to the similarly initiated change. The conversation now began to be acted out. This new process was given organisational form in August 2000 with the

[16] Quoted from their website www.americananglican.org/site/c.ikLUK3MJIpG/b.564139/k.A6A2/ How_We_Began.htm (accessed 18 December 2006).

formation of the Anglican Mission in America. The following year bishops from overseas conducted four more consecrations, this time in Denver, Colorado.[17] These consecrations were condemned by the Archbishop of Canterbury, George Carey, and he declared that he would not recognise them.

The same year the Ekklesia Society published a proposal over the names of Drexel Gomez (Archbishop of the West Indies) and Maurice Sinclair (Presiding Bishop of the Southern Cone of America) called *To Mend the Net*.[18] They proposed that the primates should take enhanced responsibility, as had been urged at Lambeth in 1998 (LC.1998,3.6). They proposed that the primates deal with issues that arise in a province to restrain innovations outside the limits of Anglican diversity and prepare guidelines for the province on how they should deal with the issue. The primates would have the power to recommend to the Archbishop of Canterbury that the non-cooperating province should be reduced to observer status in Anglican Communion institutions, and that evangelism and pastoral care arrangements should be authorised for the province. In effect the province would be expelled. This proposal did not gain traction and soon fell by the wayside.

George Carey had invited twelve bishops to meet and consult in line with a request from Lambeth 1998 and they reported in 2002. The report registered only modest movement and continuing disagreement.

ACTING OUT

However, the tide was turning. Action would begin to take the place of talk. The Archbishop of Canterbury's consultation group had met for two years but in 2002 they seemed not to be able to find a way forward. In his presidential address to the ACC in 2002 Carey lamented the deteriorating situation:

In short, my concern is that our Communion is being steadily undermined by dioceses and individual bishops taking unilateral action, usually (but not always) in matters to do with sexuality; and as a result steadily driving us towards serious fragmentation and the real possibility of two (or, more likely, many more) distinct Anglican bodies emerging. This erosion of communion through the adoption of

---

[17] The four consecrated were Douglas Brooks Weiss (retired); Thomas William Johnston Jr. who was planting a new church in South Carolina; Alexander Maury Greene, rector of the Anglican Church of the Spirit in Littleton, Colorado; and Thaddeus Rockwell Barnum who served as missionary bishop in the Anglican Mission in America in Fairfield, Connecticut.

[18] D. Gomez and M. Sinclair (eds.), *To Mend the Net* (Carrollton, Tex.: Ekklesia Society, 2001).

'local options' has been going for some thirty years but in my opinion is reaching crisis proportions today.[19]

Michael Ingham, bishop of New Westminster in Canada, reported that he was considering authorising liturgical rites for the blessing of same-sex unions. The General Convention in ECUSA had declined to do this in 2000. The new Archbishop of Canterbury, Rowan Williams, on behalf of the Primates' Meeting, issued a statement on 27 May 2003 that they could not support the authorisation of such rites. But Michael Ingham had already authorised the rites while the primates were meeting, and the first use of the rites took place the day after the statement. It was a stunning snub to the primates.

Nine days later a major crunch point came when Gene Robinson was nominated as bishop of New Hampshire. Robinson was in an open same-sex relationship. His election was confirmed at the General Convention on 5 August and he was consecrated on 2 November. It might have been possible to ignore the action of one bishop in Canada, but the Robinson nomination raised the prospect of official action by a province. The Archbishop of Canterbury called an emergency meeting of the primates at Lambeth and on 16 October they declared that Robinson's consecration, if it went ahead, 'will tear the fabric of our Communion at its deepest level, and may lead to further division on this and further issues as provinces have to decide in consequence whether they can remain in communion with provinces that choose not to break communion with the Episcopal Church (USA)'.[20] The primates unanimously reaffirmed the view of Lambeth 1998, Resolution 1.10 and asked the Archbishop of Canterbury to appoint a commission to investigate the issue of how provinces could sustain communion with each other.

Twelve days later, on 28 October, Rowan Williams appointed the Lambeth Commission to consider the issues raised by these two actions and report 'specifically on the canonical understandings of communion, impaired and broken communion, and the ways in which provinces of the Anglican Communion may relate to one another in situations where the ecclesiastical authorities of one province feel unable to maintain the fullness of communion with another part of the Anglican Communion'.[21]

[19] Presidential address to ACC-12, Singapore, 2002, quoted from www.archbishopofcanterbury.org/carey/ (accessed 18 December 2006).
[20] Quoted from the Anglican Communion website at www.anglicancommunion.org/acns/articles/36/25/acns3633.html (accessed 15 December 2006).
[21] Quoted from the mandate of the commission from the Anglican Communion website at http://www.anglicancommunion.org/acns/articles/36/50/acns3652.html (accessed 15 December 2006).

Meanwhile things were continuing in their fragmenting way. African and Asian bishops were becoming more active, and liaisons with sympathetic American bishops and parishes were developing. Dissenting parishes in ECUSA were being joined up with African bishops for 'pastoral oversight'. The Anglican Church in Nigeria established the Convocation of Anglican Nigerians in America (CANA) to provide a framework for those in the USA who wished to associate themselves with the Anglican Church of Nigeria. The Global South network continued to meet and established a wider organisational base. It looked like the beginnings of an alternative Anglican Communion.

The Lambeth Commission delivered its report in September 2004. It was published under the title *The Windsor Report*. The standing committee of the primates' meeting appointed a group to track the reception of the report across the communion. The full meeting of the primates reviewed the report in detail in February 2005 and put in place plans to establish an Anglican Covenant to hold the communion together, as had been recommended in the *Windsor Report*. They went beyond the Windsor recommendations and asked the Canadian and US churches to withdraw their representatives from the ACC. They also asked the ACC to provide for a hearing from these two churches at its meeting in June 2005, and to establish a listening process to hear the voice of gay and lesbian people. The Archbishop of Canterbury was requested to establish a panel of reference for those who were seeking alternative episcopal oversight. This all happened. They again reaffirmed Lambeth 1998, Section 1.10 and committed themselves not to encourage or initiate cross-boundary initiatives. Subsequent to the meeting, the primates of Nigeria, the Southern Cone and Uganda did in fact initiate cross-border interventions, though they claimed they were justified in the circumstances. In November 2005 the Anglican Church in Nigeria entered into a 'covenant of concordat' with two groups that had separated from ECUSA, the Reformed Episcopal Church (1873) and the Anglican Province of America (1968).

In June 2006 the General Convention of TEC met and responded to the *Windsor Report*. Before the convention met, ECUSA published a report, *To Set Our Hope on Christ*, in response to the *Windsor Report* request for an explanation of 'how a person living in a same-gender relationship may be considered eligible to lead the flock of Christ'.[22] It is a remarkably irenic exposition of the openness of ECUSA and the interpretation of the lives of

---

[22] Lambeth Commission on Communion, *The Windsor Report 2004* (London: Anglican Communion Office, 2004), para. 135.

homosexual people in the church and the teaching of scripture. It contains a long section on the experience of the Episcopal Church in striving for unity-in-difference.

After long and detailed debate the General Convention responded to the *Windsor Report*, which had asked ECUSA 'to effect a moratorium on the consecration of any candidate to the episcopate who is living in a same-gender union until some new consensus in the Anglican Communion emerges'. The General Convention resolution B033 calls on bishops and standing committees to 'exercise restraint by not consenting to the consecration of any candidate to the episcopate whose manner of life presents a challenge to the wider church and will lead to further strains on communion'. The convention also committed itself to the covenant process recommended by the *Windsor Report* and to the life of the Anglican Communion. Two days later the Council of Anglican Provinces of Africa (CAPA) responded with a statement regretting that 'your elections and actions suggest that you are unable to embrace the essential recommendations of the *Windsor Report* and the 2005 Primates' Communiqué necessary for the healing of our divisions'. The reference to election here is to that of Katharine Jefferts Schori as the new presiding bishop. On the other hand, Robin Eames, chair of the Lambeth Commission which produced the *Windsor Report*, declared the ECUSA response to be satisfactory.

In September 2006 the Global South primates met in Uganda and agreed on three things: the refusal of some of them to recognise the new presiding bishop of the TEC, Katharine Jefferts Schori, as a primate; to pursue with the Archbishop of Canterbury how some North American dioceses can receive primatial oversight from the Global South; and more radically to plan for a new Anglican Communion structure.

> We are convinced that the time has now come to take initial steps towards the formation of what will be recognized as a separate ecclesiastical structure of the Anglican Communion in the USA. We have asked the Global South Steering Committee to develop such a proposal in consultation with the appropriate instruments of unity of the Communion. We understand the serious implications of this determination. We believe that we would be failing in our apostolic witness if we do not make this provision for those who hold firmly to a commitment to historic Anglican faith.[23]

All of this meant that there were a number of streams running in world-wide Anglicanism at the end of 2006: the Anglican Communion structures

---

[23] From the Global South website, www.globalsouthanglican.org/index.php/comments/kigali_communique/ (accessed 18 December 2006).

pursuing the Windsor process; the development of a covenant; a panel to audit requests for episcopal oversight;[24] and a process to foster listening to gay and lesbian people. These came to a head at the meeting of the primates in February 2007 when extensive demands were made of the bishops of the Episcopal Church which constitutionally they were not in a position to accede to. A separate structure of episcopal oversight was proposed for TEC dissenting parishes and dioceses. These were simply impossible demands. The bishops in TEC do not have the constitutional authority to do what was asked, and at their meeting in March 2007 they said so. The president of the House of Deputies of the General Convention, Bonnie Anderson, had already made this constitutional point clear. 'The House of Bishops does not make binding, final decisions about the governance of the Church. Decisions like those requested by the Primates must be carefully considered and ultimately decided by the whole Church, all orders of ministry, together.' The primates also asked for a stop to episcopal interventions in TEC from mainly African provinces. This stand-off was the state of play at the time of writing.

SOME UNDERLYING DYNAMICS

This is a complicated and difficult story but there are some overall things that can be said about it and the way the issue is being handled, and these illustrate something about the character of worldwide Anglicanism.

The approach has been to look for ways to constrain action in order to preserve unity. Of course, at the worldwide level there is no existing constitutional arrangement which has coercive powers. It is hard to imagine what kind of coercion could be applied in this kind of community. It is hard enough in the broader political arena to obtain international purchase on individual nations apart from economic and military action. Presumably Anglican provinces could suspend clergy exchanges or refuse to recognise the ordinations of clergy in delinquent provinces. That certainly would be a significant matter, though it might not be felt very directly at the grassroots and it would mean different things to different dispositions within Anglicanism. The top-down proposals of *To Mend the Net* have not been taken up. The recent designation of, for example, the Lambeth Conference and the ACC as 'instruments of unity' implies a more persuasive and open-textured community. Even these have been subject to qualification

---

[24] The first report of this panel dealing with the diocese of New Westminster was published on 13 October 2006. See www.aco.org/commission/reference/docs/report_october.pdf (accessed 18 December 2006).

by Rowan Williams who says he 'would be much happier ... if we spoke of the "servants of Unity in the Anglican Communion", because whatever the instruments of unity are, I don't think that they are in any sense conditions to be met for Christian faithfulness'.[25] He also seems to be more comfortable with the idea of his own office as a focus of unity rather than an instrument of unity, presumably for similar reasons.

But even so the kinds of groups that have become known as 'instruments of unity' have been in fact mainly episcopal, and even primatial. This level of dominance in the structural menu eclipses the strong conciliar tradition in Anglicanism and suggests a move to a top-down model for worldwide Anglicanism. The shape of the provincial organisational hierarchy and the place of clergy and laity in that system differ somewhat around the world. The democratic model, albeit dressed in republican clothes, predominates in the USA. A more integrated assembly is more common in other places.

The covenant proposal is a quest for a mechanism of constraint. It will come into effect only with the agreement of the provinces. The strategic approach to the sexuality issue was no doubt influenced by the thought that the approach used to respond to conflicts over women's ordination was successful. It is significant that Robin Eames chaired all three of the crucial commissions: the commission on the ordination of women as bishops (called the Eames Commission); the IATDC commission which produced the *Virginia Report*; and finally the Lambeth Commission which produced the *Windsor Report*. However, in the case of homosexuality the fundamental moral issue was much more difficult and more contentious. By using Lambeth 1998, Section 1.10 as the standard, the primates kept the basic issue of homosexuality in the public life of the church out of the picture. But no matter how the current strategy develops, that central question cannot be avoided and it will come back in some way or another.

Furthermore LC.1998,1.10 was passed in the heat of contention, and a significant number of bishops subsequently dissented from it. The conflict in its institutional form is thus linked with a basis which is itself a focus of procedural conflict. Appealing to a Lambeth resolution as a 'standard' of teaching in world Anglicanism is itself a striking innovation which runs against the grain of almost all previous Lambeth Conferences. This is true even if it is for the sake of setting a point of reference in the debate. Such an appeal also begs important questions about the process of 'reception' for such a claim.

---

[25] 'One Holy Catholic and Apostolic Church', the archbishop's address to the third Global South to South Encounter, Ain al Sukhna, Egypt, 28 October 2005. Quoted from his website: www. archbishopofcanterbury.org/sermons_speeches/2005/051028.htm (accessed 18 December 2006).

The nature of the communications in the crisis has brought a new dimension to worldwide Anglicanism: this is the first crisis that has been conducted using modern electronic information systems. Dissenting groups have been able to establish websites accessible to millions around the world. Public statements could be issued and reactions given within very short periods of time. Blogs were established by the more enterprising. In all of this the debate was in large measure conducted by bishops and archbishops who had access to this technology. It gave power to webmasters and media outlets who were able to control the content of their sites. It also meant that the tone of speech in this cyber debate often lacked the constraints that usually apply in face-to-face encounters. The language of designation noticeably changed in the course of the debate. Terms like 'orthodox', 'faithful' and 'traditional' took on extra layers of meaning. On the other hand, the community-based character of Anglicanism means that processes of consultation are necessarily slow and often painfully so. Because the relevant diocesan and provincial synods do not meet very often, they have often responded after the event or not at all, and the consultative process has floundered in the new blitzkrieg cyber world.

The way in which the Anglican Communion dealt with this issue is also illuminating. It clearly blew up as a crisis after the Lambeth Conference of 1998. Action tumbled along at an increasingly rapid rate. This meant that people believed that responses to these brush fires all around the world had to be dealt with fairly expeditiously. They could not wait for discussion in provincial synods, which generally meet only every three years, or the Lambeth Conference every ten years. In any case such a large gathering had been shown at the 1998 Lambeth Conference not to be such a good forum for serious discussion. So carriage of the matter fell to smaller and more deployable groups such as the Primates' Meeting, the executive of the ACC, and the ACC itself. The Archbishop of Canterbury was necessarily at the heart of all this. Special-purpose groups were brought into being to deal with specific aspects. The Lambeth Commission which produced the *Windsor Report* was given just one year to do its work. In general this is a very short period of time for such a task and does not allow very extensive consultation. Then there were other groups dealing with alternative episcopal oversight and the development of a covenant. This whole process has been a classic case of crisis management, and like any crisis management phase it has the potential to change the power relations of the existing institutions. It can change the way in which the community thinks about itself and how it deals with important issues of principle. It has a corporatising effect so that a leadership of influence more easily turns into managerialism.

In this rush of activity it is surprising that there has been so little deployment of conflict-resolution processes. Here is a classic example of group conflict. Why would one not use some of the clearly identified processes of conflict resolution? After the manifest demonstration of conflict and division at the Lambeth Conference in 1998 a major effort could have brought together different kinds of people with different views on the question at issue to sustain some extensive exercise in conflict resolution. It would also have held out better prospects of mutual understanding. The cultural divides at relevant points are so great and the mutual ignorance so extensive that the debate struggles to get beyond the simplest terms of mutual incomprehension. It is not simply that the parties themselves do not understand, or show some consciousness of, the cultural context and perceptions of Africans, it is often that Americans do not understand the tacit cultural and historical assumptions that influence their own statements and actions. And it is manifest in all of this that even the categories 'African' and 'American' are themselves multifaceted and differentiated.

What is at stake here, however, is the nature of the catholicity of the church. The very nature of the strategy being pursued already prejudices an understanding of catholicity. The strategy implies forms of catholicity and unity which are already more primarily global. In the Anglican tradition catholicity has generally addressed the relation of the church to the apostolic origins of the faith on the one hand, and to the wider extent of the church as the extended community of believers on the other. In other words, catholicity is about relations out from the local. This strategy looks like reversing that dynamic.

It is easy to notice in this crisis underlying dynamics of a colonial past. The residual influence of the colonial missionary period and its styles and methods do not lie far below the surface. The demographics of the crisis make this apparent. The role of the Global South network, now a developing organisation, is moving from a mission and evangelism facilitator to a power bloc of churches in opposition to the churches of the former empires. The present position of the USA as the one global superpower and the style of its operation find natural resonances in aspects of the debate. The Anglican Church in Third World countries is witnessing an extraordinary growth in numbers, in line with other churches in those countries. According to Philip Jenkins, that is where the new Christendom will be located.[26] In some respects the crisis represents a new configuration of power in worldwide

---

[26] Jenkins, *The Next Christendom*, though he notes America as the one western nation where there will be future Christian growth.

Anglicanism, concerning not only its location but also its character. It could be seen as a struggle between the power of tradition and history represented by Canterbury, of money represented by New York, where the Episcopal Church Centre and Trinity Wall Street foundation are located, and of numbers represented by Lagos, the centre of the fastest-growing national Anglican Church in the world. In conflict it is easy for the graces of long-standing faithfulness, open-hearted generosity and evangelistic commitment to be corrupted into patterns of power for the supremacy of a point of view.

Some underlying theological dynamics can also be seen at work in this crisis. There is a strand of thought in the *Windsor Report* and also in the earlier *Virginia Report* which moves in a more centralising direction in the organisation of the Anglican Communion, with a more vertical conception of hierarchy.[27] The creation of the 'instruments of unity' language was the first step, but the trend appears in the way in which the *Windsor Report* speaks about local autonomy and the general strategy of seeking to establish mechanisms of constraint, rather than directly engaging with the issue causing the conflict. In the process of this development unity comes to have connotations of ordered compliance, which is not quite the unity that might be shaped by love in the language of John's gospel.

The priority of engagement appears in the determination to enculturate Anglicanism in non-English contexts. That impulse is often spoken of in terms of an incarnational strand in Anglicanism. In this crisis it is apparent in the members of the Global South group. From the seventeenth century we can see Anglicans in England engaged in a similar struggle of adjustment to a changing social context. That struggle reappeared in very sharp and reactive form in the USA after the War of Independence, and in a more compliant tone in places such as Australia, New Zealand and Canada. The particular patterns resulting from those earlier enculturations gave different nuances to Anglican understandings and expressions of church. It should not be surprising that the decolonisation of the second half of the twentieth century should take time to work itself out. The present crisis acutely demonstrates the fragmenting capacity of a theological commitment to enculturation.

---

[27] See I. T. Douglas, 'An American Reflects on the Windsor Report', *Journal of Anglican Studies* 3.2 (2005), pp. 155–80, and I. T. Douglas, P. F. M. Zahl and J. Nunley, *Understanding the Windsor Report: Two Leaders in the American Church Speak across the Divide* (New York: Church Publishing, 2005).

PART III

Beliefs

CHAPTER 12

Knowledge and authority
in the conversation

Anglicanism is riddled with reasoning activity. Anglicans are people who have traditionally reflected upon their faith and sought to understand it in their own particular circumstances. That is partly what causes them so much trouble in understanding each other across deep cultural and linguistic divisions. But the continuing reality of world Anglicanism is that there is a persistent sense of the faith as something that is reasonable: not in the sense that any reasonable person in any context would on reflection see that Anglicanism is persuasive; rather in the sense that it is capable of reasoned reflection and endeavour, which takes place in all sorts of contexts and situations and with varying styles and competences.

Theology as reasoning about the faith is pervasive and intensive in Anglicanism because it serves the vital task of nurturing an understanding faith in the church. It is that activity which enables Anglicans' love to overflow more and more with knowledge and wisdom and full insight. It is also forced upon the church because of its commitment to the historical distance of the life, death and resurrection of Jesus, whom the church continues to worship now in the present. These are also the elements which shape the kind of authority that works in Anglican faith and theology.

HOW THE CONVERSATION TAKES PLACE

The range of styles and types of theology done by Anglicans is apparent simply by identifying who is doing it and where. Obviously seminaries and theological colleges do theology in the sense that they teach theology to their students, and staff engage in theological research. There are over two hundred such institutions around the world. This is formal – perhaps we could say academic – theology. In some countries this kind of theology is also done in universities and in Anglican colleges of higher education. In some places former seminaries are becoming universities. This is happening in such diverse countries as Kenya and Australia, and in both cases as a result of changing government regulations about tertiary education generally. A number of Canadian universities were founded in the twentieth century on pre-existing Anglican colleges. There are also other research institutions which engage in specific areas of theology. The William Temple Centre in Manchester, England, focuses on social ethics in an Anglican tradition. Bible colleges and non-seminary ordination training schemes are also places where theology is done, though usually without a research component. Theological education for lay people is a different area and takes place often by extension of the kind pioneered in South America by the Theological Education by Extension (TEE) movement. There is a long tradition of parish clergy doing theology and in any case their sermons constitute a form of pastoral theology.

Theological material is delivered in a variety of ways and increasingly on the internet. Many theological journals are available electronically and blogs and websites contain theological publications which reach all sorts of people. For centuries books have been the principal means of delivering extended theological material. Anglican theology is thus very widely available and in many different formats.

There are two arenas of theological activity that are characteristically Anglican: synods, especially the Doctrine Commissions they ask to do theological work, and the tribunals and courts of the church. These two provide a rich resource for Anglican theology, and the courts have played a crucial role in a number of important issues. The Court for the Trial of a Bishop in ECUSA made very significant and highly contentious theological arguments in passing their judgment on retired bishop Walter Righter on the charge of ordaining a man who was a practising homosexual, contrary to the doctrine of that church.

The Doctrine Commissions established by provinces and also the Anglican Communion have produced reports of substantial theological significance. Allied to these commissions are ad hoc bodies set up to deal with particular and usually urgent matters. Different provinces have established such bodies as well as the Anglican Communion, and they often operate on different terms. The Doctrine Commission in the Church of England is usually given fairly general terms of reference, and each commission produces a report on the subject. This has created an extremely valuable library of material on theology in the Church of England. The reports are not authoritative statements of the church's teaching, but they do provide a very informed narrative of theological attitudes in the church.[1]

---

[1] See the discussion of this issue in the foreword by Stephen Sykes to Church of England Doctrine Commission, *Contemporary Doctrine Classics: The Combined Reports* (London: Church House Publishing, 2005), pp. xxxii f.

In Australia the Doctrine Commission is given some freedom about what it reports on, though it can be asked for its opinion on specific questions which might have arisen in the life of the church. It has not produced agreed reports but an intermittent collection of short responses which have generally not been published. In recent years the commission has published collections of essays expressing different points of view. The effect of the English pattern is to foster degrees of coherence, whereas the Australian pattern has the opposite effect.

Other provinces give power to the synod or to the bishops to make statements about the faith of the church. This power is constitutionally constrained within certain parameters. The church in Nigeria gives the bishops responsibility and authority to preserve the truth of the doctrine of the church, but the constitution gives authority to the ecclesiastical tribunals to decide on the interpretation of the 1662 Book of Common Prayer, the Ordinal of 1662 and the Thirty-Nine Articles, to which the church is constitutionally committed. Most provinces in fact have a tribunal set up under the constitution to provide for authoritative interpretation of the essential beliefs of the church set out in their constitutions. Constitutions also often set out guiding principles for the basic faith of the church, and in many cases these refer to the 1662 Book of Common Prayer and the Thirty-Nine Articles. It is often at this point that reference is made to being in communion with the Archbishop of Canterbury, or with other Anglican churches. The church in Nigeria recently changed a reference to being in communion with the Archbishop of Canterbury to being in communion with other Anglican churches who agree with the fundamental faith set out in their own constitution. This is really not that much different from many other provinces. It is entirely understandable that an independently constituted body would define its connections with other bodies in terms of its own faith commitments.[2]

Embedding doctrines in constitutions like this means that the general direction of the faith is clear. However, because the doctrines are identified in relation to historical documents from several hundred years ago, the identification of particular matters of faith and conduct must inevitably be caught up in the processes of historical interpretation. For that reason alone a theological conversation would need to be a continuing part of the life of such a church. Moreover these constitutions receive the scriptures of Old and New Testaments as the ultimate rule and standard of faith and these

[2] For a commentary on these constitutional arrangements see Doe, *Canon Law in the Anglican Communion*, pp. 197–200.

documents date back into the distant reaches of history. They notoriously invite interpretative argument. And so it has proved to be, not only in the dioceses and the provinces, but also in world Anglicanism and its current institutions.

Anglicans are thus cast in a situation of endemic conversation and argument about faith and practice. This has important implications for how Anglicans understand authority in their faith. Because they define themselves in relation to a particular tradition within Christianity and thus look back to the faith of the apostles, the texts of scripture and subsequent special texts, any authority turns out necessarily to be a question of persuasiveness in relation to these sources. It is not surprising that in this context Anglicans have often thought of their theological tradition in terms of individuals who might be thought of as standard divines[3] or as identities of the faith.[4]

Anglicans often speak of a tripod of scripture, reason and tradition as the way they work with this situation. This tripod is sometimes said to have been developed by Richard Hooker (1554–1600). It is true that Hooker worked with a combination of scripture as supreme authority interpreted in the light of the experience of the church in the past: that is to say tradition. He further argued that reason was the instrument by which we engaged with these two sources. Reason is thus not some independent authority that sits alongside scripture and tradition. It is that human facility reflecting the character of God which we see in the law of God by which the world can be seen to be an ordered creation.

Anglicans approach this area with a series of commitments which make for some real problems institutionally. Institutions can very successfully carry continuity. They exist to sustain continuing similarity of relationships between people and/or things over time. It is this continuity that enables them to serve through changing generations with such success and to sustain pervasive reliable expectations of others who inhabit the institution. But Christianity generally is also committed to change. The place of a doctrine of the Holy Spirit makes it clear that the intergenerational carriage of the faith is linked not just to institutional sources such as canons of scripture and ordered ministries, but also to spontaneity and inspiration which comes directly from God.

The degree to which this operates in Anglicanism varies according to the level we are considering, but from the local parish to the international

---

[3] See J. Booty, 'Standard Divines', in S. Sykes and J. Booty (eds.), *The Study of Anglicanism* (London: SPCK; Philadelphia, Pa.: Fortress Press, 1988).

[4] See R. Williams, *Anglican Identities* (Cambridge, Mass.: Darton, Longman and Todd, 2004).

organisations the issue presents itself with monotonous regularity. At the international level Anglicans do not have the institutional force of the Roman Catholic Church. The papacy has been established within Roman Catholicism as an international juridical force for just under a thousand years, and for over a hundred years has been declared to be infallible. The international institutions of Anglicanism are very recent creations and do not in any case have the same jurisdictional character or aspirations. Anglicans manage these tensions often with great difficulty and usually with the particular force of persuasiveness which comes from strong personal relationships. As Anglicanism has spread around the globe in the last four centuries it has been increasingly difficult to sustain such relationships between large numbers of people.

Liturgy provides a particular form of continuity for Anglicans. For a long time the almost universal use of the English Book of Common Prayer provided some basis for common liturgical experience and, more importantly, liturgical formation. It was not always as strong a force as sometimes imagined, but it was certainly a vital factor. The story of the modern revision of liturgies in world Anglicanism is in part the story of an attempt to maintain some level of commonality of liturgical experience.[5] The growing influence of the International Liturgical Consultation has been an important factor in this, in terms not of controlling change but of monitoring and influencing liturgical developments.

A similar point can be seen in the long history of texts that speak of the Anglican search for holiness of life. That search is itself a window into the nature of authority in Anglicanism. It shows authority as a lived quality. It was often remarked that during the disturbed radicalism of the 1960s Michael Ramsey carried an enormous authority in world Anglicanism, not by virtue of the brilliance of his theological insights, though his scholarship was of such substance that it came out in direct simplicity, nor yet by his organisational skills, which were not so remarkable, but rather because of his patent piety as an Anglican believer on a pilgrimage of holiness. A collection of texts on this theme dating from 1530 to 2001 entitled *Love's Redeeming Work* was published in 2001 and amply illustrates the variety and character of this journey in Anglicanism.[6] The collection was deliberately

---

[5] See, for example, Hefling and Shattuck, *The Oxford Guide to the Book of Common Prayer*, part 4, pp. 229–67, and also Buchanan, 'Liturgical Uniformity'.

[6] G. Rowell, K. E. Stevenson and R. Williams, *Love's Redeeming Work: The Anglican Quest for Holiness* (Oxford: Oxford University Press, 2001).

started at the Reformation, but it would be good to have the collection extended back to the pre-Reformation period of the Anglican tradition.

THEOLOGICAL AUTHORITY IN WORLD ANGLICANISM

There has been a good deal of discussion in the last fifty years of the nature of authority in the Anglican Communion, mostly about the authority of recently created institutions. These are the institutions that fall under the umbrella of the so-called 'official' structures of the Anglican Communion. They do not comprehend all the institutions of world Anglicanism, nor do they immediately represent all aspects of the life of Anglicans around the world. Rather they are those institutions that have been created to sustain what the Lambeth Conference has called a 'fellowship of churches'. They focus on how the national or provincial organisations of Anglicans can relate to each other. Given the tertiary level of institutions involved it is not surprising that power and authority are significant issues in the documents of the Anglican Communion.

But these documents are also interesting from the point of view of theological authority in world Anglicanism in the sense that they appeal to certain kinds of theological arguments and warrants in order to justify institutional propositions. Those theological appeals reveal something of the underlying views of the authors of these documents, or of the assumptions which could be agreed upon within the group producing them. They also reflect something of the perceptions of what assumptions are likely to be persuasive in the wider audience to which these documents are directed. They therefore provide an opportunity to gain a picture of the kind of theological authority that is generally resident in the worldwide community of Anglicans. Some of these texts mistake what is widely accepted and almost all of them are contested. One of the real difficulties in world Anglicanism is discerning when something has actually been agreed upon. That in itself says something about the open-textured character of Anglican theology and polity.

ANGLICAN COMMUNION THEOLOGICAL COMMISSIONS

Theological and Doctrinal Commissions are a very recent phenomenon in world Anglicanism. The first was established in 1981 on the initiative of the ACC meeting in 1978 and with the encouragement of the Lambeth Conference in the same year. This commission met three times: in 1981, 1983 and 1985. Its report *For the Sake of the Kingdom* was warmly welcomed by ACC-7 in 1987 and commended for study in the communion. The ACC produced a guide to facilitate widespread study of the report. The report was not the subject of a resolution at the Lambeth Conference the following year, though LC.1988,22 on Christ and Culture reflects something of the thinking in the report. The second IATDC was established on the basis of a resolution of the Lambeth Conference in 1988. LC.1988,18 called for study of the meaning and nature of communion. A preliminary consultation in 1991 produced a document entitled *Belonging Together* which was widely circulated around the communion for comment. The successor to the 1991 consultation, IATDC II, met in 1994 and 1996. They presented *The Virginia Report* to the ACC meeting in 1996 but it was not the subject of a resolution. It was welcomed by Lambeth 1998 in a long resolution which tried to express something of the theological character of the Anglican Communion. The first meeting of IATDC III was disrupted by the attacks on the World Trade Center in New York in 2001, but the commission has met three times since then and will present a report to the Lambeth Conference in 2008. It has initiated a consultative process around the communion on a series of specific questions and has presented interim reports. It has also responded to the Windsor Group process which has been dealing with unity and homosexuality issues.

There are thus two reports produced in the Anglican Communion under these arrangements and a continuing process with IATDC III. In both reports and in the work of IATDC III we can see some quite clear theological appeals relevant to a characterisation of authority in Anglican theology and also some changes in approach.

The report *For the Sake of the Kingdom* addressed the theme of 'Church and Kingdom in Creation and Redemption'. Special attention was to be given to the relationship between the actual experience of the church and the anticipated kingdom of God and also to the 'changing cultural contexts in which the gospel is proclaimed, received and lived'.[7]

The report works with two inescapable realities: the actual empirical experience of Anglican churches around the world and an extensive engagement with scripture on the theme of creation and the kingdom of God. This scriptural material shapes the argument that follows. There is little appeal to the theological tradition in Anglicanism. But the struggle in the main part of the report is with the diverse reality of Anglican churches. This leads into an

---

[7] Anglican Consultative Council and Inter-Anglican Theological and Doctrinal Commission, *For the Sake of the Kingdom: God's Church and the New Creation* (London: Church House Publishing for the ACC, 1986), p. 1.

extended and carefully honed discussion of pluralism. The report is clearly working with the two realities of the diversity of the churches' contexts and their faithfulness in those contexts. It is not surprising, therefore, that the fulcrum of the argument from a theological point of view is Christological. It is the kingdom of God as inaugurated in Christ that drives it.

This gives the argument a very strong handle to deal with colonialism. It puts all cultures on the same footing. All have within them that which enables a response to the gospel of the kingdom and all have within them a fault-line which means the gospel of the kingdom will stand in critical judgement in that culture. No culture is privileged in this formulation. This gives a kingdom basis for a notion of pluralism which in turn provides the basis for an argument for continuing interaction between the churches in these different cultural locations.

It is a little odd that at this point in the argument the report does not develop this in terms of catholicity in the church. That would be the traditional theological category to underline the interdependence of different parts of the church. The report also seems to envisage that the different cultures under discussion are located in different places. 'This means, as we have seen, that Christians in a given place and time both will and must share the cultural idiom of their geographical and social locale.'[8] This is clearly a very important part of the problem. However, even in the last quarter of the twentieth century the worldwide migration of peoples of different cultures and traditions away from their homes has meant that in almost every location there is a degree of cultural diversity. The nation-states created by decolonisation in Africa in the twentieth century amply demonstrate this. It is this phenomenon of local diversity that has created the challenge of national identities, in Africa especially.

There is not only diversity between locations; there is also diversity within locations. If we think of culture in terms of traditions of habits and attitudes then it is clear that within Anglicanism there have always been different cultures. The Catholic tradition within Anglicanism, stemming in recent times from the nineteenth-century Tractarians, is a culture that spreads across locations. The liberal instinct amongst Anglicans is part of a broader liberal culture which comes to expression in other areas of human activity. In the early part of the twenty-first century the revival of evangelical or puritan habits of thought and practice expresses itself in Anglicanism as an overlaying culture. Part of the struggle in Anglicanism in the early twenty-first century is about the relative power of these overlapping traditions.

[8] Ibid., p. 58.

Given the postcolonial context in which IATDC I was working, it is remarkable how far they were able to advance the argument in such a helpful way. It is also significant how far they were able to build into their argument a sense of the continuing hope of the anticipated kingdom of God. It gives to their consideration of the nature of the church a strong eschatological dimension.

IATDC II was established on the basis of a resolution at Lambeth 1988 that was concerned with the American proposal to ordain women as bishops, effectively in tandem with the Eames Commission which was asked to recommend pastoral guidelines for dealing with the relations within the communion in the light of the American action. IATDC was asked 'to undertake as a matter of urgency a further exploration of the meaning and nature of communion; with particular reference to the doctrine of the Trinity, the unity and order of the Church, and the unity and community of humanity' (LC.1988,18). Robin Eames chaired both groups. IATDC was to consider the underlying theological issues of communion, while the Eames Commission was to help the accommodation of women bishops by suggesting appropriate practical pastoral guidelines. It was clearly a sensible strategy, as it was also sensible to have the groups working in liaison with each other.

The Virginia Report (VP) did not challenge the focus on the doctrine of the Trinity given in the Lambeth resolution. It added some other considerations, but presented an argument that gave a particular construal of the doctrine of the Trinity a determinative role in understanding communion. Furthermore its approach to communion turned out in the end to be focused on organisational arrangements, a focus nominated from the beginning of the report.

The Commission has centered its study on the understanding of Trinitarian faith. It believes that the unity of the Anglican Communion derives from the unity given in the triune God, whose inner personal and relational nature is communion. This is our center. This mystery of God's life calls us to communion in visible form. This is why the Church is called again and again to review and to reform the structures of its life together so that they nurture and enable the life of communion in God and serve God's mission in the world. (VP.1,11)

This imitative use of the doctrine of the Trinity is striking. Despite the references to renewal and reform it gives to the whole report a static character which is in sharp contrast with the more integrated eschatology of the earlier report from IATDC I.

The context for the report is said to be modern pluralism and diversity within the church. Clearly the presenting issue is how to cope with initiatives from America which are not acceptable in other parts of the communion. The report works systematically from an exposition of a form of the doctrine of the Trinity, to some of the organisational arrangements that have been established to help churches in the communion relate to each other. It nominates the Lambeth Conference, the ACC, the Archbishop of Canterbury and the meeting of the primates, a relatively selective list. It then addresses the fact of levels of communion, or organisational cohesion, and articulates a notion of subsidiarity which suggests that only those things which cannot be dealt with locally, or at a 'lower level', should be dealt with at a 'higher level'. This leads the report to a consideration of the nature of communion, *koinonia* and principles which flow from that for the ordering of organisational arrangements. The last chapter presents the organisational conclusions said to flow from this argument. The report proposes 'instruments of unity' as a way of thinking about the organisational things that will enable the Anglican Communion to sustain what it calls 'the highest level of communion possible'.

The phrase 'highest level of communion' resonates in a number of later documents and reports and refers to the goal of this ecclesiological experimentation. Sometimes it is related to the farewell discourses and Jesus' prayer in John's gospel for added validation. But it is surely an inadequate formulation for a worldwide community. It leaves out a level of analysis that is reasonably important. Different kinds of communities require different kinds of connection, or communion. Furthermore not every community is capable of the same kind of communion. Therefore the form of communion needs to be appropriate to the kind of community under consideration. The issue in world Anglicanism is not the highest degree of communion possible in some undifferentiated quantitative sense. The issue is what pattern or character of communion is appropriate in this kind of worldwide community. *The Virginia Report* begs the question of what kind of community world Anglicanism, or the Anglican Communion, actually is, or could or should be. The form and character of communion in a parish is different from what is possible or appropriate in a diocese or a province, and even more in the globally scattered Anglican Communion. If the prior question had been addressed it would have yielded a fuller and better argument which would have been much more helpful.

The report has not been widely discussed by theologians, though it has been taken up in subsequent discussion about the structures and even the character of the Anglican Communion.[9] The report suffers significantly

---

[9] See Kaye, 'Unity in the Anglican Communion'; I. T. Douglas, 'Lambeth 1998 and the "New Colonialism"', *The Witness* (May 1998), pp. 8–12.

because it limits its horizon for Anglicanism to the sixteenth century and it shows an amazing disregard for the multitude of institutions and groups that have for centuries contributed to the unity of Anglicans around the world. The focus is peculiarly clerical and episcopal, if not prelatical.

These two IATDC reports were written in response to two quite different briefs. The first was a general theological question which touched on a widespread challenge in the churches of the Anglican Communion. The second was a theologically framed question about current relationship problems between the churches of the Anglican Communion. The first report clarified the theological character of the situation of the local churches and gave a basis for approaching the challenge. The second report gave a theological rationale for a selection of the organisational arrangements in the Anglican Communion with the hope that this would provide a basis for some confidence in those arrangements in dealing with the emerging conflict. In that sense the *Virginia Report* did not develop a theological account of the Anglican Communion, which is a great pity.

However, both reports do reflect the kind of enterprise that is needed to develop and sustain a theological rationale for the Anglican Communion. The aspects addressed by each report have a key place in such an understanding. The first report addressed a key issue of enculturation, though I would prefer to speak of engagement. That approach reflects the local and 'bottom-up' dynamic in Anglicanism. The second report addressed an aspect of the inevitable challenge of catholicity in Anglicanism which arises because of the worldwide spread of the tradition. In one sense the reports move towards the same issue but from different directions. They also show the importance of some key themes in Anglican theology: ecclesiology, incarnation and mission, Christology, and a Trinitarian doctrine of God.

CHAPTER 13

Ecclesiology

At a time when the great depression had come upon western countries and independent Anglican provinces existed in India, Japan and China, the 1930 Lambeth Conference took time to reflect on the nature of the Anglican Communion. Touched with political and economic uncertainties, the bishops nonetheless reflect the cautious optimism of the growing ecumenical movement in looking towards the unification of all churches. In that mood the report sees the Anglican Communion in somewhat transitional terms, but not altogether transitional. It envisages that distant future when if 'a council of the whole Church were to be called together, it would be assembled on a plan of autonomy and fellowship similar to that which is the basis of our Conference to-day'.[1] Earlier in this report the bishops had said that the principle which underlies the church – that is, the Anglican churches – was very clear:

There are two prevailing types of ecclesiastical organisation: that of centralised government, and that of regional autonomy within one fellowship. Of the former the Church of Rome is the great historical example. The latter type, which we share with the Orthodox Churches of the East and others, was that upon which the Church of the first centuries was developing until the claims of the Roman church and other tendencies confused the issue. The Provinces and Patriarchates of the first four centuries were bound together by no administrative bond: the real nexus was a common life resting upon a common faith, common Sacraments, and a common allegiance to an Unseen Head.[2]

In the final united Christendom there will be no place for the Roman model of church. Here clearly is a very important statement of something quite fundamental in Anglican ecclesiology. This commitment to the local is held on the assumption that each local church is committed to the Catholic faith

---

[1] Conference of Bishops of the Anglican Communion, *The Lambeth Conference, 1930. Encyclical Letter from the Bishops. With the Resolutions* (London: SPCK, 1930), p. 150.
[2] Ibid., p. 153.

in its entirety and it holds that faith in freedom. The report quotes Mandel Creighton to the effect that local churches

have no power to change the Creeds of the universal Church or its early organisation. But they have the right to determine the best methods of setting forth to their people the contents of the Christian faith. They may regulate rites, ceremonies, usages, observances and discipline for that purpose, according to their own wisdom and experience and the needs of the people.[3]

But the freedom of this local orientation 'naturally and necessarily carries with it the risk of divergence to the point even of disruption'.[4] What is seen as the complete ecclesial entity is the local province and the essential constituent unit is the diocese. The conference envisaged the possibility of a national church where that was appropriate for the provinces concerned, largely on the basis of the cultural and social entity which the nation represented.

What is remarkable about this formulation of the nature of the church is that throughout the long history of the Lambeth Conferences this point of view has been so persistently held. It is a point of view deep in the marrow of the Anglican tradition, and its consistent representation in the records of the Lambeth Conference is telling evidence for the character of the foundations of an Anglican ecclesiology. This foundational point alerts us immediately to the significance of the contemporary struggle in the Anglican Communion to gain some more precise shape to its institutional arrangements and to find some kind of theological framework for such ideas. This struggle is not new in Christianity. On the contrary, it is a perennial struggle in the church and can be seen from the fundamental challenge of ecclesiological methodology.

APPROACHING ECCLESIOLOGY

From the very earliest times Christians believed that Jesus of Nazareth was also and at the same time the Son of God incarnate. Their belonging to this Jesus Christ committed them to living according to a heavenly vocation in the earthly circumstances in which they believed God had placed them. The early Christians' struggle to understand how Jesus was both human and divine was at the same time a struggle reflected in their own lives as a group of people. Paul encouraged the Philippians, who lived in a Roman garrison town, to think of their circumstances in terms of a heavenly citizenship. Jesus told his disciples that they were to set their hearts on a treasure in heaven.

[3] Ibid., p. 154. [4] Ibid.

The point is well made in the second-century letter of Diognetus. He was concerned to show that the Christian faith appealed to all throughout the known world and therefore it underlined continuity across cultural and social differences. The continuity was provided between believers through a common heavenly citizenship.

For the distinction between Christians and other men is neither in country nor language nor customs. For they do not dwell in cities in some place of their own, nor do they use any strange variety of dialect, nor practice an extraordinary kind of life … while living in Greek and barbarian cities, according as each obtained his lot, and following local customs, both in clothing and food and in the rest of life, they show forth the wonderful and confessedly strange character of the constitution of their own citizenship.[5]

This shared vocation constitutes them as Christians and together with the character of their lives marks out the heavenly kingdom to which they belong.

Just as Christians have sought to understand the nature of their faith, that search has also been a quest to understand the nature of the community which together they are becoming. As a consequence ecclesiology has been an implicit part of the Christian conversation from the beginning. This has been so especially at times of significant social and cultural change and at times when Christians have found themselves in contact with each other across different cultural divides.

This ecclesiological method can be seen in two different Anglican approaches. Anglicans have continuously been preoccupied with the relation between the empirical reality of the church and the so-called theological ideal of the church. Michael Ramsey's influential Anglican treatment of this subject, *The Gospel and the Catholic Church*, illustrates the interdependence of the empirical and the ideational. 'Michael Ramsey wished to recall both Evangelicals dismissive of church order and legalistic Catholics to a truly catholic awareness of the continuity and interdependence of the Gospel and church order.'[6] Ramsey sought to sustain an argument that catholic order, by which he meant episcopacy in an apostolic succession, arose from the character of the gospel which he found to be focused in the death and resurrection of Christ.

---

[5] K. Lake (ed.), *The Apostolic Fathers*, English translation by Kirsopp Lake (Cambridge, Mass.: Harvard University Press, 1965), V,1.
[6] Geoffrey Rowell, 'Introduction', in M. Ramsey, *The Gospel and the Catholic Church*, second edn (London: SPCK, 1990), p. iii.

This is a different argument from that of Charles Gore who wished to argue that the same catholic order was a consequence of the institution by Jesus of an organic community, the church, and this particular order. Despite the confidence of Gore, Ramsey's argument is less vulnerable to the criticisms of historical investigation, and at the same time is a more substantial theological account of the issue. The Gore position relies for its force on a notion of legitimacy that arises from institutional pedigree.[7] In nineteenth-century England the rhetorical power deriving from the status of a bishop in the social structure of the day gave weight to Gore's point of view. No doubt there is some sense in such an argument, but it carries significantly less cultural value now than it did in Gore's time. Ramsey makes a more substantial argument precisely because he addresses the question in terms of the nature of the gospel.[8]

This is the methodological context in which we should see the significance of the work of Richard Hooker on Anglican ecclesiology. He worked with a clear theological framework, marked at key points by a concern with the centrality of the incarnation, and then sought to make sense of the empirical reality of the church community of his time. Some of the institutional arrangements he supported have had their day and no longer play a role in Anglican church life. The Anglican Royal Supremacy exists nowhere in worldwide Anglicanism except in a much diminished form in England.[9] Lay participation in church governance which Hooker insinuated into his rationale of the Royal Supremacy of his day remains, though the exact form differs around the world. This dynamic in Anglican ecclesiology highlights the vital question of the nature of institutions in church life and the significance which is given to them.[10]

We may illustrate this by reference to the question of ministerial orders. The point made generally at the Lambeth Conference in 1930 applies here in more specific terms and does so in a way that highlights the nature of institutionality in ecclesiology. On 13 September 1896 Pope Leo XIII issued his apostolic letter, *Apostolicae Curae*, in which he declared Anglican orders had been and still were null and void. The two English archbishops

---

[7] See S. Sykes, 'The Basis of Anglican Fellowship: Some Challenges for Today', *Journal of Anglican Studies* 1.2 (2003), pp. 10–23.

[8] I have used in the preceding paragraphs material developed in B. Kaye, 'Foundations and Methods in Ecclesiology', in B. Kaye, S. Macneil and H. Thomson (eds.), *'Wonderful and Confessedly Strange'. Australian Essays in Anglican Ecclesiology* (Adelaide: ATF Press, 2006), pp. 5, 6.

[9] In an ironic twist it can be seen in ecumenical form in some parts of Indonesia, the country with the largest Muslim population in the world.

[10] For an analysis of Hooker on this point, see B. Kaye, *Reinventing Anglicanism: A Vision of Confidence, Community and Engagement in Anglican Christianity* (Adelaide: Openbook, 2003), pp. 116–21.

responded the following year with a rejoinder entitled *Saepius Officio*. Leo based his conclusion on a fault in the form of the ordinal of Edward VI and a lack of intention to do in that ordinal what was necessary to secure a valid ordination, namely a priest with grace and power 'of consecrating and of offering the true body and blood of the Lord'.[11]

The modern consideration of this document has been set in the context of changing attitudes to sacraments and to the character of the institution of orders that is implied in ordination. The ordinals of 1550 and 1552 in some modified form have found their way into most Anglican church constitutions around the world. In an important preface they claim that 'it is evident unto all men diligently reading the Holy Scriptures and ancient authors that from the Apostles' time there have been these orders in Christ's church, Bishops, Priests and Deacons'. The significance of this preface has been an issue of continuing debate amongst Anglicans, and figures in Pope Leo XIII's document. If the preface intends to claim that there were these three orders from the very beginning within the testimony of the documents of the New Testament then it is not a claim that is sustained by New Testament scholarship. In the nineteenth century J. B. Lightfoot claimed that episcopacy went back to the influence of John in Asia and thus could be said to testify to the influence of the earliest apostolic times and hence to Jesus himself. It was a long bow and a considerable stretch.

However, the issue is very significant from a theological point of view. Does history validate or invalidate a theological claim about such an institution? Is it possible for the institution of a threefold order of ministry to have a theological validity or significance without being historically authorised by Jesus himself? In any case what kind of value is to be put on this institution? Here the real roots of the difference between the Anglican position and that of the papal document come necessarily to the fore. The Pope ends his encyclical with the following words:

40. We decree that these letters and all things contained therein shall not be liable at any time to be impugned or objected to by reason of fault or any other defect whatsoever of subreption or obreption of our intention, but are and shall be always valid and in force and shall be inviolably observed both juridically and otherwise, by

---

[11] The text of the section is '25. But the words which until recently were commonly held by Anglicans to constitute the proper form of priestly ordination namely, "Receive the Holy Ghost," certainly do not in the least definitely express the sacred Order of Priesthood [*sacerdotium*] or its grace and power, which is chiefly the power "of consecrating and of offering the true Body and Blood of the Lord" (Council of Trent, Sess. XXIII, *de Sacr. Ord.*, Canon 1) in that sacrifice which is no "bare commemoration of the sacrifice offered on the Cross" (Sess. XXII, *de Sacrif. Missae*, Canon 3).' Quoted from www.papalencyclicals.net/Leo13/l13curae.htm (accessed 16 February 2007).

all of whatsoever degree and pre-eminence, declaring null and void anything which, in these matters, may happen to be contrariwise attempted, whether wittingly or unwittingly, by any person whatsoever, by whatsoever authority or pretext, all things to the contrary notwithstanding.[12]

Herein lies the crux of the problem, for this paragraph speaks of an absolute authority which the Pope takes to exist in the Roman Catholic Church. The definition of the nature of the ordered ministry is similarly unambiguous in its divine authority. The Anglican theologian Stephen Sykes[13] has responded to this absoluteness by seeking to steer a middle path between easy legitimation of a social development and dismissing such developments out of hand. It is a crucial point.

The problem is that Anglicans wish to hold tenaciously to the traditional order of ministry while not being willing to regard it as part of an absolute hierarchy. But then that is what the Anglican version of Christianity is all about. It claims that our faith is built on Jesus himself as the incarnate Word of God. It claims that as a consequence of that foundation our response is always limited, partial and contingent: not limited in the sense that we can go nowhere with it, but rather that wherever we go with it we will need necessarily to go by faith. The institutionalisation of church life is inevitable, indeed necessary. However, the precise form of the institutional arrangements is always *sub specie aeternitas* and always open to reformation, which is to say change. The institutions share the pilgrimage character of the faith of the community which has created those institutions.

Many Anglican writers and theologians have expressed this instinct. Richard Hooker displayed it in Book V of his *Ecclesiastical Laws* when he began his exposition of the sacraments with a long foundational statement on Christology. He rehearsed the early church debates about the human and divine in Christ and the nature of the Christological confession which stood at the heart of the church's faith. This Christological foundation enabled him to characterise sacraments; 'Since God's Person is invisible and cannot be discerned by us, it seemed good, in the eyes of His heavenly wisdom, that we should be able, for some particular purposes, to recognize His glorious presence. He gave us a simple and reasonable token whereby we might know what we cannot see.'[14] On this basis he ascribes to 'the cooperation of His omnipotent power to make it for us His body and

[12] Ibid.
[13] S. Sykes, '"To the Intent That These Orders May Be Continued": An Anglican Theology of Holy Orders', *Anglican Theological Review* 77 (1996), pp. 48–63.
[14] Richard Hooker, *Richard Hooker on Anglican Faith and Worship. Of the Laws of Ecclesiastical Polity: Book V*, ed. P. B. Secor (London: SPCK, 2003), Book V.57, p. 218.

His blood'.[15] It is the mysterious unseen presence of God that gives the sacrament its presenting significance. The institution is thus rigorously penultimate.

This instinct about institutions in the church is deeply ingrained in Anglicanism. It combines a staunchly conservative attitude towards key ecclesial institutions while at the same time recognising the ambiguity of such institutional developments in church life. There is deeply embedded here a sense of humility and fallibility about the patterns of church life which matches the nature of our perception of the divine presence.

This fundamental conviction in Anglicanism led to special difficulty in the debates in world Anglicanism in the late twentieth and early twenty-first centuries. The Anglican ecclesiological form is generally settled at the provincial and diocesan level. The recent crisis over the ordination of women and the place of homosexuals in the public life of the church has raised in sharp form the question of the ecclesiological significance of the Anglican Communion. The maintenance of appropriate unity and fellowship between provinces, which had generally been taken to include interchangeability of ministries, created a global ecclesiological challenge. What kinds of institutional arrangements should properly be developed to enable such disputes to be satisfactorily handled? What should be done if disputes within one province lead to a breakdown of the hitherto unchallenged jurisdictional integrity of dioceses and provinces?

These are matters which call for a theological appraisal of the substantive issues involved: the nature of the ordained ministry and an evaluation of homosexuality. However, the way Anglicans respond to them is also an ecclesiological issue of some significance. The whole episode has in fact been a practical case study in the operation of an Anglican ecclesiology. By this I do not mean that what has been happening has been a straightforward expression of a clear Anglican ecclesiology which has led to the new structures that have emerged in the last forty years. Rather it is a case study of an ecclesiology which has some central and general commitments but which is constantly experimenting to discover how to respond to new and different challenges.

This ecclesiological experiment began in its current form with the question of the ordination of women and can be seen in the reports and debates at the Lambeth Conferences. The status of the Lambeth Conference and its resolutions has often been remarked upon, not least by the Lambeth Conference itself. As elsewhere in this book I am using these resolutions

[15] Ibid., Book V.67, p. 284.

here as evidence of what Anglicans generally think and not as any kind of authoritative statement of Anglican beliefs. Earlier in this book I traced the course of developments on women's ordination and homosexuality. Here I am focusing on the significance of these debates for an understanding of what Anglicans believe about the nature of the church.

THE CURRENT ECCLESIOLOGY EXPERIMENT
IN THE ANGLICAN COMMUNION

These issues are most extensively opened up in the report from the Doctrinal and Pastoral Concerns Section from Lambeth 1988. The conference was divided into four sections, each of which produced reports that were presented as part of the main report of the conference, though not themselves debated by the conference as a whole. Each section presented a number of resolutions for the whole conference on the basis of the contents of their report. The section on Dogmatic and Pastoral Concerns presented six resolutions, the longest of which concerned the identity of the Anglican Communion.

The section had before it material prepared beforehand by the St Augustine's seminar, the report of IATDC I, *For the Sake of the Kingdom*, a discussion paper on Instruments of Communion, and no doubt a lot of other things which the bishops brought with them from their dioceses. The discussion paper was printed in the official report of the conference. It was a second revision of a paper discussed at ACC-7 and prepared by a small group of church officials based in England and chaired by Robin Eames. The conference section was chaired by Keith Rayner from Australia, who had chaired the IATDC which had produced *For the Sake of the Kingdom*, and who also chaired the Design Group for the 1998 Lambeth Conference. The vice-chair of the section was Mark Dyer from the USA. Robin Eames was to become chair of the subsequent commission on women bishops and also the next IATDC which produced the *Virginia Report*. He also chaired the Lambeth Commission which produced the *Windsor Report*. Mark Dyer served on both these groups as well. There was thus within this ongoing debate a reasonably high level of continuity of personnel in key positions.

The report is interesting in that it reflects the basic thinking of the IATDC report with only a few slight differences, and it deals in specific terms with the discussion document on women bishops. The report begins with an allusion to the Trinitarian model for ecclesiology, though the argument quickly moves to the more Christological focus of *For the Sake of the Kingdom*. It also introduces, but then gives only slight consideration to, the ecumenical issue of the ARCIC reports. Clearly the real focus is on the practical question of how to deal with the issues surrounding the institutional innovation of women bishops. Women bishops appear not to be as vital a question as the related ecclesiological issues of worldwide coherence and provincial initiative.

The argument begins with the assertion that 'we are caught up into a "great pattern of relation" in the Christian Trinitarian revelation' (para. 1).[16] This is a matter of God being with us and us being with God, which in turn implies being with one another in the communion of the Spirit. This constitutes a community of the church with its own language and culture. At this point the argument turns to more directly ecclesiological issues by claiming that this initial introduction informs their approach to questions of authority and in particular decision-making in the church. A crucial step is then taken. 'The Church has to make provision for decision making, so that the transcendent gospel may be really communicated in particular cultures. This is why Anglicans have encouraged decision-making at the Provincial level, but at the same time are obliged to give expression to interdependence, a duty discharged by four embodiments and agencies of unity at the universal level' (para. 5).

It is important to notice the character of the argument here. Provincial decision-making is grounded in an understanding of Christ and culture. That understanding in turn is an expression of the meaning of the incarnation and its interpretative framework of mission and communication. Because this mission and communication necessarily take place in the particular, church decision-making must also take place in the particular context, that is to say, in the local. This theologically grounded understanding of ecclesiastical structure takes the argument to the heart of the faith. It is because this structure is understood in this fundamental way that the problem of finding a legitimation for some kind of decision-making structure at the global, supralocal level is so great.

But even at the local level decisions and communication are already ambiguous. The report claims that the church 'itself has a language and a "culture", a way of making sense of things, a way of being human; and so it can never fully be assimilated to any society in which it finds itself' (para. 13). This does not mean that this church culture is univocal in any universal sense. 'We learn the Christian way of being human *in* our being with the context where we find ourselves' (para. 18). This is true of the form of the

---

[16] The text of the report is in Secretary General of the ACC, *The Truth Shall Make You Free*, pp. 79–122. References to the report are given in brackets by paragraph number.

church, its discipline and its decision-making. 'It is right and proper that the one true faith and discipline of the Church should be "incarnate" in varied cultural forms' (para. 23).

The report moves to the universal context of the Christian's belonging and so the shape of the local is set in connection with the other locals of the Christian community. At this point we encounter a theme not often heard in these debates – that of the catholicity of the church. 'The *catholicity* of the Church is not just an abiding fact about its faith and order: it is also the reality of active exchange between diverse Christian enterprises' (para. 19). The catholicity of the church within the framework of the tradition of Anglican faith thus becomes on this basis a crucial element in sharpening the character of the interdependence between sections of world Anglicanism, especially the provinces, which in this argument have become the representative local. There is a missing element in the argument at this point, namely the sinfulness of the Christian and the Christian community, and thus the persistent fallibility of the community. That fallibility will inevitably come to visible expression in institutional decisions.

The cogency of the argument here represents a very significant statement of Anglican attitudes and approaches. It certainly reveals a quite significant ecclesiology. Its distinctiveness lies in large measure in the way in which it holds together the empirical elements of the church and its divine character. The reality of the empirical is asserted not in terms of observable facts, but on the theological grounds of the character of God as creator and redeemer. That conception finds its fulcrum in a particular framing of Christology and incarnation. The very specifically theological argument leads to a quite distinctive conception of the church. 'The Anglican communion's strength lies in what some see as its weakness: its suspicion of centralised authority, of anything or anyone claiming an absolute power of veto on what a local church (one discipline of sacramental fellowship) does' (para. 110).

It is at this crucial point in the argument that the report turns to the practicalities of decision-making and to the discussion paper that had come to them from the ACC. New elements are introduced and a discernibly different direction to the argument emerges. They acknowledge the need for 'a process of mutual consultation, discernment and criticism, for effective decision making at a universal level' (para. 113). In a situation of divided Christianity 'Anglicans judge that the unity of the world-wide Church is best served by processes of mutual consultation within world Communions as well as between separated Churches' (para. 113). This is an extraordinary claim since it assumes that the Anglican Communion should be defined in terms of other supposedly world churches. But the argument in Anglicanism has been about the nature of that worldwide connection of Anglican churches from the perspective of the history and tradition of Anglicanism itself. That tradition has consistently thought of church union at the local or provincial level. More than that it is not something that has been suggested beforehand and is in itself reasonably incoherent. Which are these world communions to which the report refers? Hardly the Orthodox families, since they have a structure as dispersed as the Anglicans. Not the Lutherans, for they have multiplied and divided much more that the Anglicans. Not the Baptists or the Pentecostal churches, for they do not believe in such a thing. The only world communion that thinks of itself as a world church is the Roman Catholic Church and it speaks of other churches as 'separated churches'. The report seems to be tiptoeing into fields that the 1930 Lambeth Conference was never even going to contemplate. Or perhaps in the way of these things this is just a sentence that someone got into the report in order to keep their own idea visible. Whatever the case, it is certainly out of step with the general run of the approach reflected in successive Lambeth reports. Even so, it pops up again later[17] and in some degree is a pointer to an underlying current in debates.

The report goes on to nominate four embodiments or agencies: the Archbishop of Canterbury, the Lambeth Conference, the Anglican Consultative Council and the meeting of primates. These are the way 'by which the autonomous Provinces of the Anglican Communion express their unity and communion and live out their interdependence today' (para. 122). The report calls for an enhanced role for the Primates' Meeting in order to take 'special care for the universal coherence of the Communion in major questions affecting its unity' (para. 127), and then considers two issues: a response to the ARCIC documents and the ordination of women as bishops. The ecclesiological approach has two elements in it. First there needs to be a process of reception. There is a delicate balance here which is illustrative of the ecclesiology of Anglicans. The process of reception is a way of the church finding coherence. The Lambeth Conference does not legislate for the communion: 'the mind of the Anglican communion expressed by the Lambeth conference still has to be received by the fellowship of churches in the Anglican Communion and by the *whole Church*' (para. 147). This is a slow and dynamic process. It is the question of how to identify the mind of the communion, or indeed of a

---

[17] It is referred to in an article in the *Daily Telegraph* by Rowan Williams following the Primates' Meeting in Tanzania, February 2007. The text was available at: www.archbishopofcanterbury.org/ sermons_speeches/070223.htm (accessed 26 February 2007).

province. A synodical majority may not necessarily indicate this. On the one hand there must be sufficient confidence in the decisions of provinces and of the Anglican Communion to do something, yet on the other hand there must be room for continuing dissent.

This is the crux of the issue for an institution. For something to be done, or a line to be drawn on the nature of the faith, there must be institutional arrangements to do this and enough confidence to act. But that action must not override continuing dissent in the process of reception. This balance is not peculiar to Anglicanism. Most civil constitutions carry a similar challenge.[18] The issue that is particularly Anglican is the insistence on the place of continuing dissent. There is a theological issue here about the nature of the church. God makes his will known in the church as a community of faithful people. That process does not guarantee success in gaining correct decisions. The Thirty-Nine Articles make it clear that councils may err. Thus synods may err. Primates' Meetings may err. Lambeth Conferences may err. Bishops may err. Individuals may err. The sensitivity in Anglicanism has to do with a belief in the fallibility of the church. As a result decision-making is always an exploration. From a social science point of view it is at best unrealistic, and most probably in general terms unworkable. That is because what is at stake here is not just decision outcomes, but a quality of life and faith in the community in this very process. The question at issue is not whether institutions can get things done. That is only subsidiary to the fundamental issue of whether within the community the love of Christ is to be found. That is a relational matter.

In that respect it is interesting to notice that the resolutions of the conference arising from the work of section 3 included a recommendation that regional conferences of the Anglican Communion should meet between Lambeth Conferences as and when the region concerned thought it appropriate. Unfortunately, apart from Africa, no such regional meetings were initiated. There were regional groupings in Asia and the Pacific but these have remained slight and tend to carry little weight in the provinces. The Council of the Provinces of Africa (CAPA), however, has grown in influence and value as a forum for African provinces. One might be tempted to say that Anglicanism in Africa has flourished because it took seriously the ecclesiological experiment proposed at the 1988 Lambeth Conference.

This 1988 Lambeth section report shows us where the modern experiment in ecclesiology in Anglicanism began to surface. The foundational

---

[18] See, for example, S. Carter, *The Dissent of the Governed. A Meditation on Law, Religion and Loyalty* (Cambridge, Mass.: Harvard University Press, 1998).

basis which had prevailed from very early times, and was expressed so clearly in the 1930 Lambeth Conference report and in the conflict over Pope Leo XIII's declaration on Anglican orders, is now being stretched. Where you have a worldwide communion of autonomous provinces within the one tradition and where the world around and within the provinces becomes much more plural and diverse, as it did in the second half of the twentieth century, sustaining reasonable connections across the world inevitably becomes more difficult. The twenty years after the 1988 report have seen the emergence of a particular strand in this ecclesiological experiment. The line of experiment through the *Windsor Report* and the Primates' Meetings has been to look for institutional arrangements to contain differences. An alternative would have been to confront the precise issues in conflict and work for relational acceptance. Given the contextual impulse in Anglicanism there is something to be learned from sociological and political studies of 'large communities'.[19]

Before looking as some other matters it might be helpful to set out in general terms what the report points to in terms of Anglican ecclesiology. It begins with a focus on the incarnation and mission as the initiative of God to engage and redeem humanity. That presence of God in Jesus Christ inevitably meant a revelation in the particular and called for a response in terms of that particular context. The Anglican ecclesiology thus works in that incarnation/mission mode. It embraces the whole of life in practices which are both liturgical and lifestyle habits. Its governance institutions tend to be conciliar in emphasis and to restrict the range of completeness of an ecclesial unit to the province, an arena where there is a reasonable prospect of relational contact. It retains a staunch conservatism in relation to the ministerial orders of bishops, priests and deacons and sustains a commitment to the influence of the early church and to the supremacy of scripture.

Given the incarnational mission character of the ecclesiology, it is open to development on all things in principle, but in practice some things move faster than others. There is no absolute authority in the empirical experience of this church and there is an abiding sense of the fallibility of the church. There is thus a prominent place for experiment and a patient process of

---

[19] On sociological method see, for example, B. B. Bunker and B. T. Alban, *The Handbook of Large Group Methods: Creating Systemic Change in Organizations and Communities*, first edn (San Francisco: Jossey-Bass, 2006); G. DeSanctis and J. Fulk, *Shaping Organization Form: Communication, Connection, and Community* (Thousand Oaks, Calif.: Sage, 1999). On a more political and literary approach see Anderson, *Imagined Communities*. See also the discussion of networking in relation to ecclesiology in Kaye, *Reinventing Anglicanism*, pp. 133–90.

reception. There is a distinction between institutional commitments and individual convictions and recognition that continuing dissent within the church must be accommodated by any institutional arrangements. Unity is thus a highly dynamic notion. It borders at times on organisational compliance, though it lurches away from it in favour of openness and acceptance. It tries to give expression to the unity which is constituted and shaped by love. It struggles with interdependence, but the underlying driver in its persistence with such interdependence is an intense commitment to catholicity in the local church.

In the light of this Anglican experimental ecclesiology I want to draw attention to two other particular experiments in different parts of the world. These are experiments at the provincial or national church level and in that respect have not attracted any special attention in world Anglicanism. However, each has shaped the ecclesial world in which these two churches now operate, and that in turn has influenced the way in which they understand their Anglicanism and thus how they relate to other Anglican churches around the world.

A BAPTISMAL MISSION ECCLESIOLOGY IN ECUSA

Anglicanism in America existed from the earliest colonial days of settlement. Services had been held by English clergy on both the east and the west coast of America before the 1607 settlement at Jamestown brought the first resident presence of Anglicans. Anglicans developed an extensive church life which survived the War of Independence despite the fact that the first bishop to serve in America was Samuel Seabury who was consecrated in Scotland for service in the United States in 1784, just 177 years after the Jamestown settlement. From the beginning there were differences of view about the role and status of bishops. Seabury stood for a more central and determinative role, William White for a more functional role.[20] The constitution was cast in ways which included this spectrum of views. The 'democratic' temper of the early days has been formative and appeared again in the 1970s with the revision of the liturgical standard in the church.[21]

It is important to remember that changes in liturgical practice in Anglican churches are relatively recent. The origins of the Liturgical Movement may

---

[20] See W. White, *The Case of the Episcopal Churches in the United States Considered* (Philadelphia, Pa.: Printed by David C. Claypoole, 1782).
[21] For an analysis of ECUSA liturgies in relation to the character of episcopacy envisaged, see Spinks, 'An Unfortunate Lex Orandi?'

go back to the impulse of the Oxford Movement in the nineteenth century, but effectively liturgical renewal came in the second half of the twentieth century. In America this process began with the increased lay participation in services and a tendency to make the Eucharist the central weekly service. In the two decades after the Second World War congregations were encouraged to join in some of the prayers, such as the prayer of humble access and the post-communion prayer. They also began to participate in an offertory which included the gifts of the congregation and the elements for the communion. Until 1952 lay readers were not authorised to read the epistle, and women were not permitted to do so for another decade. In this period the long and strong tradition in ECUSA of weekly morning prayer as the central service was eroded in favour of the Eucharist.

The weekly celebration of the Eucharist with active lay participation increasingly became the identity marker for the Christian community. This worked very well in the social upheavals of the 1960s and provided a clear point of reference for the Anglican community. Ruth Meyers claims of this period: 'when the foundations of Christendom were crumbling, the corporate act of Eucharist became a primary means by which the Church's identity was established'.[22] But these very changes pointed up the need for prayer book revision, which became the project of the 1970s.

Changes in baptismal practice had already taken place in the 1960s: baptism in the weekly service, the font in a prominent position, the concentration of baptisms on Easter with catechumenal preparation for parents and godparents. However, it was the process of revision of the prayer book that led to the baptismal ecclesiology which is such a distinctive mark of the Episcopal Church in the USA.

A new prayer book was authorised in 1979. Under Article X of the constitution there is only one authorised prayer book and that is the standard approved by the General Convention after preliminary reference to the dioceses. Amending the prayer book is thus a significant matter affecting the standard and content of worship throughout the church. In the new 1979 prayer book a very significant ecclesiological change was made. Leaving aside the ambiguity of the 1662 Book of Common Prayer, ECUSA committed itself to a new reformation in the nature of the church. In the reports and arguments that led to this change it was clear that this was a very significant development and was seen by many as a new and realistic way of demonstrating the position of the church in the broader society.

[22] R. A. Meyers, *Continuing the Reformation: Re-Visioning Baptism in the Episcopal Church* (New York: Church Publishing, 1997).

The whole church was framed within a concept of baptismal covenant. The church was the community of the baptised and a baptismal covenant provided the context for all that the church was to do and be. This meant a reconfiguring of the role and significance of confirmation, and also the participation of children in the Eucharist. Up until this time the ECUSA definition of membership generally meant that you had to be baptised and confirmed, to be in good standing, and to have attended communion three times in a year. This pattern was broadly in line with Anglican churches elsewhere. Under the new model membership was established by baptism. A new category was created of confirmed member, a status required for ordination candidates.

Here was an attempt to define who was a member of the church clearly and by reference to baptism. For many in ECUSA this was a distinct move away from the idea that the church was the religious aspect of society and the assumption that all in society were members of the church, at least implicitly. This meant not only that all who were baptised shared the responsibilities of church membership in mission and witness, but that all the baptised were entitled to all the benefits of membership. This cove-nantal framework is not prominent in the 1662 Book of Common Prayer baptism services.[23] The revisions in ECUSA recognised this and set out to change the pattern. Baptismal covenant was to be the determining category for understanding membership, and thus by implication the character of the church as a free-standing independent community within the host society rather than as a state church. This was not just a continuation of the reform of the true nature of the church from state church to free church. It was also a challenge to the long-held sentiment in ECUSA that the Episcopal Church was a national church, if not in some sense *the* national church.

The developments in thinking about a national conception of the Episcopal Church during the late nineteenth and early twentieth centuries reached a climax at the 1919 General Convention. This convention organ-ised the Episcopal Church under one central body, soon referred to as the National Council, with a full-time presiding bishop and a fund-raising campaign to support the new organisational arrangements. 'For the first time in its history the Episcopal Church saw itself as being a unified body with a unified mission.'[24] The church identified itself with the democratic

---

[23] There is a slight hint in the service for the baptism of those of riper years, which may owe something to Herbert Thorndike; see K. Stevenson, *The Mystery of Baptism in the Anglican Tradition* (Norwich: Canterbury Press, 1998), p. 144.

[24] Douglas, *Fling out the Banner*, p. 139.

values of the USA, and far from being dispirited after the First World War saw victory in the war as the triumph of democratic principles, and was fortified in its commitment to a national church ideal and a strong missionary direction. In similar vein George Marsden has argued that the unexpended energy generated by America's brief involvement in the First World War turned in upon the nation after the war and expressed itself in a variety of social oddities such as prohibition and, within the Christian community, the birth pangs of biblical fundamentalism.[25] A similar kind of nationally shaped triumphalism emerged in ECUSA, which encouraged overseas missions and influenced the retention of strong control in its mission areas. Ian Douglas describes it as essentially 'colonialistic'.[26]

These tendencies did not persist to the end of the twentieth century, but they are residually visible in the collection of former mission areas in the General Convention as Province X and are faintly echoed in the change of name from ECUSA to the Episcopal Church. The definition of membership of the church established at the 1979 General Convention set in place a notion of the church community which was fundamentally open and democratic. If you were a member you had rights and privileges. However, just as many other Anglican churches around the world had discovered, it is not very easy to discipline lay members of the church other than by a system of ostracism, which in an open society and a market place of churches is not really a strong sanction. The 1979 changes to the prayer book and the new baptismal ecclesiology it provided are significant in that they gave a theological framework within which the underlying democratic and individual rights instincts could be expressed.

This change also gave ECUSA a new basis for the mission of the laity and a new way of seeing the coherence and unity of the church in the authorised liturgical practices. It was, in Ruth Meyers' terms, part of a continuing reformation. It was a reformation that directly related to the place of the church in modern society. 'Increasingly baptism is no longer viewed as a mark of citizenship in the world, but rather signifies entry into a distinctive community that has experienced the power of the risen Christ and so chooses to live as Christ's people in the world.'[27] Furthermore it provided the basis for a redefinition of the relationship between the ordained and the lay. All in the church had a ministry arising out of their baptism. Thus lay

[25] G. M. Marsden, *Fundamentalism and American Culture: The Shaping of Twentieth Century Evangelicalism, 1870–1925* (New York: Oxford University Press, 1980).
[26] Douglas, *Fling out the Banner*, p. 149.
[27] Meyers, *Continuing the Reformation*, p. xvi.

people participated at all levels and one of the central tasks of the clergy and bishops was to provide the necessary training for lay people to fulfil their ministry in the church. Church members were now citizens in the church and like citizens in the wider society they had rights and responsibilities for the life of the church. The baptismal covenant provided the basis for a democratic church, which saw itself as a distinct group within the wider society. This 'reformation' was clearly an ecclesiological experiment to give expression to the Anglican tradition in the context of modern America.

Such a presentation of the situation means that in the present debates, when gay and lesbian people are said to be members of the church, this has a much more significant connotation in ECUSA than in other parts of the Anglican Communion, where membership is less precisely defined and more loosely conceived and where the democratic spirit is not so rigorously in place.[28] In ECUSA membership underwrites the claim of dissenting or minority groups to recognition and standing.

AN EPISCOPAL MISSION ECCLESIOLOGY IN NIGERIA

The second ecclesiological experiment is located in Nigeria and has to do with the use of bishops in mission. The first Anglicans to arrive in Nigeria were freed slaves from Sierra Leone. In 1900 there were 35,000 Anglicans in Nigeria, or 0.2 per cent of the population. In 2000 this figure had grown to 20 million or 18 per cent of the population and Anglicans formed the largest Christian church in the country.[29] The mission context in Nigeria has changed significantly during the last hundred years. At the beginning of the twentieth century the population was roughly divided as follows: Muslim 48 per cent, traditional African worshippers 48 per cent, Christians 4 per cent. At the end of the century these figures had been totally transformed: Muslim 41 per cent, traditional African worshippers 6 per cent, and Christians 53 per cent. Furthermore the country is divided roughly on religious grounds: the north is 90 per cent Muslim, the Middle Belt is 43–45 per cent Muslim and 47–48 per cent Christian, and the south is 75 per cent Christian.[30]

Early in the twentieth century the British replaced the Fulani Islamic empire with a system of emir surrogates. The sultan of Kokoto was retained

---

[28] Membership became an issue as soon as Anglicans moved out of England. When the Australasian bishops met for the first time in 1850 the first question they discussed was who members of the church were.
[29] Ward, *History of Global Anglicanism*, p. 132.
[30] Idowu-Fearon, 'Anglicans and Islam in Nigeria', p. 40.

and across northern and middle Nigeria a system of emirs represented political authority. The British concordat with these Muslim rulers limited Christian missionary activity. While this was theoretically removed at independence in 1960, the tradition of ruling the whole country from the Muslim north continued. The coming of a more militant form of Islam and attempts to impose Shariah law has been the focus of civil violence against Christians in the middle and north of the country. The dramatic expansion of Christian numbers during the twentieth century must also have been a considerable threat to the Muslim population. After independence in 1960 the Church of Nigeria (Anglican Communion) expanded and dioceses multiplied.

In 1990, at a time when Christians were feeling the pressure of Muslim leadership in the nation, Archbishop Adetiloye ordained eight missionary bishops in St Michael's Cathedral as well as a bishop for Kaduna. These missionary bishops were to engage in the rapid and direct evangelisation of the Muslim north. Within the year eight new missionary dioceses had been established as a result of the work of these missionary bishops. The 1990s was also the Decade of Evangelism in the Anglican Communion and in the course of that decade nearly thirty new dioceses were established in Nigeria. According to the Archbishop of Canterbury, George Carey, it was the fastest-growing church in the communion.

There is quite a history to the idea of missionary bishops in modern Anglicanism and it came to the fore in the 1830s in America where a distinct missionary situation had arisen. The church was not able to keep up with the westward spread of the population, and the idea of a bishop who was appointed by a group of established churches and who could sustain the episcopal ministry simply did not work. In order to respond to this situation the General Convention began to raise money in its parent institution, the Domestic and Foreign Missionary Society, and, with enough resources, it resolved to appoint missionary bishops at its 1835 meeting. These bishops would be supported by funds from the society and would minister in the far-flung reaches of the west. The proposal won support for its missionary impulse from evangelicals, and from High Church members for its focus on the bishop.[31]

At the consecration of Jackson Kemper, the first of the missionary bishops, the preacher was G. W. Doane who declared in his sermon the bishop is '*sent forth* by the Church … going *before* to organise the church, not waiting till the Church had been partially organised – a leader, not a

---

[31] See Prichard, *A History of the Episcopal Church*, ch. 5.

follower'.[32] Possibly through the writings of Doane, Samuel Wilberforce, the bishop of Oxford, became an exponent of the idea of missionary bishops amongst the English Tractarians. The idea sat very comfortably with the Tractarian emphasis on the apostolic authority of the bishop's office. It was taken up in England as part of their reaction to the control of the church by parliament. This impulse led to the consecration of Charles MacKenzie as bishop to the Universities Mission to Central Africa in Zambezi, though not much else.

CMS, in the person of Henry Venn, took a quite different point of view. He argued that missionaries should evangelise in such a way as to create a self-sustaining local church which could then, at an appropriate time, appoint a bishop. That appropriate time was always to be sooner rather than later. Rather than wishing to be free of the constraints of English law which came through the letters patent, he saw this connection as restraining bishops from excesses. In general the appointment of bishops in the British colonies followed the CMS pattern simply because they came through government decisions and were appointed to colonial situations. There were exceptions to this, including Samuel Ajayi Crowther when he was appointed bishop on the Niger, that is in the 'countries of Western Africa beyond our dominions'. But the Venn model had been eclipsed when Crowther died in 1891, deeply disappointed with CMS who planned to give the leadership of the Niger mission to European missionaries.[33] There was no tradition of appointing bishops *in partibus infidelium* as the Roman Catholic Church began to do in the nineteenth century.

There are two interesting features of the Nigerian missionary bishop strategy from an ecclesiological point of view. First, this is a church deeply influenced by the evangelical CMS tradition and the reasons which so engaged Wilberforce and the Tractarians on the idea of missionary bishops hardly bear on the subject. Rather the American situation of seeking to provide some missionary outreach which would carry with it the ecclesial features of Anglican ministry and practice is more relevant. Given the highly charged political situation in which this initiative took place it is entirely understandable that a bishop as protector of the flock might have been a good idea right from the beginning. Secondly, the structure that is implied in the office of the bishop of an ordered ministry would resonate in

---

[32] G. W. Doane, *The Missionary Bishop* (Burlington, NJ: Missionary Press, 1835), quoted from T. E. Yates, 'The Idea of a "Missionary Bishop" in the Spread of the Anglican Communion in the Nineteenth Century', *Journal of Anglican Studies* 2.1 (2004), p. 54.

[33] Reed, *Pastors, Partners, and Paternalists*, pp. 8–11.

the authoritarian culture of the Muslim north and provide recognisable resonance in that culture.

There is yet another ecclesiological issue raised by the Nigerian experience. It is not just that missionary bishops were sent to the north as shock troops of evangelism. The very idea of sending bishops somewhere else is itself a novel ecclesial action. The appointment of bishops by election of the people, so much part of the wider Anglican model, simply cannot apply. However, in the constitution of the Church of Nigeria such action is entirely feasible since the people in a diocese do not elect or appoint their bishops; rather bishops are appointed by the synod of bishops. The constitution provides for a synod with clergy and lay representatives and this synod is the supreme governing body in the church. However, when the bishops meet separately from the synod they are called the synod of bishops and they have the responsibility of appointing all bishops.[34] Here is a version of Anglican polity which retains strong conciliar elements but also contains a very distinctive role for the bishops. That role is given to them under the constitution which is itself established on the basis of the authority of the whole people through their representatives. The Nigerian model is thus a form of conciliar delegation. The conciliar role of the General Convention in appointing missionary bishops from 1835 is here delegated to the bishops collectively and extended to all episcopal appointments. There may be cultural issues at work here. There certainly were in the formation of the constitution of ECUSA and elsewhere in the world, which according to Anglican approaches is entirely appropriate.[35]

That is precisely the point. Here we have two experiments in relation to the office of the bishop responding to a particular missionary situation set in different cultural and political contexts. These differences raise directly the question of how far cultural and contextual considerations should play a role in shaping the ecclesial structures. But from an ecclesiological point of view the question is not so easily settled. The inside of the matter cannot be adequately dealt with in general terms which cut across the particular. That is both the freedom and the frustration of Anglican ecclesiology. You only know the answer to the question in relation to the particularities of the local situation in the context of mutual interdependence and some humility

---

[34] Church of Nigeria (Anglican Communion) Constitution, chapter 10 section 43: 'Every Diocesan Bishop of this Church shall be elected by the Episcopal Synod in accordance with the procedure laid down in the Canons and Regulations made under this Constitution but such election shall not take effect until the same is confirmed by the Archbishop, Metropolitan and Primate.' The constitution is available on the Church of Nigeria website, www.anglican-nig.org/home.htm.

[35] On Australia see Kaye, 'Strange Birth of Anglican Synods'.

about the details of the decisions made in each particular. That has been part of the lesson Anglicans have been invited to learn in the tumultuous years since 1998.

These two examples of ecclesiological change in the USA and Nigeria highlight the experimental character of institutional formation in Anglican ecclesiology. The two experiments were worked out in their own particular local contexts. That is the Anglican priority. The institutional experiment being conducted in worldwide Anglicanism since 1998 lacks any natural support in the historical pedigree of Anglicanism. Inevitably that means there are greater risks of false starts. In such a situation it is incumbent on all involved to keep open the possibility of retracing steps and trying again.

In the ecclesiological experiment going on in the Anglican Communion there is no 'local' as in the Nigerian and American examples. These provincial experiments reflect the traditional ecclesiological parameter of the province. It has a reasonably identifiable 'local'. That is not to say that from an ecclesiological standpoint institutions beyond the province are impossible in this theological tradition. Rather it means that any moves in this arena are literally radical innovations and therefore call for careful justification. They will also need to be very tentative and exploratory.

The details of the Anglican Communion experiments have already been traced in the discussion of the issues of women's ordination and homosexuality in the public life of the church. In terms of ecclesiology it is worth noting that both the *Virginia Report* and the *Windsor Report* found the transition from general theological principles to specific institutional proposals to be very difficult. The argumentation between specific institutional proposals in the last chapter of the *Virginia Report* and the preceding argument is paper-thin and hardly visible. The argument in the *Windsor Report* in favour of the specific proposal for a covenant is virtually non-existent. Making such arguments is not easy, especially given that the underlying current of Anglican ecclesiological and its more general theological tradition tends towards the local and against moves beyond the provincial. At root the question is how to construe catholicity in this tradition and how that might be best sustained and made creative and effective in the life of the church. The question is not whether the Anglican Communion is a catholic body. In the terms of the Anglican tradition the question is how the supra-provincial arrangements foster effective catholicity in the provinces, dioceses and parishes.

CHAPTER 14

Other themes in the contemporary agenda

It should not be surprising that Anglicans share the general range of Christian doctrine that has emerged in the history of Christianity. Anglicans are part of that tradition and make a specific claim to trace their religious pedigree back to the apostles and Jesus Christ. It is commonly said that Anglican churches are not confessional in the sense that they adopt a legal statement of doctrines to which the church is committed. This is only partially true. All Anglican churches adopt certain texts or formulations of authority which are legally embedded in their constitutions or canons. Most Anglican churches adopt in one way or another the Book of Common Prayer, the ordinal and the Thirty-Nine Articles of 1662. Furthermore the canons and constitutions state that these doctrines are grounded in scripture and in the teachings of the early church fathers that are compatible with the scriptures.

In Australia the unalterable parts of the constitution assert that the church is 'part of the One Holy Catholic and Apostolic Church of Christ, and holds the Christian Faith as professed by the Church of Christ from primitive times and in particular as set forth in the creeds known as the Nicene Creed and the Apostles Creed'.[1] This part of the constitution also receives the scriptures as the ultimate source of authority, commits to Christ's commands, doctrine and discipline, and preserves the three orders of ministry. Its commitment to the Reformation documents is contained in a further section of the constitution which can be changed by appropriate majorities.

This represents a mediating position between those churches which commit to the Reformation texts such as the Church of England, and those which commit to the apostolic and early church texts in the first instance. An example of this latter model is the province of South-East Asia,

---

[1] Anglican Church of Australia, Constitution, Part I: see www.anglican.org.au/docs/ACAConstitution-2003.pdf (accessed 12 March 2007).

which 'holds the Faith of Christ as taught in the Holy Scriptures, preached by the Apostles and summed up in the Catholic Creeds and confirmed by the Councils of the undivided Catholic Church'.[2] Having said this all Anglican churches in some sense look to the documents of the English Reformation as authoritative sources for Anglican doctrine. In 1789, after the War of Independence from Great Britain, the Episcopal Church in America adopted a constitution, but it was not until 1801 that they adopted the Thirty-Nine Articles in a slightly changed version to take account of the different political situation they were in. A proposal to drop them from the proposed prayer book revision in 1924 was reversed in the light of huge petitions from church members when it came back to the convention for confirmation in 1928.

This canonical evidence suggests what history already indicates: that Anglicans see themselves as being in the mainstream of Christian faith. Clearly there are some distinctive Anglican elements, but they are set within a large framework of commonality. Having said that, it is not surprising that Anglicans are influenced by the interest in particular doctrines at different times that can be seen in other churches. Theologians who spread their interests on a wide canvas of trends in civilisation and large cultural traditions are sometimes drawn to particular aspects of Christian theology in order to address cultural changes and challenges to Christian faith. It was widely said that the twentieth century would be the century of the Holy Spirit, and also of the church. Certainly there was a lot of theological writing on ecclesiology in the twentieth century, and in the second half of the century on the doctrine of the Trinity, led by such influential theologians as Karl Barth and Karl Rahner. Anglicans are part of these broader streams.

The Thirty-Nine Articles illustrate the theological position of Anglicans. They are pre-eminent texts which are themselves set in and addressed to particular historical contexts. This can easily be seen from Article 37 which refers to the Royal Supremacy in England. Clearly this would not be an article directly applicable to the United States just after a war to secure independence from the king. Indeed it could not be immediately applicable anywhere in the world, and not even in England after parliament had asserted a secure hold over government power. The article is plainly of use only insofar as it might point to some underlying principles about relations between Christians and government. In other words the text calls for obvious historical interpretation. While less obviously so, this is also true

---

[2] Quoted from Doe, *Canon Law in the Anglican Communion*, pp. 197–9.

of all the articles. Each of them reflects the issues and debates of their day.[3] Some of those debates lie more on the surface of the text, such as the reference to Anabaptists in Article 38, while others are more discreetly located between the lines and behind the terminology such as the reference to the 'visible church' in Article 2.

Having said all that, it remains of interest to notice the order of the articles. The first five are about God, the next three deal with the sources of our knowledge of God, followed by some which deal with issues in debate at the time of the Reformation, particularly how Christians are saved and what that means. Article 18 declares we are saved not by the doctrine of our sect but only by Christ. Then follow eight articles on the church and seven on the sacraments of baptism and the Lord's Supper. The last group of articles deals with more social and political matters. Some articles are introduced in a polemical way, such as Article 22, 'The Romish doctrine concerning Purgatory'.

Even taking into account the particularities of the historical context which is addressed by these articles, it is clear enough that there is a strong emphasis on Christ as the incarnate revealer of God and the representative and only redeemer of humans. Set within a framing doctrine of God's sovereign providence this provides the bones of the particular shape of an Anglican approach to the central doctrines of Christianity.

We have already seen that ecclesiology is the strategic element in recent Anglican theology. This is because Anglicans have been engaged in an important and interesting ecclesiological experiment. However, theology is not like a recipe book where you choose what you need from a menu and then prepare the meal. The whole process is much more interactive and the arguments that are used in one area of concern may be, and often are, drawn from the whole range of theological beliefs. That is what one would expect in a faith that sees the whole of life as subject to the grace and providence of God. The themes of theology that have figured in the recent work of Anglicans as they have struggled to relate to the changing modern world and the changing profile of their churches around the world thus give some indication of the character of the theological method and approach of Anglicanism. We gain some insight on this from the reports of the Doctrine Commissions of the Anglican Communion. We have already looked at these reports for clues about the place of theology and the nature

---

[3] See O. O'Donovan, *On the Thirty Nine Articles: A Conversation with Tudor Christianity* (Exeter: Paternoster Press for Latimer House, Oxford, 1986).

of authority in world Anglicanism; here we are concerned with the range of themes deployed in these reports.

DOCTRINE COMMISSION REPORTS IN THE ANGLICAN COMMUNION

In treating the reports of the Doctrine Commissions of the Anglican Communion as evidence for the kinds of theological interests and concerns of worldwide Anglicanism we need to be cautious on a number of scores. First these are commissions of the world body and therefore concerned with issues that appear on that horizon. They do not deal with the more immediate issues of polygamy in Africa, the treatment of indigenous peoples in Australia, Canada or New Zealand, or the heritage of slavery in the USA. It is vital to acknowledge that these local concerns have priority for Anglicans, not just for practical reasons but for reasons of the nature of their faith. Nonetheless, in looking at the phenomenon of world Anglicanism, the broader concerns of these Doctrine Commissions provide valuable material. Secondly, the work of these commissions is shaped by the terms of the brief given to them. There has been a clear change in the kind of concerns the commissions have had to grapple with. The first commission was given a very broad task which arose from the general situation of churches in the communion. The second was asked to deal with a more specific issue about the nature of the communion and how it could be held together, and the third commission was asked to continue this work.

It is interesting to note how the first Doctrine Commission with its broader brief directs its attention to issues not greatly touched on by the second commission. Asked to look at the nature of the church and the kingdom of God with special reference to the changing cultural context in which the gospel is proclaimed, the first commission directly addressed the issue of enculturation. How were Anglicans to frame their approach to living faithfully in the church and the kingdom in such different cultural assumptions? The commission elaborated the context in terms of the colonial heritage.

This focus gave them a basis for speaking of relativism and the central commitment to Christ. They reject relativism that sees culture and language as closed entities jostling each other. They also reject the relativism that sees all expressions of human experience as equally valid for Christians. They reject the idea that there is no limit within the Christian community to the interpretation of the foundational events of the faith in scripture. Thus they end up saying 'that there is indeed a "sovereign" truth, something beyond our fashions and fancies, but that it is to be known only in the continuation of active human encounter'.[4] Out of plurality comes catholicity. The effect of this formulation of the question is to affirm the diversity that exists and continues to be created in the local circumstances of Anglicans around the world. There is a strong sense of dynamism in this formulation. The kingdom of God is announced in Jesus, preached in the gospel and lived out in the church community wherever it is located. Engagement with each other across cultural differences will be the way in which Anglicans will be able to glimpse the 'sovereign' truth of the kingdom of God. Thus catholicity becomes the servant of the integrity of the local and particular.

It is probably not too much to say that this report opened up the crucial theological issue facing Anglicans worldwide. They put their trust in engagement and 'active human encounter' to sustain the faith of Anglicans. This was the path along which catholicity could flow and also it would give enough coherence to enable there to be such a thing as an Anglican Communion.

When we move to the report of the second commission we not only enter different territory and encounter different challenges, we also move into a different world of theology. We have already outlined the context in which the second Doctrine Commission produced the *Virginia Report*. Unlike *For the Sake of the Kingdom* this report was addressing a pressing issue caused by dissent and conflict between provinces, and of course within them. The *Virginia Report* is a sustained piece of theological argument. It makes assumptions and omits considerations for which it has been criticised. However, there is no mistaking the drive of the argument. It builds a notion of the church as a community which reflects the community of life within the Holy Trinity. For this purpose it develops a particular representation of the doctrine of the Trinity which has honourable antecedents in the theology of the Cappadocian fathers of the early church and draws on work that had more recently been developed within the Orthodox tradition. This portrayal highlights the communion between the persons of the Trinity – Father, Son and Holy Spirit – which in the classical formulation is described as a *perichoresis* – an interacting movement, a kind of 'dance'. The church as the creation of this God, it is said, reflects this *perichoretic* character. The church is a community of interacting persons and provides an image of how we belong together in the Anglican Communion.

---

[4] ACC and IATDC, *For the Sake of the Kingdom*, para. 78.

The report is concerned with questions of decision-making and thus turns to levels at which decisions are appropriately made in the church. In order, apparently, to acknowledge the commitment to the local in Anglicanism, it employs a doctrine of subsidiarity. This was a doctrine developed by reformers in the Roman Catholic Church in the twentieth century to argue against all decisions being made at the apex of decision-making authority in that church. The hierarchical structure in Anglicanism, however, moves in the opposite direction to the Roman model, which is not to say that there is not a proper authority of the hierarchy to exercise power in Anglicanism.[5] But it is to say that the capacity to exercise that power is given by the community in which it is expressed. In the *Virginia Report* the principle of subsidiarity is introduced to make the opposite point to that argued by the Roman Catholic reformers, namely that there are indeed some decisions which need to be made at a higher level in the order of the church. Which questions should be dealt with at this higher level should be restrained by the subsidiarity principle.

It is not the conclusions of the report that we are concerned with here, but rather the theological hinterland which has shaped the argument. Clearly it is built on two key theological themes: a particular version of the doctrine of the Trinity and a theology of *koinonia* or communion. It has moved away from the more eschatologically shaped notion of the kingdom of God and also from the strong and dynamic notion of catholicity seen in IATDC I. The impression given by the report is of a theological interpretation of worldwide Anglicanism which is static. It lacks the drive of the enculturation theme of *For the Sake of the Kingdom*, and at the same time seems to be so internally occupied that it leaves little or no opening for mission. A focus on the incarnation and its surrounding categories of redemption and repentance would have brought this to light, but is not to be found in the report. Clearly the brief given to the commission, and the urgency and importance of the practical challenge facing the communion at the time, have had an understandable influence on the work of the commission. Indeed the terms of reference for the commission set out the theological themes they should consider. One wonders what the commission might have come up with if it had simply been asked for some theological advice about the crisis itself.

---

[5] See the argument made for this in S. Sykes, *Power and Christian Theology* (London: Continuum, 2006).

OTHER ANGLICAN COMMUNION REPORTS

There are two other important recent reports from the Anglican Communion which provide evidence of the kind of theological thinking current in Anglicanism at the beginning of the new century. The first is the Eames Commission report, *Women in the Anglican Episcopate*, which addressed pastoral guidelines for dealing with disagreements over the ordination of women as bishops, and the *Windsor Report* which was produced by the Lambeth Commission. Following the Eames report a monitoring group was set up to watch over the process of reception of the ordination of women as priests and bishops throughout the communion. Robin Eames, the primate of Ireland, chaired the Eames Commission, the monitoring group Inter-Anglican Theological and Doctrinal Commission which produced the *Virginia Report*, and the Lambeth Commission which produced the *Windsor Report*. That is to say he has chaired every one of the key commissions that have dealt with the two crises presented in the communion by the ordination of women and of homosexuals. It is an interesting question as to whether these reports represent a kind of Eames theology of the communion. It is not easy to answer that question. It is much easier to report that he was a natural for this kind of work because of his considerable chairing and negotiating skills honed in the conflicts of Ireland where he was the primate.

The Eames Commission and the subsequent Eames Monitoring Group provide a consistent approach to the conflict which emerged in the communion over the ordination of women as priests and bishops. The group was established to set out pastoral guidelines for dealing with the conflict that was expected over the steps to ordain women. The commission issued four reports, the last being that of the monitoring group which followed the main commission. Throughout all these reports there is a continuous theme of respect and courtesy. These were qualities called for by the 1988 Lambeth Conference.

Within that framework of courtesy and respect the commission described the theological framework they planned to use: the nature of communion as revealed in the mystery of God the Trinity and the nature of *koinonia* within the Anglican Communion.

This report introduces the theme of the communion which exists within the Godhead and relates it to the nature of the church. The images of the church in the New Testament, such as a chosen race, a royal priesthood, a holy nation, 'speak of a communion with God; Father, Son and Holy Spirit. This communion determines theologically our relationship with one another. Communion with God and one another is both gift and divine expectation for the Church' (para. 22).[6] Structures thus become 'instruments for maintaining and strengthening the visible communion of the Church' (para. 26). This is not a new thing, they say, for from the earliest times the church has found ways of maintaining the 'highest degree of communion possible in the face of sharp doctrinal disagreement and diversity of practice' (para. 32).

When the report comes to the Anglican Communion it states that while the 'Provinces are autonomous in matters of order and discipline, and they are held together by the visible bonds of communion and thus in a real sense they belong to one another; they are interdependent' (para. 36). They go on to say that 'certain issues, particularly those which affect the bonds which hold the Communion together, namely, the faith, the sacraments, and the ministry, or issues which concern changes in the relationship of Anglicans to another world Communion need the reflection of the whole Communion; they need a Communion wide mind' (para. 37). This somewhat surprising misunderstanding of the situation of the provinces of the Anglican Communion enables the commission to proceed on the assumption that there are material and organisational connections which have the effect of limiting the autonomy of the provinces and that this autonomy is located in the area of order and discipline only. In almost every case the provinces have constitutions which give them authority over the whole range of matters to do with the faith, including making statements and decisions about the content and meaning of that faith. The framework within which such statements and decisions can be made is laid down in the fundamental elements of the constitutions of the provinces. Even where these constitutions contain matters which are not able to be changed, such as core elements of the faith, that restraint arises from the constitutions themselves and not from any outside relationships or history, thereby indicating yet again that the provinces by their own constitutions are autonomous.

Despite some misunderstandings, the eminent good sense of the commission takes it a very long way towards providing the kind of advice that would enable the fulfilment of their desire for the highest degree of communion between and within the provinces in the face of significant disagreement over the ordination of women. They consider a form of parallel jurisdiction in dioceses where there is a woman diocesan bishop and find it just bearable as an extraordinary anomaly in preference to schism. It is in this frame of thinking that the commission makes a

---

[6] ACC, *Women in the Anglican Episcopate*.

profound and critical observation: 'If Anglicans mean what they say by an "open process of reception", such ambiguities will be accepted as one of the growing pains of living in a church where there are no binding central decision making structures' (para. 61). They return to this important notion of reception in subsequent reports and in the last report they spend time outlining the origins of the idea in the Grindrod report of 1988 and track through its role in the course of the debate from 1988 to 1997.

Reception is not just putting up with dissent from a decision or action until people come to accept it. Nor in the Anglican context is it a matter of waiting until all the faithful come to accept some decision or action by a higher authority, although it has something of that sense in the Roman Catholic Church. Reception for Anglicans is rather a way of speaking about the tentativeness and experimental character of decisions about new situations or problems. It may mean equally that the initiative is found not to be acceptable. This is a very long-range idea and, as the Commission constantly repeats, it calls for patience and charity. 'During the process of reception we need to make space for each other and to listen to each other in charity and patience' (para. 261). We might say that reception in an Anglican context means something about the long-range providence of God, the fallibility of the church and the experimental character of ecclesial formation especially in the formation of institutions.

The Lambeth Commission had a different task and its *Windsor Report* reflects this in its conclusions, though the theological themes are similar. Again the Commission was chaired by Robin Eames. We find here the theme of *koinonia* or communion, though it is nuanced in a more relational direction than in the *Virginia Report*. Much greater emphasis is given to the place of scripture in the operation of authority in Anglican churches, though it is done in such a way that interpretation of scripture is an essential part of any use of the texts of scripture. They set out a proforma for discernment of theological debate, formal action and extensive consultation.

However the significant new discussion in this report concerns the notion of the autonomy of the provinces. It suggests that 'speaking of their autonomy came to refer to their disengagement from' the Royal Supremacy in England (para. 73). That is to say they were granted their autonomy. This hardly fits the USA or those provinces that were never English colonies. When provinces established their own constitutions they gained a form of self-determination which was expressed in different ways in the constitutions of the provinces. That, says the report, 'raises the key question of how much diversity is to be allowed or encouraged, on what matters, and under what conditions' (para. 74). The report then engages in a discussion of terms and concludes that autonomy means 'not an isolated individualism, but the idea of being free to determine one's own life within a wider obligation to others' (para. 76). Thus an autonomous body 'is capable of making decisions for itself in relation to its own affairs at its own level. Autonomy then is linked to subsidiarity' (para. 77). The argument gives every appearance of claiming some kind of 'reserve powers' for the long-since-dead Royal Supremacy.

One wonders where such a curious argument is going. Why not speak about the catholicity that churches are committed to out of the core of their Christian faith? Why not speak about the inherent drive of fellowship or *koinonia*, or of the bonds of a shared heritage of faith? This logical definitional argument seems to serve the purpose of providing a basis for the proposal for a covenant but it lacks historical cogency and any clear and substantiated relation to the covenant proposal. Instead the covenant is presented as a way that would give shape to the obligations presented in this report. As with the *Virginia Report* the move from theological argument to institutional proposal has not proved easy.

The covenant is the other major innovation in the flow of reports. Here is a notion with an extensive theological history. It is clearly found in the biblical texts. The Old Testament is replete with covenants as a way of speaking about the relationship of God to Israel. In the New Testament Jesus alludes to this usage by referring to the new covenant of his blood and that language is taken up by some of the New Testament writers. These references generally refer to relations between God and his people. However, in Anglicanism covenant has not been a prominent theme in theology. The new baptismal theology in ECUSA, introduced in the 1979 prayer book revision, is set within a covenantal idea of baptism, but that is not the usual pattern in the wider Anglican experience. Covenants have also been used in ecumenical relationships between Anglicans and others.

The covenant proposal has prospered in recent meetings of the primates, and a drafting group presented a preliminary version of a covenant to the meeting of the primates in February 2007 with a view to it being developed further for the Lambeth Conference in 2008. At the theological level, which is our concern here, this is a significant new theme in the Anglican debate. It remains a question, not solved at the time of writing, as to whether such a covenant will in fact turn out simply to harden the conflict and draw other theological differences into the orbit of the current debate. So a question about homosexuals in the public life of the church might turn into a question about a wider range of growing differences current in the communion which have to do with other and broader theological issues. To use a First World War image, this may turn out to be a little like moving from the significant battle at Anzac Cove to the horrors of the battle at the Somme.

It is one thing to say that the presenting question of homosexuality in the public life of the church is related to a range of other matters such as biblical authority or interpretation, or the tradition of orders, or the nature and extent of orthodoxy, or the structure of Christian theology and the character of its coherence, or any number of other things. It is quite another thing to say that the resolution of the presenting problem requires that all, or even some, of these issues must be settled either before or at the same time as the presenting issue is resolved. Human communities do not work like that. They more characteristically deal with the actual issue. Linking a controversial matter to all the different reasons why people might agree or disagree on the point at issue is generally a way of destroying communities, not restoring them. At this point in the debate the covenant looks as though it will broaden the range of issues to be resolved and therefore seems to be a very risky strategy. At the time of writing, attempts to provide a rationale for such a covenant have tended to revert to biblical examples which, however, seem to be addressed to different kinds of relationships. There has not been very much to show that this is a category that has significant consonance with the Anglican tradition of theology and practice.

EVIDENCE FROM THE PROVINCES

The material reported above reveals the kinds of theological themes that are currently used in dealing with the divisions and conflicts in the Anglican Communion. The strategy in these reports has not been to confront the substantive issue of sexuality. The strategy has been to address the question of how to deal with such divisions and conflicts that have arisen or might arise in the communion. The theological themes therefore have focused on the nature of the Anglican Communion and especially the relations between the provinces. It has been in this respect an attempted experiment in ecclesiology of a very particular kind.

However, there have been other issues facing the provinces, and there has also been a very significant body of Anglican theological literature produced during this time. We can gain some purchase on this wider theological material which has taken the attention of Anglicans in the provinces by reviewing two examples from England and Africa respectively. Such a review will necessarily be brief, but nonetheless suggestive of what is going on in world Anglicanism.

Church of England Doctrine Commission reports

Throughout the twentieth century the Church of England has regularly appointed a Doctrine Commission. Such a commission was first established in 1922 and published its report in 1937 entitled *Doctrine in the Church of England*. The reports of 1976 (*Christian Believing*) and in 1981 (*Believing in the Church*) focused on what it meant to believe, or, to put it another way, they focused on the method of theology. These reports were published as a collection of essays on different aspects of the theme and usually represented different perspectives. In 1987 a new approach was begun. This new programme was to focus on the content of Christian belief and three unanimous reports were published in 1987 (*We Believe in God*), 1991 (*We Believe in the Holy Spirit*) and 1995 (*The Mystery of Salvation*). In 2005 a combined edition of the reports was published in a similar format to the fourth in the series which had been published in 2003 (*Being Human*).[7] These reports therefore set out to discuss what the Doctrine Commission of the Church of England thought was the content of Anglican belief at the end of the twentieth century, or rather what they thought it ought to be.

In the foreword to the combined edition Stephen Sykes raised the question of the authority of such reports in terms which resonate with the discussions in the Anglican Communion. He refers to the fact that the report *We Believe in God* was welcomed by the House of Bishops, commended to the church and published 'under its authority'. Sykes says that this commendation must mean at least that the bishops did not think there was anything misleading in the report. The discussion in the church meant that it went to the General Synod for study and debate, and presumably to the dioceses and parishes and theological colleges if for no other reason than that it was published and in the public domain. But the fact that it came from the Doctrine Commission of the church and that the House of Bishops commended it and published it under their authority must, according to Sykes, mean something. Precisely what is hard to tell. However, Sykes quite rightly says in relation to the synod and wider study and debate that 'both these stages constitute the reception of the teaching contained in the report, and their reception likewise becomes part of their authority'.[8] The degree of authority yielded by the process of reception would depend on the degree to which the reports gained acceptance. In this sense final authority resides in the church at large. Though the example also demonstrates that subsidiary authorities also operate in winning

---

[7] Church of England Doctrine Commission, *Contemporary Doctrine Classics*.   [8] Ibid., p. xxxiii.

acceptance, the standing of the commission and the commendation of the House of Bishops and the General Synod nonetheless play a certain role.

This example of reception applies to a doctrine report, not institutional action by one province among a number. Nonetheless this more localised example perhaps sheds light on the operation of a process of reception in the more distantly dispersed provinces of the Anglican Communion. It highlights that conversation and argument are the precursors to reception by the church at large, and that in the end this is the basic point of acceptance and authority.[9]

The three reports deal with crucial issues in the Anglican tradition, but interestingly do so in somewhat different ways. The first and second reports begin with an analysis of the context in which the theology is to be developed, whereas the third report on the Holy Spirit enters into the subject immediately from the contents of the traditions. Such context-setting as does occur in the development of this report turns to a more internal church matter, namely the charismatic movement that has had such an influence on the churches. The first report begins with an extended consideration of the historical context in which the commission is working. Even in the development of the material on the doctrine of God the commission works this out in interaction with the modern scientific enterprise. The report then moves to the scriptural material and the theological tradition, which introduce the doctrine of the Trinity. The commission accesses the substance of the doctrine by exploring the encounter with God in prayer and from that point moves out into the whole of life. The third report follows a very similar line of development. It is noteworthy that this is such an integrated approach to the writing of theology. The second report refers directly to the charismatic renewal in the opening chapter and then returns to this theme in its discussion of structures and power, though the report does turn outwards to discuss mechanistic versions of science in relation to the Holy Spirit and creation.

The reports thus show a characteristically Anglican preoccupation with integrating theological work with the context in which the faith is to be lived out, indeed in which the very terms of the faith are to be understood. The second report may have shaped its argument differently, but the same concern is present there, though not as strongly as in the first and third reports. It is also clear in these reports that the rather more exuberantly

---

[9] The pattern of argument is consonant with earlier presentations from Stephen Sykes. See, for example, S. Sykes, *The Integrity of Anglicanism* (London: Mowbray, 1978), and S. Sykes, *Unashamed Anglicanism* (London: Darton, Longman and Todd, 1995).

open, even liberal, style and direction of some of the earlier and controversial report, *Christian Believing*, have been left behind.

Stephen Sykes has drawn attention to three themes in these reports which are significant signs of the beliefs of Anglicans in this period. First, and not surprisingly in the light of our earlier discussion of theology reflected in Anglican Communion documents, is the doctrine of the Trinity. The reports consistently affirm in a straightforward way the traditional doctrine of what Christians mean when they speak of believing in God. Sykes puts this in the context of the empiricist attack on theological claims about the non-empirically verifiable reality of God. In the mid-twentieth century this affected many, epitomised perhaps by Bishop John Robinson who used to say that he did not like to preach on Trinity Sunday because he did not know what to say. These were currents which traversed the western world. In England there were more local examples of doubt about belief in this central doctrine of God. Liturgical revision was going on in the Church of England at the time of these public uncertainties, but the liturgies being proposed expressed traditional understanding of Christology and the Trinity. 'Controversies about radical proposals are not necessarily a reliable indicator of how theology is developing in a new era, and the doctrine of a necessary development in the direction of greater theological liberalism simply seems untrue.'[10] It may be that the reactions in the wider Anglican Communion to North American initiatives point to the same conclusion. In these reports statements about God are not in mythological language, or about the depth of our being or as part of our perspective on the world. Rather the language of this doctrine refers to a reality, God, even though this and our language generally do not and cannot describe God completely.

There was also a broader Christian context for the fate of the doctrine of the Trinity in the mid-twentieth century. The challenge of empiricism, while it may have had its specific English manifestation in Oxford analytical philosophy, was a much more general trend in western culture, and beyond. Karl Barth in a Reformed tradition and Karl Rahner in a Roman Catholic tradition were theologians who responded to this challenge by giving the doctrine of the Trinity a central place in their theological endeavour.

Essentially this strategy was not just about language and what it refers to. It was about the way in which we imagine God to be when we try to express our apprehensions in theological formulations, prayer or daily living. Barth especially was responding to the impact of the First World War and the rise

---

[10] Church of England Doctrine Commission, *Contemporary Doctrine Classics*, p. xxv.

of the Nazis in Germany where he was teaching in the 1930s. The aftermath of European cities in ruins and people massacred only added to the sense of overwhelming suffering which cried out for some kind of articulation of how God might relate to this human disaster.

Sykes draws attention to the eclipse in the English reports of the doctrine of the impassibility of God. This doctrine underlines that God is not fickle like humans. This has come to be regarded as inadequate to the human condition and indeed to the implications of Jesus' passion and suffering. Again we see here another marker about the way in which God is seen in relation to the created world and the actual circumstances of the human condition. That is precisely the issue at stake in the principle of encultura-tion and mission to which we have already drawn attention in regard to the Anglican focus on the incarnation.

The third theme Sykes notes is a more critical embrace of scriptural authority. The diversity within scripture itself demands interpretation for Christians who live in different circumstances. These reports do not yield at all on the supremacy of scripture in the formation of the Christian faith community. Nor do they restrict the use of scripture to its function in theological endeavour. Scripture plays its role in liturgy and meditation and in sundry other ways. Its role and function in the life of the church is multifaceted. This is an attempt to retain the demand of interpretation made from within the texts themselves which is not captured by the dismissive tendencies of much twentieth-century biblical criticism. In a word, interpretation is not a captive of liberal theology but rather is the demand of scripture itself. In this respect these reports represent very much where biblical studies by and large had moved by the end of the twentieth century.

These themes seem to me to be well taken by Sykes and point to an Anglican theology which is prepared to take on substantial and controversial issues. The reports also highlight the crucial significance of method in theology, even when the focus is directly upon the content of the faith. They also demonstrate a highly engaged form of thinking which is charac-teristic of the Anglican tradition and which we have seen is related to the singular place given to the doctrine of the incarnation conceived of in redemptive and mission terms.

The reports also display some marked continuity with the work being done in the Anglican Communion studies and thus probably display two things. First, that the issues facing Anglicans around the world have some clear points of contact with those being faced in England. They also suggest that these theologians seem to be talking to each other, or at least reading each other's writings and engaging with them. Of course these reports come from within one province, England. That province has been going through significant cultural changes, but those changes have taken place within a continuing and stable political and legal framework. That gives a certain constancy of context for these theologians. That is by no means true elsewhere in the world, and by way of contrast we will now look at a province where political change in the last part of the twentieth century has been both dramatic and calamitous.

Apartheid and reconciliation in southern Africa

At hearings of the Truth and Reconciliation Commission held in East London in November 1997, and presided over by the former Anglican archbishop of Cape Town, the Anglican Church found itself in the dock and apologising for its failures during the apartheid period. Bishop Michael Nuttall:

(a) acknowledged the complicity of the Anglican Church in apartheid by, for example, appointing chaplains to pastor only white conscripts in the Defence Force and appointing ministers to congregations in accordance with the notorious Group Areas Act.

(b) noted that many members and leaders of the Anglican Church remained silent in the face of injustice.

(c) apologised to black members of the church for failing to acknowledge and prevent actions within the church that perpetuated the same racial, social and economic divisions existing in the country – for example by paying stipends on a racially different basis.[11]

How did it come about that Anglicans found themselves representing both the healing of the nation in the post-apartheid period and the failures of the church during that terrible time? The answer is complex and bound up with the mixture of black and white members in the Church of the Province of South Africa (CPSA), and with the internal dynamics of the church in its relations with other churches in South Africa. It is also part of the story of the leadership of successive archbishops. The history of apartheid has been well rehearsed but something of the length and depth of the policy over many years cannot be forgotten in trying to understand the

---

[11] Statement read by Bishop Michael Nuttall to the Truth and Reconciliation Commission Faith Community Hearings in East London on 17–19 November 1997. The transcript is available at www.doj.gov.za/trc_frameset.htm.

response of Anglicans.[12] Dutch settlers first came to South Africa in 1651 and exploited both the land and the people. British missionaries arriving in 1810 were critical of what they called the racist actions of the Boers. The independence constitution gave only limited rights to blacks, and in 1912 the African National Congress was formed. Repressive laws were passed during the 1950s which forced Africans into specific areas, took away their political rights and compelled them to carry passes. Between 1948 and 1973 more than ten million Africans were arrested for pass offences. An anti-pass demonstration in Sharpeville in 1960 led to the death of sixty-nine people and the banning of the ANC. In 1963 Nelson Mandela, head of the ANC, was jailed. Five hundred and seventy five people were killed in a civil disobedience riot in Soweto in 1976. This horror precipitated international sanctions against South Africa. In 1990 the new President F. W. de Klerk announced the end of apartheid and the release of Nelson Mandela. Elections were held in 1994 under a new constitution and Mandela was elected president.

Within South Africa the struggle against this evil regime was sustained and fearfully costly for those involved. The churches played a role mainly through the South African Council of Churches (SACC). Archbishop Joost de Blank became very outspoken against the government. He campaigned for the expulsion of the Dutch Reformed Church from the World Council of Churches if it did not renounce apartheid. It did not do so and left the WCC in 1961. His successor Robert Selby-Taylor was less public in opposition to the government, but during his time the Board of Social Responsibility was established. He also pressed for fair wages for its entire non-clergy staff, which would have put the church at odds with the rest of the community. Bill Burnet became archbishop in 1974 and did less public advocacy than his predecessors. Social action thus moved more to the Board of Social Responsibility which had been reconstituted to include more blacks. At this time white clergy were in the vast majority of parishes, though membership of the church increasingly included more blacks. The church was developing its own internal problems. Nonetheless the Board of Social Responsibility continued to work in the political arena and several of its staff were detained by the police for their political activities.

The turning point for the CPSA was the election in 1986 of Desmond Tutu as archbishop. Tutu had worked for the SACC and had been deeply involved in the mass democratic movement. He was already a seasoned

---

[12] See J. W. De Gruchy and S. De Gruchy, *The Church Struggle in South Africa*, twenty-fifth anniversary edn (Minneapolis, Minn.: Fortress Press, 2005).

campaigner, and in 1984 he had been awarded the Nobel Peace Prize. From his position as archbishop he thus became the 'symbol of resistance and hope of the black constituency of the CPSA'.[13] Tutu's position was strengthened by his alliance with Allan Boesak, Frank Chilane and Beyers Naude, and he played a crucial role in the mass confrontation with the state in the second half of 1989. His work at the SACC and his leadership during the transition to the new democracy made him a natural choice to direct the work of the Truth and Reconciliation Commission.

What is not so widely recognised is the theological basis of his actions and its particular blend of African and Anglican elements. Three themes come together for Tutu to create a powerful dynamic that arose from his Anglican formation: his African conception of human solidarity and connection which informed how he thought about the church, a clear conception of humanity created in the image of God, and a blended notion of forgiveness. These themes bring out a dynamic basis for reconciliation, private and public. Not least amongst the reasons for taking account of this African-Anglican version of the theme is that in the present turmoil in the Anglican Communion reconciliation is a mounting challenge in the conflicts that are so manifest around the world.

Writing in 1999 Desmond Tutu tried to explain why South Africa did not go the way of Nuremburg and seek punishment for all those involved in the terrors of apartheid, or, on the other hand, simply declare a general amnesty in order to put the period behind them. Rather, a third way was taken of granting amnesty to individuals if they fully disclosed their crimes. That third way was pursued through the Truth and Reconciliation Commission which Tutu chaired. This 'was consistent with a central feature of the African *Weltanschauung* – what we know in our language as *ubuntu*, in the Ngumi group of languages, or *botho*, in the Sotho languages'.[14] *Ubuntu* means 'We belong in a bundle of life. We say, "A person is a person through other persons." It is not "I think therefore I am." It says rather: "I am human because I belong. I participate, I share."'[15]

Out of this African understanding of humanity Tutu developed an explanation of the need for forgiveness.

Harmony, friendliness, community are great goods. Social harmony is for us the *summum bonum* – the greatest good. Anything that subverts, that undermines this

---

[13] B. Haddad, 'Neither Hot nor Cold. The Church of the Province of Southern Africa as an Agent of Social Transformation in the Western Cape, 1960–1990', *Journal of Theology for Southern Africa* 101 (1998), p. 66.
[14] D. Tutu, *No Future without Forgiveness* (New York: Doubleday, 1999), p. 31.   [15] Ibid.

sought after good, is to be avoided like the plague. Anger, resentment, lust for revenge, even success through aggressive competitiveness, are corrosive of this good. To forgive is not just altruistic. It is the best form of self interest.[16]

In Tutu's formulation there is another dimension to this conception of the human, namely the image of God. This is not an individualist concept but is worked out in terms of the claim that we are made for ultimate fellowship with God. The image of God is what constitutes our identity and all share in the image of God equally. Thus the traditional Christian notions of humanity, person and the image of God are caught up in terms of the African communitarian understanding of *ubuntu*. This formulation at once gives a solidarity with others which the more individualist western formulations find more difficult to establish.

This way of differentiating conceptions of the human does not lead Tutu to think that one approach is better than another. They are just different and more than that they are both from God.

Unlike Westerners, Africans have a synthesizing mind set, as opposed to the occidental analytical one. That doesn't mean Africans are better or worse; it just means that God is smart. Westerners have analysis. We have synthesis. Westerners have a very strong sense of individualism. We have a strong sense of community. Because Westerners have a strong sense of the value of the individual, they are able to take personal initiatives. It's not so easy, when you are a community-minded person, to go against the stream ... This feel for religious and spiritual realities has made it difficult for atheistic and materialist ideologies such as communism, to attract many African adherents.[17]

There is, however, a consequential difference of some importance between these western and African approaches. The western model speaks about the human condition in a theoretical way. Such a general theory is capable of detachment from the particular concrete condition of human living. It is a theory, even a theology, which is framed conceptually. That way of thinking means that the relation between this universal or theoretical and any particular decision or action in life is sharpened and made problematical. How to transform the general into the particular is thus a challenge to which the western intellectual tradition has offered a number of faltering answers. What is true of the western intellectual tradition is also true of western theology insofar as it has been worked out in relation to that

---

[16] Ibid.
[17] From an address by Desmond Tutu to Trinity Institute, 1989, diocese of East Oregon, 'Where Is Now Thy God?' Quoted here from M. Battle, *Reconciliation: The Ubuntu Theology of Desmond Tutu* (Cleveland, Ohio: Pilgrim Press, 1997), p. v.

intellectual tradition. In Tutu's African approach that is not the case. Tutu's theology is not theoretical in that sense, nor general. It is always concrete. It is located in the context in which the theologian is living and acting. That very fact makes a western characterisation of his theology quite difficult.

It is not that this linkage is not to be found in western theology, but that in Tutu's case the linkage is foundational in a way that it is not generally in western theology. In western terms we might say that Tutu is not a theologian in the traditional academic sense, but perhaps more what a westerner would think of as a reasoning activist priest. However, within the western tradition the Anglican method and understanding have tended towards the engaged. We can see this in the way Anglicans often look to persons and personal holiness rather than theological systems, and also in the tradition of disciplined theological activity outside the academy and often linked to parish ministry.[18]

It is thus all the more important to recognise that Tutu's Anglican formation came from a particular strand of that Anglican tradition represented by the work of the Community of the Resurrection in South Africa. Tutu is a Khosa, born in 1931 in Klerksdorp, Transvaal, and at the age of twelve his family moved to Johannesburg. He was greatly influenced by the members of the Community of the Resurrection and their Anglo-Catholic habits. 'Life with them taught me that prayer, meditation, retreat, devotional reading, and Holy Communion were all utterly central and indispensable to an authentic Christian existence.'[19] This influence was reinforced by engagement with the ascetic tradition of the Desert Fathers.

This tradition of Anglicanism matched the whole of the person and life tradition which he brought from his African background. Its emphasis on affect, discipline, prayer, meditation, liturgy and especially the Eucharist all provided the lifespring of Tutu's life. What was true of Tutu's personal life was also true for the life of the church community. It was the worship of the church which both motivated and inspired life. It was also the most telling political act of the church because it drew attention to another world. Indeed it drew attention to God who is the creator and redeemer, present to give identity and purpose to life in the here and now. Drawing on a more eastern style of theology Tutu focused on the work of Christ to draw us into the life of God. Worship pointed to this transformation and inspired testimony to Christ in the harsh realities of politics and the struggle for

---

[18] See the remarks of Rowan Williams on persons in the introduction to Rowell *et al.*, *Love's Redeeming Work*, and the essay by Booty, 'Standard Divines'.
[19] Tutu, 'Where Is Now Thy God?' Quoted in Battle, *Reconciliation*, pp. 131f.

justice. In that sense the church was a direct agent of change in society and looked forward to a final vision of humanity in the purposes of God. 'It was God's intention to bring all things in heaven and on earth to a unity in Christ, and each of us participates in this grand movement.'[20]

This incorporating image – what Tutu calls God's centripetal movement – means that he is always looking for ways of retaining relationships. He was thus more willing than some to compromise with others. He was more ready to extend forgiveness in order to hold to the other. This tendency was often criticised, not least in 1990 at the Rustenberg conference of the churches in southern Africa when Tutu was ready to respond immediately to the pleas of the Dutch Reformed Church for forgiveness for its involvement in the apartheid regime.[21] Tutu's theologically shaped vision of God drawing all to himself lies behind this generous attitude. He wants, by forgiveness, to be able to reconcile all who will come for forgiveness. It was this that motivated him in his work as chair of the Truth and Reconciliation Commission. The commission enabled people to seek an amnesty for themselves by coming forward and seeking forgiveness through full acknowledgement, confession, and the award of reparations for the victims. Perpetrators had to face victims or victims' families. 'The way of amnesty and reparations is the path that our nation elected to walk, crossing from a blighted past to the promise of a better future.'[22]

Tutu's approach to reconciliation is thus shaped out of his particular Anglican formation, his African heritage about the human condition, *ubuntu*, a sense of the ultimate eschatological purposes of God, and patience. He repeats regularly that reconciliation is a long process and requires good leaders, restrained language and a profound understanding of the suffering of the victims. It calls for a vision of the nation and of the church of which he was a part, and the affirmation of diversity.

In 1989 Tutu preached at a gathering in the cathedral after the security police had blockaded a service in the Methodist church at which Beyers Naude was to speak. The huge crowd in the cathedral came together as an alternative and then moved to the town hall. Tutu spoke about the peace which they sought. He refused to say there is nothing wrong with this country except for the perpetrators of apartheid. No, there is nothing wrong with this country except for apartheid, except for injustice, except for the

---

[20] Tutu, *No Future without Forgiveness*, p. 265.
[21] D. Tutu and J. Allen, *The Rainbow People of God: The Making of a Peaceful Revolution*, first edn (New York: Doubleday, 1994), pp. 221–6.
[22] Tutu, *No Future without Forgiveness*, p. 65.

violence of apartheid. The perpetrators of apartheid were to be reconciled. The crowd was a mixed multitude, black and white. 'Come see, Mr de Klerk', Tutu called. 'This country is a rainbow country! This country is technicolour. You can come and see the new South Africa.' And outside to the wider crowd he declared: 'We say we are the rainbow people! We are the new people of the new South Africa.'[23]

This is a staggeringly powerful gospel of reconciliation. It emerges from the formation of Anglican faith and worship and African life and practice. It highlights precisely the nature of the Anglican tradition in its interaction with the particular in which the believer is placed. It is particular, it is concrete, it is traditional and it grows out of the completeness of a life in Christ. It does not detract from Tutu's example to note that there are other cases of such engagement and creative expression; nor to point out the similarities that can be found in other cultures to what is known in Africa as *ubuntu*. While differently construed, such solidarity is to be found in the culture of Australian Aborigines, and in the familial shape of a number of Asian cultures. That only goes to show the particularity of the western model which, of course, has its place in the rainbow, but is not itself the rainbow.

[23] Tutu and Allen, *The Rainbow People of God*, pp. 187f.

CHAPTER 15

Quo vadis?

The Apocryphal Acts of Peter tells the story of an encounter between Peter and the risen Christ on the outskirts of Rome. The church had encouraged Peter to leave the city because of the persecution breaking out there so that:

> thou mayest yet be able to serve the Lord. And he obeyed the brethren's voice and went forth alone … And as he went out of the gate he saw the Lord entering into Rome; and when he saw him, he said, 'Lord, whither (goest thou) here?' And the Lord said unto him, 'I am coming to Rome to be crucified.' And Peter said to him, 'Lord, art thou being crucified again?' He said to him, 'Yes, Peter, I am being crucified again.' And Peter came to himself.[1]

Having come to himself Peter returned to Rome to meet his death.

The history of the Christian church is full of examples of the church community getting the direction of the calling of Jesus wrong. Here the church wanted to keep Peter for further service in the gospel. A very sensible judgement. The sort of thing a synod, a mission board or a bishop might conclude. Such further service might be to protect the Anglican Communion as it has developed so far. It might be to insist on my, or our, clear perception of the truth of some matter. It might be the desire to see a pure church, or a church so open as to be free and welcoming to all without restraint. It might be a church or group of church leaders who do not wish to engage too closely with others with whom they disagree. What Peter and the church concluded was to them very reasonable and also an act of faith. But it turned out not to be the calling of the crucified Christ.

It has been part of the argument of this book that in the Anglican tradition of Christianity the church is fundamentally on pilgrimage and that it is bound to get things wrong. Central to its faith is a belief that the

---

[1] The Acts of Peter quoted from E. Hennecke *et al.*, *New Testament Apocrypha*, ed. W. Schneemelcher, English trans. ed. R. Mcl. Wilson, a translation by A. J. B. Higgins and others of *Neutestamentliche Apokryphen*, edited by E. Hennecke, revised by W. Schneemelcher (London: Lutterworth Press, 1963), vol. II, p. 318.

incarnation of the Son of God in the person of Jesus of Nazareth was a radical and missionary engagement with the human condition. This incarnation is the foundation and inspiration for the Anglican vocation to engage with the realities of the world around them. That very engagements carries with it ambiguities. How far is that engagement to take the believer, or the church community? The formation of institutions, essential for the sustaining of faith practices over time, is itself an expression of that engagement. But the challenge for both the believer and the community is to understand when this engagement detracts from their witness to the kingdom of God and when it is truly an expression of Christian vocation. This is not new in Christianity. It is precisely the point faced by Paul: how not to conform to this world, but to be transformed by the renewing of our minds in order to discern the will of God. But a lot of water has flowed under the bridge since Paul wrote Romans, and the situation for Anglicans in the twenty-first century is at one level much more complicated, while yet being still the same essential challenge.

It has also been the argument of this book that Anglicanism is best thought of as a tradition, a conversation in a community of people over time. Such a conversation is about responding to the redeeming incarnation of God in Jesus of Nazareth. That incarnation in the particular circumstances of first-century Palestine calls for a faith response in the particular circumstances of the believer that would witness to Jesus Christ. Such a vocation for fallible and sinful people was fulfilled in the light of the eschatological coming of the kingdom of God. The Anglican tradition has been formed through a story which began in the memory of Celtic Christianity, came to clearer expression in the imagination of Bede, and has come to fuller and more extensive shape in the life of Anglican churches around the world. That tradition is present for contemporary Anglicans in the practices and beliefs of the community. The core focus on a living response to the crucified Christ means that the instruments of this tradition exist to enable and support that faith response. The 1662 prayer book sets out very clearly the task of the ordained ministry. The minister is to serve the community so that there is such an 'agreement in the faith and knowledge of God', and a 'ripeness and perfectness of age in Christ', that there is no place left in the community for 'error in religion or for viciousness in life'. The language may be old and the categories not quite contemporary, and there may be some variations around the world, but the general ambition for the character of the church is clear and profoundly Anglican.

This way of focusing the tradition gives Anglicanism its local priority, though it is a local priority in which the catholicity of the church is a vital element. For practical purposes that element is set at the institutional limit of the province as providing a reasonable degree of relational connection and extension. It is this element in the tradition that makes the development of theological arguments in favour of global institutions of any significance so difficult to develop out of the tradition, while, on the other hand, the drive in the tradition to sustain self-correction and encouragement from the contactable wider church makes such institutions seem appropriate in a global village. But what kind of institutions would be appropriate? That has been what world Anglicanism has been experimenting with in recent decades. It has been doing a very Anglican thing: testing out the possibilities to see what is the vocation of Christ at this stage in human history. It would be more than optimistic to imagine that the experiment has advanced to a conclusion. The latest experiment of a covenant, arising out of the *Windsor Report*, represents a strategy of constraint which is more than adventurous in the light of the tradition of the status of provinces in Anglican ecclesiology. A more reflective appreciation of the tradition might have suggested a strategy which worked directly with the issue in conflict for some kind of relational way forward.

Viewing world Anglicanism as a tradition draws attention to the nature of institutions as both contingent and limited. They can do certain kinds of things and are especially good at sustaining continuity in nurturing beliefs and values. They do not, however, comprehend the whole life of the community. That is more extensive, different in character and more profoundly important in witnessing to the kingdom of God. The vast array of other relationships in world Anglicanism beyond those of the 'official' judicature-like institutions also shape and influence the life of Anglicans around the world. The judicature serves to provide for a ministry of word and sacrament in the community, and in the present Anglican model that means they inevitably focus on the ordained ministry. Perhaps that is why in the present crisis the conciliar element in the institutional heritage has been more or less sidelined. It looks as though it has become a clerical argument.

At the time of writing it is impossible to be confident about how the present crisis will develop. Speculation is easy, and forms part of the rhetoric of the current arguments. However, there are some contextual factors to this crisis. We live in a time of considerable international anxiety. Terror as a weapon of protest has re-emerged in human history. That fact reflects underlying tensions and the response to it has not shown much deftness of touch. We are on the cusp of a number of monumental changes for human life. Global warming currently attracts increased attention and concern. The approaching end of the oil era probably threatens the fabric of industrialised societies in more immediate terms. There is clearly the ongoing adjustment to the collapse of communism in Europe and Russia and its apparent transformation in China. Twentieth-century communism was the centralist political experiment of the Enlightenment and it has proved unsuccessful in meeting the needs of a population. The implications of this have been chiefly seen in the end of the Cold War and the survival of the USA as the one superpower in the world. But the USA has been the site of the individualist version of the Enlightenment political experiment, and whether it will prove to be enduring in the longer term is probably still an open question.

Kevin Ward puzzles as to why sexuality should have become the presenting issue in the crisis and has pointed out that the response to modernity is a factor. 'Modern Christian understandings of sexual relations – being primarily between individuals and based upon mutual attraction and affection, rather than on more social or economic considerations – are precisely the conditions which erode more traditional attitudes to sex and marriage in non-western societies.'[2] He thinks that the current crisis is not so much about a conflict between a liberal North and a doctrinally and ethically conservative South. Rather it is more like a 'spill-over of the mounting civil war within American society between liberal and conservative religion'.[3] Furthermore he suggests that the 'ethical dimensions of the specific issue of homosexuality are themselves likely to change radically in the south itself'.[4] The issues of modernity are certainly present in Africa and Asia. The recent rise and fall of globalism has in part been an early foray into a global experiment in modernity probably made possible by the vacuum created by the fall of European communism.[5] It was always something of an irony that western industrialised nations should be exporting the terms of their experiment with modernity when it was becoming doubted in their own cultures.

Perhaps we are seeing in the present international Anglican crisis the tectonic cultural grindings brought about by the proximity within Anglicanism of different experiences of the encounter with Enlightenment modernity. In that sense the conflict could be seen as a spillover of the conflict within the USA, overlaid with all sorts of baggage on all sides from a postcolonial world. It could and should also be seen as part of the ongoing struggle by Anglicans to find the appropriate engagement with the world in which they live. If there is truly no precise and definitive form to that relationship then the problems for cross-cultural understanding and catholicity

---

[2] Ward, *A History of Global Anglicanism*, p. 310. [3] Ibid., p. 313. [4] Ibid., p. 318.
[5] See Saul, *The Collapse of Globalism*.

become vexed and difficult if what is being sought for that catholicity is a significant level of constraining conformity. IATDC I, with its report *For the Sake of the Kingdom*, was on the right track all along in focusing on the local context and plurality set within the framework of eschatology.

Whatever may be the case, it is clear that the issues at stake here are profound and have to do with deeply embedded elements in the Anglican tradition and in the social and cultural contexts in which Anglicans around the world live out the terms of that tradition. That must mean that this is a long-haul issue and that a priority in the present circumstances would be to slow the process down. 'Talk talk, not walk walk' might be a useful motto for the prominent players in this game. The issue in the end is not, as has often been claimed, that there should be 'the highest degree of communion possible', but rather the identification of that kind of communion which is appropriate to this kind of Christian tradition for relations between the provinces. What appears not to have been achieved so far is a high level of relational understanding and respect. A strategy of constraint is unlikely to advance that situation.

But how might Anglicans respond if the current Anglican Communion institutions fracture? What if we finish up with two versions of the Episcopal Church in the USA and a variety of relationships to these two bodies around the world, not least of course in Africa? What should Anglicans think has happened? Would it mean that their church had been destroyed? Would that be the end of Anglicanism? Clearly that would not be the case. There are, of course, already two breakaway versions of the Anglican tradition in the USA, with whom the province of Nigeria has established a concordat. The difference in this case would be the size of the split and the demands that each party might make on other provinces around the world.

It is clear that such a split would be a very great disaster. Not because the global organisations might collapse. It might just mark the end of that experiment as a dead end. On any construal of reception it would carry some implications that would take time to evaluate. But most of all it would be a disaster because of the failure of relationships that it would indicate. It would be even worse if such a split was carried through with hostility and venom. That would be shameful as a piece of Christian witness. It would probably mean the loss of any hope for being seen as a global church like the Roman Catholic Church which was hinted at in the *Windsor Report*. But in any ultimate sense that would not be such a loss in terms of the longer history of Anglican ecclesiology. The Lambeth Conference report in 1930 was right. This structure is not the Anglican form of ecclesiology.

The tradition would go on. It witnesses to something fundamental in the Christian understanding of God. But it would be institutionally more scattered and to that degree the tradition would be somewhat fractured. Much would depend on what happened in the provinces and how far they internally divided. Currently connection is facilitated beyond the provinces by a multitude of institutions which provide channels for catholicity to have its effect. In a world that is increasingly divided and fractious, as the intensity of the occupation of the planet increases and we struggle to find a way past the primordial individualism of modernity, the absence of a more manifest Anglican witness to the Christian God would be a sadness hard to bear, and a loss to humanity and to the gospel hard to sustain.

Bibliography

This bibliography contains those printed sources referred to in the footnotes and a small selection of other titles. The development of the internet has led to a vast amount of material on world Anglicanism being available electronically. Most of the Anglican provinces and many of the dioceses and parishes maintain websites which provide documentation about the host institutions. There are also innumerable other independent groups who put forward their points of view on their websites.

The Anglican Communion Portal has been greatly enhanced in recent years and is an excellent starting point for links to other sites within the Anglican Communion. This portal keeps an increasing array of documentation. It provides important records of the groups that exist under the umbrella of the Anglican Communion and provides access to the website of the Archbishop of Canterbury and the Anglican Communion Office. A complete list of the resolutions of the Lambeth Conference and the Anglican Consultative Council can be found there. The reports of the Lambeth Conference and the Anglican Consultative Council are important documents and have usually been published by the Church of England Information Office and latterly by the Anglican Consultative Council. The complete list of these reports is not included in this bibliography, except those to which special attention has been drawn.

Anglican Communion Portal: www.anglicancommunion.org/index.cfm.
Anglican Consultative Council Resolutions: www.aco.org/acc/downloads.cfm.
Lambeth Conference Resolutions: www.lambethconference.org/resolutions/index.cfm.
'Afro-Anglicanism: Identity, Integrity and Impact in the Decade of Evangelism: Second International Conference Report', *Anglican Theological Review* 77 (1995).
Albright, R., 'Conciliarism in Anglicanism', *Church History* 33 (1964), pp. 3–22.
Allchin, A. M., *The Theology of the Religious Life: An Anglican Approach* (Oxford: SLG Press, 1971).
Allen, R., *Missionary Methods: St Paul's or Ours?*, second edn (Grand Rapids, Mich.: W. B. Eerdmans, 1962).
Anderson, B., *Imagined Communities* (London: Verso, 1991).
Anglican Consultative Council, *The Time Is Now*, First Meeting, Limuru, Kenya, 23 February–5 March 1971 (London: SPCK, 1971).

Partners in Mission, Second Meeting, Dublin, Ireland, 17–27 July 1973 (London: SPCK, 1973).

Women in the Anglican Episcopate: Theology, Guidelines and Practice: The Eames Commission and the Monitoring Group Reports (Toronto: Anglican Book Centre, 1998).

Anglican Consultative Council and Inter-Anglican Theological and Doctrinal Commission, *For the Sake of the Kingdom: God's Church and the New Creation* (London: Church House Publishing for the ACC, 1986).

Anglican Religious Communities, *Anglican Religious Communities Year Book. Fifth International Edition 2006–7* (Norwich: Canterbury Press, 2005).

Anglican/Roman Catholic International Commission, *Mary: Grace and Hope in Christ: The Seattle Statement of the Anglican–Roman Catholic International Commission; the Text with Commentaries and Study Guide* (London: Continuum, 2006).

Ansom, P., *The Call of the Cloister. Religious Communities and Kindred Bodies in the Anglican Communion* (London: SPCK, 1964).

Arnold, T., Jackson, M. J. and Rogan, J., *Principles of Church Reform* (London: SPCK, 1962).

Avis, P. D. L., *Anglicanism and the Christian Church: Theological Resources in Historical Perspective*, second revised and expanded edn (London: T&T Clark, 2002).

Beyond the Reformation?: Authority, Primacy and Unity in the Conciliar Tradition (London: T&T Clark, 2006).

Battle, M., *Reconciliation: The Ubuntu Theology of Desmond Tutu* (Cleveland, Ohio: Pilgrim Press, 1997).

Batumalai, S., *Islamic Resurgence and Islamization in Malaysia* (Perak: St John's Church, Jalan, Ipoh, 1996).

Bayne, S. F. and Advisory Council on Missionary Strategy, *Mutual Responsibility and Interdependence in the Body of Christ, with Related Background Documents* (New York: Seabury Press, 1963).

Bede, *A History of the English Church and People* (London: Penguin, 1968).

Bede's Ecclesiastical History of the English People: A Historical Commentary, ed. J. M. Wallace-Hadrill (Oxford: Clarendon Press, 1988).

Binns, J., *An Introduction to the Christian Orthodox Churches* (Cambridge: Cambridge University Press, 2002).

Black, A., *Political Thought in Europe 1250–1450* (Cambridge: Cambridge University Press, 1992).

Black, J. and Gregory, J., *Culture, Politics, and Society in Britain, 1660–1800* (Manchester: Manchester University Press, 1991).

Blake, G., 'Child Protection and the Anglican Church of Australia', *Journal of Anglican Studies* 4.1 (2006), pp. 81–106.

Bless, E., Gracey, J. T., Grant, W. H., Jackson, S. M. and McBee, S. (eds.), *Ecumenical Missionary Conference, New York, 1900* (New York: American Tract Society, 1900).

Bolt, P., Thompson, M. D. and Tong, R., *The Faith Once for All Delivered: An Australian Evangelical Response to the Windsor Report* (Camperdown,

NSW: The Australian Church Record in conjunction with the Anglican Church League, 2005).

Bonner, G., 'Bede and his Legacy', *Durham University Journal* 78.2 (1986), pp. 219–30.

Booty, J., 'Standard Divines', in S. Sykes and J. Booty (eds.), *The Study of Anglicanism* (London: SPCK, 1988), pp. 163–73.

Buchanan, C., 'Liturgical Uniformity', *Journal of Anglican Studies* 2.2 (2004), pp. 41–57.

Historical Dictionary of Anglicanism (Lanham, Md.: Scarecrow Press, 2006).

Bunker, B. B. and Alban, B. T., *The Handbook of Large Group Methods: Creating Systemic Change in Organizations and Communities*, first edn (San Francisco: Jossey-Bass, 2006).

Burns, A., *The Diocesan Revival in the Church of England c.1800–1870* (Oxford: Clarendon Press, 1999).

Bursell, R., *Liturgy, Order and the Law* (Oxford: Clarendon Press, 1996).

Calvani, C., 'The Myth of Anglican Communion', *Journal of Anglican Studies* 3.2 (2005), pp. 139–54.

Carnley, P., *Reflections in Glass: Trends and Tensions in the Contemporary Anglican Church* (Pymble, NSW: HarperCollins, 2004).

Carpenter, E., *Cantuar. The Archbishops in their Office* (Oxford: Mowbray, 1988).

Carter, S., *The Dissent of the Governed. A Meditation on Law, Religion and Loyalty* (Cambridge, Mass.: Harvard University Press, 1998).

Chiwanga, S., 'Beyond the Monarch/Chief: Reconsidering Episcopacy in Africa', in I. T. Douglas and K. Pui-Lan (eds.), *Beyond Colonial Anglicanism: The Anglican Communion in the Twenty-First Century* (New York: Church Publishing, 2001), pp. 297–317.

Church of England Board for Social Responsibility, *From Power to Partnership: Britain in the Commonwealth; The Church of England in the Anglican Communion* (London: Church House Publishing, 1991).

Church of England Doctrine Commission, *Contemporary Doctrine Classics: The Combined Reports* (London: Church House Publishing, 2005).

Church of England House of Bishops, *Issues in Human Sexuality* (London: Church House Publishing, 1991).

Some Issues in Human Sexuality: A Guide to the Debate (London: Church House Publishing, 2003).

Church of the Province of Kenya, *About the Anglican Church in Kenya: A Brief History of the Anglican Church in Kenya on the Occasion of the Tenth Anniversary of the Church of the Province O* ([Nairobi]: CPK, 1980).

Clarke, H. L., *Constitutional Church Government in the Dominions Beyond the Seas and in Other Parts of the Anglican Communion* (London: SPCK, 1924).

Clarke, W. K. L., *Liturgy and Worship: A Companion to the Prayer Books of the Anglican Communion* (London: SPCK, 1932).

Cnattingius, H., *Bishops and Societies. A Study of Anglican Colonial and Missionary Expansion, 1698–1850* (London: SPCK for the Church Historical Society, 1952).

Coleman, R. (ed.), *Resolutions of the Twelve Lambeth Conferences 1867–1988* (Toronto: Anglican Book Centre, 1992).

Coleridge, S. T. and Barrell, J., *On the Constitution of the Church and State According to the Idea of Each* (London: Dent, 1972).

Colley, L., *Britons: Forging the Nation, 1707–1837* (New Haven, Conn.: Yale University Press, 1992).

Conference of Bishops of the Anglican Communion, *The Lambeth Conference, 1930. Encyclical Letter from the Bishops. With the Resolutions* (London: SPCK, 1930).

Cowdrey, H. E. J., *Lanfranc: Scholar, Monk, and Archbishop* (Oxford: Oxford University Press, 2003).

Cranmer, T., *A Defence of the True and Catholic Doctrine of the Sacrament of the Body and Blood of Our Saviour Christ, with a Confutation of Sundry Errors Concerning the Same, Grounded and Stablished Upon God's Holy Word, and Approved by the Consent of the Most Ancient Doctors of the Church* (Appleford, Berks: G. Duffield, Courtenay Library of Reformation Classics, 1964; first published 1550).

Cross, C., *Church and People 1450–1660. The Triumph of the Laity in the English Church* (London: Collins, Fontana Press, 1976).

Cuming, G. J., *A History of Anglican Liturgy*, second edn (London: Macmillan, 1982).

Curtis, M., 'The Hampton Court Conference and its Aftermath', *History* 46 (1961), pp. 1–16.

Day, P. D., *Dictionary of Religious Orders* (Tunbridge Wells: Burns and Oates, 2001).

De Gruchy, J. W. and De Gruchy, S., *The Church Struggle in South Africa*, twenty-fifth anniversary edn (Minneapolis, Minn.: Fortress Press, 2005).

Doe, N., *Canon Law in the Anglican Communion: A Worldwide Perspective* (New York: Oxford University Press, 1998).

Douglas, I. T., *Fling out the Banner. The National Church Ideal and the Foreign Mission of the Episcopal Church* (New York: Church Hymnal Corporation, 1996).

'Lambeth 1998 and The "New Colonialism"', *The Witness* (May 1998), pp. 8–12.

'Anglicans Gathering for God's Mission: A Missiological Ecclesiology for the Anglican Communion', *Journal of Anglican Studies* 2.2 (2004), pp. 9–40.

'An American Reflects on the Windsor Report', *Journal of Anglican Studies* 3.2 (2005), pp. 155–80.

Douglas, I. T., Zahl, P. F. M. and Nunley, J., *Understanding the Windsor Report: Two Leaders in the American Church Speak across the Divide* (New York: Church Publishing, 2005).

Dyer, M. J., Gbonigi, E., Rumalshah, M., Etchells, R., Symon, R. and Clark, E. G. (eds.), *The Official Report of the Lambeth Conference, 1998* (Harrisburg, Pa.: Morehouse, 1999).

Elton, G., *The Tudor Revolution in Government* (Cambridge: Cambridge University Press, 1969).

Ferguson, N., *Empire: The Rise and Demise of the British World Order and the Lessons for Global Power* (New York: Basic Books, 2003).

Figgis, J., *The Divine Right of Kings*, second edn (Gloucester: Peter Smith, 1970).

Fletcher, B., 'Anglicanism and Nationalism in Australia, 1901–1962', *Journal of Religious History* 23.2 (1999), pp. 215–33.

Fortescue, Sir J., *The Governance of England Otherwise Called the Difference between an Absolute and a Limited Monarchy*, ed. C. Plummer (Oxford: Clarendon Press, 1885).

On the Laws and Governance of England, ed. S. Lockwood (Cambridge: Cambridge University Press, 1997).

Frame, T., 'Agreeing on a Common Accountability: What Can the Anglican Communion Learn from Ernst Troeltsch?' *Journal of Anglican Studies* 2.2 (2004), pp. 106–20.

Gaddis, J. L., *The Cold War: A New History* (New York: Penguin, 2005).

Gee, H. and Hardy, J. (eds.), *Documents Illustrative of English Church History* (London: Macmillan, 1921).

Gibson, P., *International Anglican Liturgical Consultations. A Review* (2000), available at: www.aco.org/liturgy/docs/ialcreview.html.

Giles, K., *The Trinity and Subordination: The Doctrine of God and the Contemporary Gender Debate* (Downers Grove, Ill.: InterVarsity Press, 2002).

Jesus and the Father: Modern Evangelicals Reinvent the Doctrine of the Trinity (Grand Rapids, Mich.: Zondervan, 2006).

Gitari, D., *In Season and out of Season: Sermons to a Nation* (Oxford: Regnum, 1996).

Goddard, A., *Homosexuality and the Church of England: The Position Following 'Some Issues in Human Sexuality'* (Cambridge: Grove Books, 2004).

Gomez, D. W., *True Union in the Body?: A Contribution to the Discussion within the Anglican Communion Concerning the Public Blessing of Same-Sex Unions: A Paper Commissioned by the Most Revd Drexel Wellington Gomez, Archbishop of the West Indies* (Oxford: Anglican Institute, 2002).

Gomez, D. W. and Sinclair, M. (eds.), *To Mend the Net* (Carrollton, Tex.: Ekklesia Society, 2001).

Grandsen, A., 'Bede's Reputation as an Historian in Medieval England', *Journal of Ecclesiastical History* (1981), pp. 397–425.

Green, I. M., *The Christian's ABC: Catechism and Catechizing in England c.1530–1740* (Oxford: Clarendon Press, 1996).

Griffiths, D. N., *The Bibliography of the Book of Common Prayer, 1549–1999* (New Castle, Del.: Oak Knoll Press, 2002).

Grudem, W. A., *Biblical Foundations for Manhood and Womanhood* (Wheaton, Ill.: Crossway Books, Foundations for the Family Series, 2002).

Haddad, B., 'Neither Hot nor Cold. The Church of the Province of Southern Africa as an Agent of Social Transformation in the Western Cape, 1960–1990', *Journal of Theology for Southern Africa* 101 (1998), pp. 59–68.

Hansen, H., 'The Colonial State's Policy Towards Foreign Missions in Uganda', in H. Hansen and M. Twaddle (eds.), *Christian Missionaries and the State in the Third World* (Oxford: James Currey, 2002).

Harris, M., *The Challenge of Change: The Anglican Communion in the Post-Modern Era* (New York: Church Publishing, 1998).

Hastings, A., *The Construction of Nationhood. Ethnicity, Religion and Nationalism* (Cambridge: Cambridge University Press, 1997).

Heer, F., *The Holy Roman Empire* (London: Phoenix, Orion Books, 1995).

Hefling, C. C. and Shattuck, C. L. (eds.), *The Oxford Guide to the Book of Common Prayer: A Worldwide Survey* (Oxford: Oxford University Press, 2006).

Hill, C. and Yarnold, E., *Anglicans and Roman Catholics: The Search for Unity* (London: SPCK, 1994).

Hobsbawm, E. J., *Nations and Nationalism since 1780* (Cambridge: Cambridge University Press, 1990).

Holeton, D., *Liturgical Inculturation in the Anglican Communion: Including the York Statement 'Down to Earth Worship'* (Bramcote, Nottingham: Grove Books, 1990).

Holton, R., *The Transition from Feudalism to Capitalism* (London: Macmillan, 1985).

Howe, J. and Craston, C., *Anglicanism and the Universal Church: Highways and Hedges, 1958–1984* (Toronto: Anglican Book Centre, 1990).

Idowu-Fearon, J., 'Anglicans and Islam in Nigeria: Anglicans Encountering Difference', *Journal of Anglican Studies* 2.1 (2004), pp. 40–51.

Inter-Anglican Standing Commission on Mission and Evangelism 2001–2005, *Communion in Mission: Report of the Inter-Anglican Standing Commission on Mission and Evangelism 2001–2005 to the 13th Meeting of the Anglican Consultative Council in Nottingham* (London: Anglican Communion Office, 2006).

Ion, A. H., 'The Cross under an Imperial Sun. Imperialism, Nationalism, and Japanese Christianity, 1895–1945', in M. R. Mullins (ed.), *Handbook of Christianity in Japan* (Leiden: Brill, 2003), pp. 69–96.

Ipgrave, M., *The Road Ahead: A Christian–Muslim Dialogue: A Record of the Seminar Building Bridges Held at Lambeth Palace, 17–18 January 2002* (London: Church House Publishing, 2002).

Scriptures in Dialogue: Christians and Muslims Studying the Bible and the Qur'an Together: A Record of a Seminar 'Building Bridges' Held at Doha, Qatar, 7–9 April 2003 (London: Church House Publishing, 2004).

'Anglican Approaches to Christian–Muslim Dialogue', *Journal of Anglican Studies* 3.2 (2005), pp. 219–36.

Bearing the Word: Prophecy in Biblical and Qur'anic Perspective: A Record of the Third 'Building Bridges' Seminar Held at Georgetown University, Washington DC, 30 March–1 April 2004 (London: Church House Publishing, 2005).

Jenkins, P., *The Next Christendom: The Rise of Global Christianity* (Oxford: Oxford University Press, 2002).

Joint Committee of the Convocation of Canterbury, *The Position of the Laity* (London: SPCK, 1902).

Jordan, W. K., *The Development of Religious Toleration in England from the Accession of James I to the Convention of the Long Parliament (1603–1640)* (London: G. Allen and Unwin, 1936).

Kaye, B., 'The Authority of the Church and the Ordination of Women', *St Mark's Review* 125 (1986), pp. 53–58.

A Church without Walls. Being Anglican in Australia (Melbourne: Dove, 1995).

'"Classical Anglicanism" A Necessary and Valuable Point of Reference', *Reformed Theological Review* 56.1 (1997), pp. 28–39.

Web of Meaning (Sydney: Aquilla Press, 2000).

'Unity in the Anglican Communion: A Critique of the Virginia Report', *St Mark's Review* 184 (2001), pp. 24–32.

(ed.), *Anglicanism in Australia – A History* (Melbourne: Melbourne University Press, 2002).

Reinventing Anglicanism: A Vision of Confidence, Community and Engagement in Anglican Christianity (Adelaide: Openbook, 2003).

'The Strange Birth of Anglican Synods in Australia and the 1850 Bishops' Conference', *Journal of Religious History* 27.2 (2003), pp. 177–97.

'Power, Order and Plurality: Getting Together in the Anglican Communion', *Journal of Anglican Studies* 2.1 (2004), pp. 81–95.

Kaye, B., Macneil, S. and Thomson, H., *'Wonderfully and Confessedly Strange': Australian Essays in Anglican Ecclesiology* (Adelaide: ATF Press, 2006).

Knowles, D., *Christian Monasticism* (London: Weidenfeld and Nicolson, 1969).

Lake, K. (ed.), *The Apostolic Fathers*, English translation by Kirsopp Lake (Cambridge, Mass.: Harvard University Press, 1965).

Lambeth Commission on Communion, *The Windsor Report 2004* (London: Anglican Communion Office, 2004).

Leggett, R. G., 'Anglican Ordinals', in C. Hefling and C. Shattuck (eds.), *The Oxford Guide to the Book of Common Prayer* (Oxford: Oxford University Press, 2006), pp. 528–37.

Locke, J. *The Reasonableness of Christianity: as delivered in the Scriptures*, ed. J. C. Higgins-Biddle (Oxford: Clarendon Press, 1998).

McAdoo, H. R., *The Spirit of Anglicanism. A Survey of Anglican Theological Method in the Seventeenth Century (Hale Lectures)* (London: Adam and Charles Black, 1965).

Anglicans and Tradition and the Ordination of Women (Norwich: Canterbury Press, 1997).

MacIntyre, A., *After Virtue. A Study in Moral Theory* (London: Duckworth, 1981).

Whose Justice? Which Rationality? (Notre Dame, Ind.: Notre Dame University Press, 1988).

Three Rival Versions of Moral Enquiry (Notre Dame, Ind.: Notre Dame University Press, 1990).

Marschin, J., 'Culture, Spirit and Worship', in I. T. Douglas and K. Pui-Lan (eds.), *Beyond Colonial Anglicanism: The Anglican Communion in the Twenty-First Century* (New York: Church Publishing, 2001), pp. 318–36.

Marsden, G. M., *Fundamentalism and American Culture: The Shaping of Twentieth Century Evangelicalism, 1870–1925* (New York: Oxford University Press, 1980).

Marshall, P. V., 'A Note on the Role of North America in the Evolution of Anglicanism', *Anglican Theological Review* 87.4 (2006), pp. 549–57.

Mason, A., *History of the Society of the Sacred Mission* (Norwich: Canterbury Press, 1993).

Mayr-Harting, H., *The Coming of Christianity to Anglo-Saxon England* (University Park, Pa.: Pennsylvania State University Press, 1991).

Meyers, R. A., *Continuing the Reformation: Re-Visioning Baptism in the Episcopal Church* (New York: Church Publishing, 1997).

Milbank, J., Pickstock, C. and Ward, G. (eds.), *Radical Orthodoxy. A New Theology* (London: Routledge, 1999).

MISSIO, Johnson, E. and Clark, J., *Anglicans in Mission: A Transforming Journey: Report of Missio, the Mission Commission of the Anglican Communion, to the Anglican Consultative Council, Meeting in Edinburgh, Scotland, September 1999* (London: SPCK, 2000).

More, P. E. and Cross, F. L., *Anglicanism: The Thought and Practice of the Church of England, Illustrated from the Religious Literature of the Seventeenth Century* (London: SPCK, 1957).

Morton, R. L., *Colonial Virginia* (Chapel Hill, N.C.: University of North Carolina Press for the Virginia Historical Society, 1960).

Mullins, M., *Handbook of Christianity in Japan* (Leiden: Brill, 2003).

Neill, S., *Anglicanism*, fourth edn (New York: Oxford University Press, 1978).

Nichols, A., *The Panther and the Hind: A Theological History of Anglicanism* (Edinburgh: T&T Clark, 1993).

O'Connor, D. (ed.), *Three Centuries of Mission. The United Society for the Propagation of the Gospel, 1701–2000* (London: Continuum, 2000).

O'Donovan, O., *On the Thirty Nine Articles: A Conversation with Tudor Christianity* (Exeter: Paternoster Press for Latimer House, Oxford, 1986).

Office of Communication, Episcopal Church Centre, *To Set Our Hope on Christ: A Response to the Invitation of Windsor Report Para 135* (New York: The Episcopal Church, 2005).

Okorocha, C. C., *The Cutting Edge of Mission: The Report of G-Code 2000, Global Conference on Dynamic Evangelism Beyond 2000: Mid-Point Review of the Decade of Evangelism from 4 to 9 September 1995 at the Kanunga Conference Center Hendersonville, North Carolina, USA* (London: Anglican Communion, 1996).

Parkes, M. B., *The Scriptorium at Wearmouth Jarrow* (Jarrow Lecture in Durham Cathedral, 1982).

Parratt, J. (ed.), *An Introduction to Third World Theologies* (Cambridge: Cambridge University Press, 2004).

Pato, L., 'Anglicanism and Africanisation. The Legacy of Robert Gray', *Journal of Theology for Southern Africa* 101 (1998), pp. 49–67.

Pato, L. and Trisk, J., 'Conversation: New Ways of Seeing: Theological Issues in Post-Apartheid South Africa', *Journal of Anglican Studies* 1.2 (2003), pp. 81–91.

Paton, D. M., *The Life and Times of Bishop Ronald Hall of Hong Kong* (Hong Kong: Diocese of Hong Kong and Macao and the Hong Kong Diocesan Association, 1985).

Pattison, M. and Nettleship, H., *Essays by the Late Mark Pattison, Sometime Rector of Lincoln College* (Oxford: Clarendon Press, 1889).

Peterson, M. D., Vaughan, R. C. and Virginia Foundation for the Humanities and Public Policy, *The Virginia Statute for Religious Freedom: Its Evolution and Consequences in American History* (Cambridge: Cambridge University Press, 1988).

Pickard, S., 'Innovation and Undecidability: Some Implications for the *Koinonia* of the Anglican Church', *Journal of Anglican Studies* 2.2 (2004), pp. 87–105.

Platten, S., *Anglicanism and the Western Christian Tradition: Continuity, Change and the Search for Communion* (Norwich: Canterbury Press, 2003).

Porter, M., *Women in the Church: The Great Ordination Debate in Australia* (Ringwood, Vic.: Penguin, 1989).

Prichard, R., *A History of the Episcopal Church* (Harrisburg, Pa.: Morehouse, 1991).

Primates' Working Group on the Ordination of Women to the Episcopate, *Report of the Working Party Appointed by the Primates of the Anglican Communion on Women and the Episcopate: To Aid Discussion in Preparation for the Lambeth Conference 1988* (London: ACC, 1987).

Ramsey, M., *The Gospel and the Catholic Church*, second edn (London: SPCK, 1990).

Ray, R. D., 'Bede the Exegete as Historian', in G. Bonner (ed.), *Famulus Christi* (London: SPCK, 1976), pp. 125–40.

Rayner, K., 'Australian Anglicanism and Pluralism', *Journal of Anglican Studies* 1.1 (2003), pp. 46–60.

Reed, C., *Pastors, Partners, and Paternalists: African Church Leaders and Western Missionaries in the Anglican Church in Kenya, 1850–1900* (Leiden: Brill, 1997).

Rivers, I., *Reason, Grace, and Sentiment: A Study of the Language of Religion and Ethics in England, 1660–1780* (Cambridge: Cambridge University Press, 1991).

Rosenthal, J. and Erdey, S. (eds.), *Living Communion. The Official Report of the 13th Meeting of the Anglican Consultative Council, Nottingham 2005* (New York: Church Publishing, 2006).

Ross, C., *Edward IV* (London: Book Club Associates, 1974).

Rousseau, Jean-Jacques, *Émile*, trans. Barbara Foxley (London: Dent, 1969).

Rowe, J., 'Mutesa and the Missionaries: Church and State in Pre-Colonial Buganda', in H. Hansen and M. Twaddle (eds.), *Christian Missionaries and the State in the Third World* (Oxford: James Currey, 2002).

Rowell, G., Stevenson, K. E. and Williams, R., *Love's Redeeming Work: The Anglican Quest for Holiness* (Oxford: Oxford University Press, 2001).

Sabar-Friedman, G., *Church, State and Society in Kenya: From Mediation to Opposition, 1963–1993* (London: Frank Cass, 2002).

Sachs, W., *The Transformation of Anglicanism. From State Church to Global Communion* (Cambridge: Cambridge University Press, 1993).

Sanneh, L. O., *Whose Religion Is Christianity?: The Gospel Beyond the West* (Grand Rapids, Mich.: W. B. Eerdmans, 2003).

Saul, J. R., *The Collapse of Globalism: And the Reinvention of the World* (London: Atlantic, 2005).

Secor, P. B. (ed.), *Richard Hooker on Anglican Faith and Worship. Of the Laws of Ecclesiastical Polity: Book V* (London: SPCK, 2003).

Secretary General of the Anglican Consultative Council, *The Report of the Lambeth Conference 1978* (London: Church Information Office, 1978).

ACC-5, Fifth Meeting, Newcastle upon Tyne, England, 8–18 September 1981 (London: ACC, 1981).

Many Gifts, One Spirit: Report of ACC-7 Singapore 1987 (London: ACC, 1987).

The Truth Shall Make You Free. The Lambeth Conference 1988 (London: Church House Publishing, 1988).

Women in the Anglican Episcopate: Theology Guidelines and Practice. The Eames Commission and the Monitoring Group Reports (Toronto: Anglican Book Centre, 1998).

Shils, E., *Tradition* (London: Faber and Faber, 1981).

Society for Promoting Christian Knowledge, *Pan-Anglican Papers: Being Problems for Consideration at the Pan-Anglican Congress, 1908* (London: SPCK, 1908).

Speed Hill, W. (ed.), *Studies in Richard Hooker: Essay Preliminary to an Edition of his Works* (Cleveland, Ohio: Case Western Reserve University Press, 1972).

Spinks, B., 'An Unfortunate Lex Orandi? Some Comments on Episcopacy Envisioned in the 1979 ECUSA Ordinal', *Journal of Anglican Studies* 2.2 (2004), pp. 58–69.

Stephens, J. N., 'Bede's Ecclesiastical History', *History* 62 (1977), pp. 1–14.

Stevenson, K., *The Mystery of Baptism in the Anglican Tradition* (Norwich: Canterbury Press, 1998).

Strayer, R. W., *The Making of Mission Communities in East Africa: Anglicans and Africans in Colonial Kenya, 1875–1935* (London: Heinemann, 1978).

Strong, R., 'An Antipodean Establishment: Institutional Anglicanism in Australia, 1788–c.1934', *Journal of Anglican Studies* 1.1 (2003), pp. 61–90.

Stubbs, W., *The Constitutional History of England: In its Origin and Development* (Oxford: Clarendon Press, 1887).

Sundkler, B. and Steed, C., *A History of the Church in Africa* (Cambridge: Cambridge University Press, 2000).

Sykes, S., *The Integrity of Anglicanism* (New York: Seabury Press, 1978).

'Foundations of an Anglican Ecclesiology', in J. John (ed.), *Living the Mystery* (London: Darton, Longman and Todd, 1994), pp. 28–48.

Unashamed Anglicanism (London: Darton, Longman and Todd, 1995).

'"To the Intent That These Orders May Be Continued": An Anglican Theology of Holy Orders', *Anglican Theological Review* 77 (1996), pp. 48–63.

'The Basis of Anglican Fellowship: Some Challenges for Today', *Journal of Anglican Studies* 1.2 (2003), pp. 10–23.

Power and Christian Theology (London: Continuum, 2006).

Sykes, S. and Booty, J. E., *The Study of Anglicanism* (London: SPCK; Philadelphia, Pa.: Fortress Press, 1988).

Sykes, S. and Gilley, S., 'No Bishop, No Church: The Tractarian Impact on Anglicanism', in G. Rowell (ed.), *Tradition Renewed* (London: Darton, Longman and Todd, 1986), pp. 120–39.

Tang, E., 'East Asia', in J. Parratt (ed.), *An Introduction to Third World Theologies* (Cambridge: Cambridge University Press, 2004), pp. 74–104.

Tanner, M., 'The ARCIC Dialogue and the Perception of Authority', *Journal of Anglican Studies* 1.2 (2003), pp. 47–61.

Thomas, P. H. E., 'Unity and Concord: An Early Anglican "Communion"', *Journal of Anglican Studies* 2.1 (2004), pp. 9–21.

Tierney, B., *Church Law and Constitutional Thought in the Middle Ages* (London: Variorum, 1979).

Turrell, James F., 'Catechisms', in C. Hefling and C. Shattuck (eds.), *The Oxford Guide to the Book of Common Prayer* (Oxford: Oxford University Press, 2006), pp. 500–8.

Tutu, D., *No Future without Forgiveness* (New York: Doubleday, 1999).

Tutu, D. and Abrams, D., *God Has a Dream: A Vision of Hope for our Time* (New York: Doubleday, 2004).

Tutu, D. and Allen, J., *Rainbow People of God: South Africa's Victory over Apartheid* (New York: Doubleday, 1994).

Twaddle, M., 'The Character of Politico-Religious Conflict in Eastern Africa', in H. Hansen and M. Twaddle (eds.), *Religion and Politics in East Africa: The Period since Independence* (Athens, Ohio: Ohio University Press, 1995), pp. 1–15.

Van de Weyer, R., *The Anglican Quilt: Resolving the Anglican Crisis over Homosexuality* (Winchester: O Books, 2004).

Walsh, J., Haydon, C. and Taylor, S., *The Church of England, c. 1689–c. 1833: From Toleration to Tractarianism* (Cambridge: Cambridge University Press, 1993).

Wand, J., *The Anglican Communion. A Survey* (London: Oxford University Press, 1948).

Ward, K., 'Eating and Sharing: Church and State in Uganda', *Journal of Anglican Studies* 3.1 (2005), pp. 99–120.

A History of Global Anglicanism (Cambridge: Cambridge University Press, 2006).

Ward, K. and Stanley, B. (eds.), *The Church Missionary Society and World Christianity, 1799–1999* (Grand Rapids, Mich.: W. B. Eerdmans, 2000).

Watson, F. and Australia Parliament Library Committee, *Historical Records of Australia* (Sydney: Library Committee of the Commonwealth Parliament, 1914).

White, W., *The Case of the Episcopal Churches in the United States Considered* (Philadelphia: printed by David C. Claypoole, 1782).

Williams, R., *Anglican Identities* (Cambridge, Mass.: Darton, Longman and Todd, 2004).

'Theological Education in the Anglican Communion', *Journal of Anglican Studies* 3.2 (2005), pp. 237–40.

Wingate, A., *Anglicanism: A Global Communion* (London: Mowbray, 1998).

Woolverton, J. F., *Colonial Anglicanism in North America* (Detroit, Mich.: Wayne State University Press, 1984).

Wright, J., 'Anglicanism, *Ecclesia Anglicana*, and Anglican: An Essay on Terminology', in S. Sykes and J. S. Booty (eds.), *The Study of Anglicanism* (London: SPCK, 1988), pp. 424–9.

Quadrilateral at One Hundred: Essays on the Centenary of the Chicago–Lambeth Quadrilateral 1886/88–1986/88 (Oxford: Mowbray, 1988).

Yates, T., 'The Idea of a "Missionary Bishop" in the Spread of the Anglican Communion in the Nineteenth Century', *Journal of Anglican Studies* 2.1 (2004), pp. 52–61.

Venn and Victorian Bishops Abroad: The Missionary Policies of Henry Venn and their Repercussions upon the Anglican Episcopate of the Colonial Period 1841–1872 (Uppsala: Swedish Institute of Missionary Research; London: SPCK, 1978).

Zizioulas, J., *Being as Communion* (Crestwood, N.Y.: St Vladimir's Seminary Press, 1985).

Index